SALTWATER, WEBBED FEET, AND BLACKPOWDER

TRACING THE HISTORY OF WILDFOWLING AFLOAT ON TIDAL WATERS INCLUDING SIR RALPH PAYNE-GALLWEY'S WILDFOWLING DIARY

Researched and
written by
John Richards and
Julian Novorol

First edition privately published by

John Richards and Julian Novorol in Great Britain in 2018

ISBN 9781904784876

All rights reserved. Except as permitted under copyright legislation no part of this work may be photocopied, stored in a retrieval system, published, performed in public, adapted, broadcast, transmitted, recorded or reproduced in any form or by any means without the prior permission of the copyright owners,
John Richards and Julian Novorol.

Designed by William Smuts
32 Rhyddyn Hill
Caergwrle
Flintshire
Wales
LL129EB

Printed by Cambrian Printers

Every effort has been made to secure permission from the copyright holders of the images included within this work. The publisher would welcome notification of any deficiencies.

In the interests of authenticity, the spelling, terminology and grammar used in this book by the authors, has been retained.

Distributed by
Coch-y-Bonddu books
www.anglebooks.com

Dedicated to Philippa Humphreys neé Richards.

Her heart beat to a different drum but Philippa was passionate in her pursuit of her sport of eventing

16 November 1982 - 14 May 2016

Illustrations

All paintings and sketches are by Julian Novorol with the exception of the picture on page 36 which is by C.M. Paddy

The illustrations of Belan Fort are reproduced by kind permission of the Merseyside Maritime Museum

Contents

Foreword by Lord Newborough	XIV
Acknowledgements	XVI
Introduction	XVIII

Chapter 1
Colonel Peter Hawker's Legacy	22

Chapter 2
The East Coast professionals	28
Dodd's adventure afloat on the East Coast	31

Chapter 3
The Victorian collectors	34

Chapter 4
Cometh the age of the railway	38
'Marshman' recounts his adventure with Gaffer Gilson on an East Coast estuary	39

Chapter 5
The increasing influence of the written word	42

Chapter 6
Sport on board a shooting yacht	46

Chapter 7
A time for innovation	52
The electric gunning punt	52
The steam-propelled semi-submersible gunning punt	53
Cometh the steam launch	54
Lewis Clement recounts a steam launch adventure on the South Coast	55

Chapter 8
Legendary amateur gentlemen wildfowlers on the Essex Coast	60
'Havoc' a sister to 'Tyche'	64

Chapter 9
Gunning punt design — 68
Hawker's punt design — 68
A motor-driven punt design — 71

Chapter 10
The Gentlemen head for sport abroad — 72

Chapter 11
The effect of duck decoys at home and abroad — 72

Chapter 12
Sir Ralph Payne-Gallwey and Captain George Gould — 82

Chapter 13
The Wildfowling Diary of Sir Ralph Payne-Gallwey Bart. 1874-1916 — 88
Southern Ireland. The formative years 1874-1881 — 88
1882 RPG and Captain Gould aboard '*Crescent*' — 92
Fowling on Continental waters — 94
RPG's vision of a breech-loading double punt gun — 96
1884 Exploring the Humber estuary — 100
1884 RPG joins George Gould in Holland and then returns to Spurn Point — 101
1885 Trials with the new double Holland and Holland punt gun — 104
1885 The International Inventions Exhibition — 106
1885/86 wildfowling season — 107
1887 Exploring Holy Island, Northumberland — 110

An account by Abel Chapman when he was amongst the
brent geese on the Holy Island Slakes — 111
Tension between Abel Chapman and RPG — 113

RPG's Diary continued — 115
1887 RPG's new wildfowling headquarters at Fenham le Mill — 115
1887 RPG visits Friesland, Northern Holland — 116
1888/89 Holy Island revisited — 117
1889 Autumn. Remarkable sport off the coast of Holland — 119

1890 An account by Thomas Mayer Pike; punting in severe weather conditions, Veere Gat, South Holland	123

RPG's Diary Continued — 128

1889/90 RPG returns to Holy Island	128
1890/91 wildfowling season. Fenham le Mill, Holy Island	129
1891 February. RPG visits Beaulieu Lodge, Hampshire	130
1891 Testing W.W.Greener's repairs to the double gun	132
1891 RPG with George Gould aboard *Watergeus*	132
1892 Back to Holy Island	134
1892 RPG's correspondence with Abel Chapman	135
1892 Unresolved problems with the double Holland and Holland punt gun	138
1893 RPG and George Gould return to Southern Ireland	138
1893 An account by Walter H. Pope and George Gould punting from Chateau De Truscat in the Gulf of Morbihan	141
1893 The hazards of travel in search of sport	145

RPG's Diary continued — 146

1893 The New Year at Fenham le Mill	146
1893. A royal salute and a shot at starlings with the double gun	148
1894 Holy Island with Steven Shuttler	148
1894 Pigeon shooting with the double Holland and Holland punt gun	149
1895 Holy Island with a new puntsman	149
1895 RPG visits Broomfleet Island on the Humber Estuary	153
1896 RPG visits Fenham le Mill with Sam Croutear, puntsman	153
1896 The opening of Holland and Holland's new shooting school and RPG completes his new book, 'Letters to Young Shooters'	154
1896 RPG visits Glynllifon, North Wales	154
1897 RPG acquires Colonel Hawker's scale model of his punt and gun	158
1897 A new duck punt commissioned	159
1897 Converting the Bentley and Playfair punt gun into a breech-loader	160
1897 Early season visit to Belan Fort	160
1897 RPG visits Adare Manor, Southern Ireland	162
1898 RPG explores Anglesey	162
1898 George Gould visits Holland	165

1898 RPG visits Anglesey, Malltraeth and the Inland Sea	165
1899 Anglesey after Christmas	169
1899-1900 RPG revisits Valley, Anglesey	170
1900 The Mersey Estuary explored	172
1900 RPG's crossbow feat	174
1900 The Inland Sea, Anglesey revisited	174
1901 10 January, RPG's personal record shot at Valley, Anglesey	176
1901 Punting the Mersey Estuary with George Gould	176
Mr Thomas Mayer Pike recounts his adventure of fowling in Holland with Mr Hugh Leyborne–Popham in the winter of 1901/02	178
RPG's Diary continued	181
1902 Belan Fort, RPG's favourite retreat	181
1902/03 RPG returns to Valley, Anglesey	182
1903/04 RPG returns to the Humber estuary staying at Patrington Village	183
1905 RPG's failing health	185
1905 Wildfowling regulations introduced in Holland	185
A curious coincidence	188
Tom Pike's Bag record	188
1908/09 RPG at Belan Fort and the road to recovering his health	189
1909/10/11 seasons. RPG feels his age	196
1912 RPG's recovery	197
1913 Belan Fort with Evan Roberts as puntsman	199
1914 Back to Belan Fort	201
1914 Death of William, RPG's only son	204
1915 Repairs to the punt before going afloat	205
1915/16 RPG returns to the Caernarvon Bay Hotel	207
1916 RPG visits Laughton Lodge, Lincolnshire	209
1916 January, Bodfuan Hall snipe shooting on the famous bog	210
Death of RPG	210
Epitaph	211

Chapter 14

The history of Sir Ralph Payne-Gallwey's punt gun collection	218
Colonel Hawker's double punt gun	218

The Bentley and Playfair and Clayton punt guns	223
The 'Gallwey' double Holland and Holland punt gun	223

Chapter 15
The historical importance of the Wildfowlers' Association of Great Britain and Ireland	240
Stanley Duncan's legacy	245
The Peter Scott conundrum	246
1963 Hunting methods under scrutiny from Europe	248
1967 Protection of Birds Act	249
1981 Wildlife and Countryside Act	251

Chapter 16
The 1990 Lindisfarne National Nature Reserve Inquiry	254

Chapter 17
Christopher Dalgety's account of an early wildfowling adventure with Peter Scott in December 1929	260

Chapter 18
The story of 'Irish Tom' and adventures with James Robertson Justice	266
James Robertson Justice's story	269
James' fowling HQ at the Bull Hotel	270
1953 James' account of his holiday on the Wash, afloat with 'Irish Tom'	270
James' Drama on the Wash a year later, January 1954	275

Chapter 19
Julian Novorol recounts the story of a day afloat on the East Coast that brings 'Double Trouble'	278

Conclusion	284
Bibliography	286
Appendix 1 Holland and Holland Punt gun Records	292
Appendix 2 Holland and Holland Punt gun Bore Sizes	293

Foreword

The winter migration of wildfowl and waders to coastal intertidal waters has always been eagerly anticipated by the foreshore gunner. In years gone by their arrival marked the opportunity to harvest wild birds that could then be sold, often at the local market; their sale either boosted a meagre income or provided a useful source of food for their families. This form of shooting did not appeal to anyone who hesitated to go forth on a cold winter dawn or at dusk on a windy moonlit night. But these old fisherman fowlers were a hardy breed and relished the challenge of bringing home wild birds for the table.

In 1814 Colonel Peter Hawker was the first exponent to write extensively about the art of wildfowling afloat. His book, 'Instructions to Young Sportsmen' gave all manner of advice to the wildfowler. The book ran to nine editions in his lifetime and by 1844 the sport of wildfowling was attracting the attention of wealthy gentlemen who wanted either to try their hand at punt gunning or hire a shooting yacht to pursue wildfowl on estuaries all around our coast. This book recounts the adventures of many of these men.

My great grandfather's brother The Hon. Frederick Wynn enjoyed shooting and sailing and it comes as no surprise that he invited Sir Ralph Payne-Gallwey to shoot at Glynllifon, our family home, in 1896. There is no doubt thereafter they struck up a firm friendship. It was in January the following year that RPG went to stay at Fort Belan, a fort built at the southern entrance to the Menai Straits, first constructed in 1775 and developed by my family for the strategic defence of the Straits.

On reading Payne-Gallwey's wildfowling diaries it becomes apparent that he loved Belan and he returned each winter, health permitting, right up to his death in 1916. His diaries recount the many punt gunning adventures he had in the Foryd Bay and on the coast of Anglesey. Before his death his punt and gun had already been gifted to Frederick and were left in the warehouse alongside the dock, along with many other artefacts related to the maritime history of the fort.

In 1986 the Merseyside Maritime Museum took charge of the collection of boats and historic objects that were in store at Belan; this collection, known now as the Wynn collection, included the punt and gun formerly belonging to Payne-Gallwey and a massive wooden Ballista (catapult) he had constructed to throw projectiles across the Menai Straits.

The Fort was eventually sold by our family but today it appears to be in good hands and some restoration work is underway with the help of Cadw, who assist with the responsibility for the maintenance and repair of historically important buildings in Wales.

In 1908 Payne-Gallwey became the first President of The Wildfowlers' Association of Great Britain and Ireland and this book traces some of the hitherto untold history of the Association. With a change of name to The British Association for Shooting and Conservation (BASC) does much today to ensure that shooting is conducted in a responsible and sustainable way.

In the latter part of the book you will find some wonderful wildfowling stories that have never before been told. These stories cannot fail to convey the compelling elements of going afloat in a gunning punt in pursuit of truly wild quarry. Today wildfowling clubs all around our coast help to ensure that the shooting is carried out in a responsible manner. The Y Foryd Wildfowl and Conservation Association maintain this tradition where Sir Ralph Payne-Gallwey Bart. once spent many happy fowling seasons staying at Fort Belan.

This book evokes a fine record of a bygone era and a binding relationship between Sir Ralph Payne-Gallwey and the Hon Frederick Wynn brought together by their passion for wildfowling

Lord Newborough

Acknowledgements

It would not have been possible to write this book without the very considerable help and co-operation we have received from a great many people, some of whom are close friends, and many others who have kindly given of their time and advice to assist us.

We would very much like to thank Lord Newborough for agreeing to write the foreword to the book.

We owe a deep debt of gratitude to Anthony McEntyre with whom we have both spent many memorable days in a gunning punt. Anthony initially gave us access to the Sir Ralph Payne-Gallwey (RPG) Diaries which later led to a meeting with Sir Phillip Payne-Gallwey resulting in permission to use the unique notes contained in RPG's Wildfowling Day Book. Where better to start to write a book about punt gunning? But, it was the help of many others that awakened us to the importance of the broader social history story associated with wildfowling afloat.

Many of the following names will appear when you read this book. These people have all played an important part and contributed much valuable information: Rev'd Hugh Burgess, Jeremy Herrmann, Arthur Credland, Emrys Heard, Peregrine Armstrong Jones, John Bishop, Kevin Thatcher, David Baker, Colin Teago, Keith Scott, Peter Avery, Rupert Foley, David Frost, Sir James Vernon Bart., Jim Spalding, David Conway, Archie Moore, Donald Dallas, David and Paul Upton, Ron Terry, Ginger Blaney, Andrew St. Joseph, Michael Gordon-Jones, David Grayling, Jack Hoy, Richard and Christopher Zawadski, Marjory McKee, Jean Skinner, Frances and Glen Thompson, Paul Morgan, Bob Watcham, Roy Kitcher, Angela Dorrington, Kathryn Rose and family. We thank them all.

Sadly, the passage of time associated with the research necessary to compile this book has meant we have lost some dear friends. They have, 'gone ahead', but they are not forgotten and we must pay tribute to them here. John Humphreys, John Rippingall, Keith Shackleton M.B.E. P.P.R. S.M.A.,S.W.L.A., Nick Frearson, Laurence Thompson, James Dorrington, Claude Oxley and Trevor Field. All were punt gunners who shared our passion for the sport.

We would like to thank the following individuals and organizations that provided us with information, contacts, leads or an insight into the history of particular families. Diana Cooke and John Wright of the Blakeney Area Historical Society for information about the Long family; Paul Mosse for extensive research in Southern Ireland; Alexander and Susan Dalgety for access to Christopher Dalgety's diaries; Bill Harriman for information about Stanley Duncan; Ann Charlton and Matt Lowe, staff in the museum of the department of zoology at Cambridge University and staff at the Cambridge University Library.

Acknowledgements

In addition a number of individuals and organizations allowed us access to archive information in their care; Sue Allison at the British Library Boston Spa; Ben Whittaker, Curator of Maritime History and Technology at Merseyside Maritime Museum; Lynne Moore at the Royal Commission in Ancient and Historical Monuments of Wales; Caroline Hampton, access to The Sammy White Archives; the late Lord Home, former President of BASC; Tim Russell and John Swift, access to Association Archives; Daryl Greatrex, Managing Director, Holland and Holland and Shan Davies, access to Company Archives; The University of Reading; the Curator of the Museum of Rural Life; The Caernarvon Records Office.

Throughout the book we have always tried to acknowledge the source of any findings which have been the result of our research. In addition, we are grateful for permission to reproduce extracts from older journals and magazines particularly The Shooting Times and The Field magazines.

To anyone whom we have unwittingly omitted, we sincerely apologise.

We thank all those fellow punt gunners who have given us encouragement to put on record, and share with others, the wildfowling adventures of coastal longshoremen and gentlemen gunners who enjoyed fowling either on home waters or abroad. We have tried to accurately document many of the important social history events of coastal resorts in British, Irish and Continental waters.

To the special group of people with whom we have shared a day in a gunning punt, we thank you for your company. No wildfowler can go afloat with another without learning something new about the birds of the estuary. Such days have been very special for us.

Finally, and by no means least, our sincere thanks to our wives Gill and Mo. We have been exceedingly lucky to have found two wonderful people who have allowed us the freedom to go wildfowling whenever we wished. They have also provided us with unending support and encouragement to complete this book for which we are eternally grateful.

Introduction

One hundred years ago, 'Saltwater, Webbed Feet and Blackpowder' was a traditional wildfowler's toast. At the end of a successful day in pursuit of ducks, geese, or waders, fowlers gathered in their local tavern and raised their glasses to celebrate success. Each winter all around the coast, when weather and tides permitted, fowlers went afloat in gunning punts carrying a large bore shotgun known as a punt gun. This book is about their adventures, reflecting on the fascinating social history and tradition of punt gunning. Initially, when we discussed the content it was to focus on the legendary wildfowler and famous Victorian author Sir Ralph Payne-Gallwey Bart. (RPG). Like so many other wildfowlers, we avidly read his classic fowling books which included: 'The Fowler in Ireland' 1882, 'Shooting Moor and Marsh' in the Badminton Series 1896, and 'Letters to Young Shooters', 1890/1892/1896. These books were the foundation upon which we built our interest in punt gunning.

After much research it became obvious that we could not write a book about wildfowling which started at 1875 (the year RPG first recorded notes about wildfowling) and ignore the social history associated with, and immediately after the publication of Colonel Hawker's, 'Instructions to Young Sportsmen' in 1814. Hence, in the early chapters we endeavour to give the reader an insight into how life around our coast evolved as a result of Colonel Hawker's influence. Fowling was accepted as an important part of rural living. It provided local communities with food which was highly prized and employment for longshoremen during the winter months, all of which helped to sustain the economic viability of coastal resorts. But, by 1870, unprecedented change to modes of travel had come about by the rapid expansion of the railway network, enabling an ever larger number of folk with guns to reach the coast and try their hand at fowling. With it came the inevitable increase in shooting pressure on wintering wildfowl populations. Adding to this pressure was the number of ducks that were being trapped in decoy ponds at home and abroad, (along the coast in Germany and Holland), reducing the migratory wildfowl populations.

Gun design was also rapidly changing. The gun trade was quick to recognise that with the coming of the breech-loading shotgun, there was an opportunity to capitalise on a new market. Gentlemen had money and they demanded better guns. Consequently gun makers reacted, introducing many new patent designs and the muzzle-loader became outdated. Innovation was not confined to guns and quickly extended to boats and particularly to gunning punt design. New tactics were devised to shoot wildfowl. Interspersed throughout the pages of the book are carefully chosen accounts of classic fowling adventures. We recount stories about shooting aboard sailing yachts, explore the working of an electric gunning punt, examine the merit of steam launches which were designed to pursue fowl far out at sea and look at the first semi-submersible steam driven gunning punt, which was in operation on the south coast in 1888. In some respects these adventures reflect our own nostalgia for a bygone era, but we tell them for a different reason. They all reflect 'real time' social history of wildfowling afloat, as it was, at home and abroad.

After Colonel Hawker's death in August 1853 the sport of wildfowling continued to be widely written about by authors such as John Henry Walsh (Stonehenge), Henry Coleman Folkard (Hoary Frost) and Lewis Clement (Wildfowler). Perhaps it was the romantic and exciting tales contained in these books and articles in the sporting press that attracted Sir Ralph Payne-Gallwey and other gentlemen sportsmen to become wildfowlers? We were privileged to have access to hitherto unseen documents and a unique personal diary written by RPG and much of the book is devoted to his life and travels in Southern Ireland, England, Wales, Germany and Holland.

When RPG died in November 1916 his widow Edith decided to dispose of many of the items in his gunroom. RPG's extensive sporting library, which included his diaries, was dispersed in 1927 when Thirkleby, the ancestral home of the Frankland family, was demolished. Extracts from RPG's Game Book and Diaries did appear in a series of articles in the Shooting Times and Country Magazine starting in October 1969 and it was clear that most of his wildfowling was done with punt and gun. The finer detail of RPG's wildfowling adventures remained obscure until 1985, at which time correspondence we had with Sir Phillip Payne-Gallwey O.B.E., M.C. (who died on 8 February 2008 aged 72) revealed the existence of a Wildfowling Day Book. This remarkable book contained the following introductory comments to his diary,:

> *"This book contains a history of my wildfowling shooting career. All entries of sport and shots in this book are written down on the same day they occurred. This makes the book much more interesting to me, than it might otherwise be. It records disappointments and a few great successes. Whether, to obtain the latter, the time and money, and hard work expended was worth the results would be doubted by nine ordinary shooters out of ten. Personally I wish I could live every moment over again that I have passed wildfowling, with the exception of when my life has been at risk."*

Gaining access to RPG's Day Book with permission to reproduce the content was a real breakthrough. We now had all the information that was required to document RPG's lifetime wildfowling adventures. But of course RPG was never alone, accompanied always by a puntsman and often with his friend Captain George Gould, and we wanted to find out more about these characters.

In 2010 David Grayling, a much respected specialist field sports antiquarian book seller telephoned to say he had discovered an interesting collection of letters and other correspondence addressed to RPG which had come from the Thirkleby Hall library. Arrangements were made to see the letters and it transpired that in this collection were letters from Captain George Gould, with whom RPG had shared many weeks each season wildfowling at home and abroad over a period of thirty years. The exchange of letters between Gould and RPG revealed the extent of their friendship, the places they visited and much about the sport of punt gunning they had enjoyed together as well as details of the professional puntsmen they employed.

The information required to document more than forty years of Payne-Gallwey's wildfowling adventures forms a large section of the book. We also researched sufficient information to write another book about his game shooting career, although the latter subject we have chosen largely to ignore, except for some amusing anecdotal stories which are included.

In August 2013 we lost one of our wildfowling friends and this galvanised our resolve to set about sharing the information we had researched. James Dorrington was a great character and wonderful company, whether you were with him in a gunning punt or together on a more formal shooting day. James held an opinion on everything and, between each puff on his cigarette, he did not hold back in giving advice. His wife Angela said, "with James there are only two ways of doing anything, James' way and the wrong way".

He undertook any project with total commitment. One such project involved the acquisition of the two halves of Payne-Gallwey's double Holland and Holland punt gun. Stanley Duncan, founder of the Wildfowlers' Association of Great Britain and Ireland (WAGBI) split the gun into two single guns in 1920. James had every intention of rebuilding the double gun to its former glory but due to failing health he was never able to complete this project. We tell the story of how this was eventually achieved and also discuss other punt guns which were owned by RPG.

In later chapters there are more stories written by the giants of wildfowling, including Abel Chapman, James Robertson Justice and Christopher Dalgety. It also seemed appropriate that we should look at post-war wildlife legislation because changes which were brought about by this legislation undoubtedly changed the history of wildfowling. We have therefore looked closely at the passage through Parliament of the 1954 and 1967 Protection of Birds Act and the 1981 Wildlife and Countryside Act. In so doing we have tried to pay, a long overdue, tribute to those WAGBI Executive Committee members and later the small dedicated staff who fought like tigers to resist overzealous legislation that might have affected many more of the traditions of the sport of wildfowling. Through their foresight they have shown how shooting and conservation, can and does today, go hand in hand.

John Richards and Julian Novorol

I

Colonel Peter Hawker's legacy

"The grand and glorious sport of great gun shooting.

Age does not wither nor custom stale its infinite variety."

Stanley Duncan

Generally speaking the diaries of sportsmen are not documents of exceptional historical value. Nevertheless, we are indebted to a number of notable men whose writings have given a full and vivid picture of sport and recreation since the early part of the 19th century.

Colonel Peter Hawker may fairly claim to be the first to write clear, detailed instructions on wildfowling and in particular wildfowling afloat. Others followed and no library would be complete without the volumes written by later authors of such eminence as Henry Coleman Folkard, Captain Lacy, Henry Sharp, Sir Ralph Payne-Gallwey, Abel Chapman and John Henry Walsh, (editor of The Field from 1858 to 1888). All these important names will become familiar as the book progresses.

Peter Hawker was born on 24 December 1786 in London, the son of Colonel Peter Ryves Hawker. He was first and foremost a soldier and as early as 1801 was gazetted cornet to the first Royal Dragoons; he exchanged into the 14th Light Dragoons in 1803 and obtained his troop in 1804. In 1809 he served heroically with his regiment in Portugal and Spain under the command of Arthur Wellesley, later to become the Duke of Wellington. On 28 July 1809, at the Battle of Talavera a bullet pierced his thigh bone and as a result of this wound he was invalided home. Eventually, in 1813, he was compelled to resign his Commission.

The Colonel devoted the remaining forty years of his life to family duties and the pleasures and recreation of a country gentleman; managing his estate at Longparish. He also maintained a house in London, initially at 2, Dorset Place and latterly at 134, Upper Gloucester Place, Marylebone. He established his wildfowling headquarters at Wigeon Cottage, Keyhaven. He married his first wife Julia in Lisbon in 1811, she being the only daughter of Major Hooker Barttelot. Four children followed, their first son Richard died at a young age, a second, Peter William Lanoe survived him and there were two daughters Mary and Sophy. After the sad death of his first wife he married Helen Susan in 1844, the widow of his late friend, Captain John Symonds R.N. Throughout his life he travelled frequently to the Continent, keeping diary notes on all he saw and the cost of his travels.

The Colonel loved music, he studied musical composition and played the piano. In August 1820 he wrote in his diary, "was detained in town this month on account of my new invention for playing the scales of a pianoforte by mechanical means." But, above all else, he was obsessed with shooting. In 1814 he published, 'Instructions to Young Sportsmen in All that Relates to Guns and Shooting.' The book was originally compiled for the benefit of a few friends and published privately. It eventually ran to nine editions during the author's lifetime. Peter, his son, published an abridged 10th edition in 1854 and an 11th edition appeared in 1859. There were two American editions, 1846 and 1853, both based on the English 9th edition to which the Colonel added, 'The Hunting and Shooting of North America— descriptions of animals and birds ' by William T. Porter. Each was published in Philadelphia by Blanchard and Lee. In 1922 a further edition was published by Herbert Jenkins Ltd., edited and with an introduction by Eric Parker.

It is undoubtedly true that during Hawker's lifetime and for many years after his death, his book remained the standard work on shooting. Plenty of books and treatise existed but Hawker dealt with the whole subject in every detail. Each edition was revised to show the stages of development reached by gunmakers, identifying innovation and all that was new in the London gun trade.

We venture to suggest that until Hawker published the first edition of his book, coastal wildfowling per se was regarded as a lowly sport, conducted in remote areas on the coast where ill-disciplined local gunners roamed the marshes in the hope of obtaining the odd bird to supplement the family diet. In the main they were professional fishermen by trade or men of the sea, who either skippered or sometimes crewed yachts and working boats. Some would turn their hand to wildfowling in the winter when the weather prevented them from putting to sea. Most shot with muzzle-loading shoulder guns but the more adventurous had heard about punt gunning and were prepared to try their hand with punt and gun. The more successful gunners sold their quarry to the village poulterer for meagre gain. If the bird was rare, a ready market existed amongst the bird collectors and taxidermists who were always on the lookout for an unusual migrant. This was a time when the typical fabric of a close knit coastal community largely remained undisturbed by people outside the neighbourhood. If an incomer was seen to threaten the livelihood of a fisherman/fowler he certainly would not be welcome. As late as 1886 Lewis Clement writing in the 'Shooting Times and Kennel News' recalls an occasion when professional wildfowlers fired off their shoulder guns in order to put the fowl up when he was setting to them in his punt. He stated, "it has been nothing out of common to even fire with swan shot and even bullets at those whom the men looked upon as poaching on their preserves." This was the status quo in the middle of the nineteenth century.

It is necessary to look closely at Hawker's 1844 9th edition to understand why he was attracted to wildfowling and wrote at length about the sport. In the Preface he writes, "So much indeed has been published, by more able writers, on field sports of every description that little more remains to be said on the subject. The pursuit of game is already too well known to require much instruction. The author has, therefore, thought it far better, instead of treating too copiously on that head, better, to give particular directions for (what gentlemen least understand)

GETTING ACCESS TO WILD BIRDS OF EVERY DESCRIPTION." So there you have it! Hawker was encouraging gentleman to take up wildfowling because wildfowl and waders were the wildest of all quarry species and provided truly challenging sport.

The origin of gunning for fowl using a boat can be traced back to the late eighteenth century. However, the design of punts in use today owes much to the ingenuity of Colonel Peter Hawker who, writing in 1822, first described a design for a punt that is readily recognisable as the type widely in use today. This punt is often referred to as the Keyhaven Canoe and is illustrated in the frontispiece of the 9th edition of Hawker's book, 'Instructions to Young Sportsmen.'

Colonel Hawker based his design upon punts used by a family of punt gunners from Essex. In Captain Lacy's book, 'The Modern Shooter' published in 1842, he states that partially decked canoes or punts were originally invented by the Buckel family who were widely regarded as, 'Superior' skilled gunners. The family worked their canoes/punts out of Maldon at the head of the Blackwater estuary in Essex and had been wildfowling using this design of punts for an estimated half a century.

Lacy writes, " The plan was more recently conveyed to Southampton by their descendant Elijah Buckel, who is most cognoscenti in everything relative to the construction and management of shooting punts, stanchion guns and in short the whole arcana of wildfowl shooting."

But boat design has a habit of changing and Buckel's design was no exception. The Southampton/Keyhaven canoe was materially improved by Colonel Hawker and the broad design for Hawker's punt was set out, for all to follow, in the eleventh edition of his book.

Again Lacy writes, "When I commenced gunning, after having viewed a variety of canoes, the one upon which I fixed as the best model to copy from, was that of Colonel Hawker's plan of the late Captain Ward, R.N. and which had just been built by Mr Blaker of Southampton, under the superintendence of Buckel." Interestingly Lacy then goes on to state that, "it was not long after that I found the canoe susceptible of improvements both externally and internally." And so it is with punt building, you learn from experience and make alterations to your craft according to the conditions that prevail on the punting grounds where you go afloat.

Innovation was not confined to punts alone, with all wildfowling equipment coming under his scrutiny. Stanchion guns and their recoil apparatus were much improved and punting tactics were debated. Thus it can be said that although Colonel Hawker was not the father of wildfowling, he was probably the first person to introduce an element of intellect to the sport which he complained in 1844 was followed by people he referred to as, "rabbles of tit-shooters and popping vagrants."

Before we leave Hawker we must reflect briefly on the discovery of his personal diaries some forty years after his death in August 1853. They were in the possession of his family, unread and unknown to the wider public until Sir Ralph Payne-Gallwey gained permission to publish a portion of the legendary manuscripts which Hawker called, 'Memorandas on Shooting, Fishing and Other Sports (and of my journal from place to place)'. Here was the Colonel's methodical record of his daily thoughts and doings which gave an accurate picture of his lifestyle. In 1893

Payne-Gallwey set about editing extracts from the extensive diaries. In doing so he chose to make alteration and unaccountable changes to Hawker's notes, which were only to become apparent some years later.

In the 1920s Eric Parker (Editor of The Field) sought to revisit the Hawker diaries. He knew that there was much unpublished material and contacted Hawker's grandson who was living in France. The original diaries had apparently been lost and only the Payne-Gallwey transcript could be found. Parker set about creating a truer picture of the diaries by rewriting many passages. The story does not finish here for, soon after Parker's newly edited edition appeared in 1931, the complete diaries appeared, offered for sale by a London bookseller. An enthusiastic American sportsman was visiting London at the time and purchased thirty three volumes of the diaries. Fortunately Mr David Wagstaff, the purchaser, was extremely knowledgeable about sporting matters and treasured his find. He eventually added a thirty fourth volume which completed an even more comprehensive understanding of Hawkers' life from 1792 to 1802. In 1945 Mr and Mrs David Wagstaff presented the Hawker Diaries to the Yale University Library. They remain in the care of the library to this day and are profoundly important when considering the history of wildfowling and in particular punt gunning.

Hawker was an accomplished writer who makes no pretence of inventing or devising any form of shooting, rather he perfected many aspects of the sport, documenting detail, experimenting and developing ideas. He was a soldier, sportsman, author, musician and above all a country gentleman and his book, 'Instructions to Young Sportsmen' inspired many of the aristocracy and the better off to try their hand at wildfowling. But before exploring this chapter in wildfowling history we will look more closely at the simple life of the fisherman fowler who inhabited every coastal village throughout the land in Hawker's time.

Returning home, Colonel Hawker and punts at Keyhaven

2

The east coast professionals

"For while the tired waves, vainly breaking

seem here no painful inch to gain,

Far back, through creeks and inlets making,

come silent, flooding in the main."

Arthur Hugh Clough

Every estuary along the east and south coast that held wildfowl had its attendant wildfowlers supplementing a living from shooting during the winter. We have chosen to describe one such place, Hamford Water, as we have local connections and experience of the place and its people.

The economy of Walton Backwaters, or Hamford Water as it is more commonly known today, has always been linked to the sea where fishing and fowling have played a prominent role in the lives of local people. Families depended on the sea for their livelihood. On this coast the landscape consists of low lying saltmarsh, islands with interlinked winding channels to the north and west of Walton-on-the-Naze. Working in this hinterland you will find longshoremen, barge pilots, sailors, fishermen, oystermen, dredgermen and, with an abundance of fowl in the area, there have been generations of punt gunners. Familiar names included Bloom, Oxley, Hammond and Canham. These men pursued the fowl in single punts which were typical of the Essex coast. Built locally they would have been seventeen to eighteen feet in length, decked fore and aft and carrying a gun of 1¼ inch bore loaded with between 10 and 16 ounces of shot. Muzzle-loaders would have been common but a few of the better-off puntsmen owned a breech loader. The Eagles were a family of landowners at Walton and the brothers, Woodruffe and Frank were keen amateur punt gunners, using a double-handed punt and 1¼ inch muzzle-loading gun firing a pound of shot.

Competition amongst the puntsmen was keen, such that few wildfowl remained in the Backwaters during the hours of daylight but, when the wind was in the east and cold weather swept in from the Continent, it would bring fresh birds and the gunners went afloat with every chance of a shot. Under normal conditions most of the punting had to be done at dawn or dusk and the most favoured tides would have been when high water coincided with their dawn and dusk raids. Frank Bloom spoke of both his father and grandfather having good success in a certain area of the marsh, just as the wigeon were feeding on the front of the tide. Their stalk was under cover of darkness and they fired by sound alone!

The Wade is a large mudflat between Horsey Island and the village of Kirby-le-Soken. During the nineteenth century it was covered by a dense carpet of Zostera grass (eel grass), a favourite food for wigeon. Claude Oxley remembered vividly hearing the sound of wigeon lifting at dawn from the feed. He recalls standing in his garden two miles from where the wigeon were feeding and as it grew light there was a sound like an express train passing the station. The westerly wind carried the sound of the rising birds and minutes later he heard the approaching wigeon whistling and growling as thousands, in great waves, swept over his house. The birds passed over the low lying area of Walton known as the Bath House and headed out to the open sea where they rested in vast rafts and grazed on the floating eel grass, carried out on the ebbing tide. When dusk came, or the flood tide offered security they flighted back to their feeding grounds, more often than not under the cover of darkness.

The Zostera beds were so vast that during the autumn equinoxial gales they would be torn out by the action of the waves and washed up in large quantities all along the lee shore. It was in such abundance that longshoremen rolled up as much of the Zostera they could gather from the strand line, hung it up on posts and lines to dry out and thereafter it was sold as stuffing for furniture such as settees and armchairs!

The professionals were opportunist and shot at small groups of fowl usually feeding at high water amongst the flooded saltings. Large shots were rare; Frank Bloom noted his best shot was 28 wigeon shot on Crabknowe Spit at the mouth of the Backwaters. It was October and the newly arrived birds were tired and this allowed a close approach by Frank's punt.

Some of the punt gunners operated in pairs and Claude Oxley's best shot was with his uncle Ted. They successfully picked up 29 wigeon with single shots fired from two punts. Claude fired as the birds stood on the ice and Ted took his shot as they lifted.

Ted Oxley and Sid Canham also worked as a team and on one occasion they set to a great gathering of brent geese. The story goes that it was after sunset as the two punts approached the geese and there was a strong east wind blowing. The geese were intent on sheltering for the night in Cormorant Creek. Once again the first shot was fired at the sitting and the second as they rose. The result was 94 geese picked up by the fowlers.

It was normal for about twelve punts to be operating from the hard at Walton, plus one or two making out from neighbouring villages such as Kirby-le-Soken and Landermere. The Bull family

A professional fowler of the 'Old School'

were wildfowlers on the north side at Little Oakley. James Bull was a professional punt gunner whose nickname was Deacon Bull, as he was a close friend of the Rev. Max Wontner, also a keen amateur wildfowler.

Unlike today, seals were not welcome in the estuaries and were shot on sight if they encroached on local fishing grounds. It was hard enough to make a living from fishing and no fisherman wanted to share his catch with seals or have his nets wrecked by these powerful animals. On one occasion Tom Poole from Brightlingsea was punting in Brightlingsea Creek when he observed a seal at close quarters. He waited his moment, shot it, and promptly hauled it into his punt taking it for dead and no doubt congratulating himself on a job well done. Perhaps his thoughts were of a new seal skin hat or a skin to cure for a winter coat, both were common apparel of the fisherman/fowler. Sailing home and watching the wind in his sail rather than the guest he had hauled into his punt, he was caught unaware when the seal suddenly came back to life and showed every sign of seeking revenge. Unfortunately the seal lay between him and his gun and he recounts the tale, "that it bared its teeth and started to come for me. I reckoned there wasn't room for the two of us and as I couldn't tip him over I went in myself and swam ashore. I clambered up the mud and ran down to the hard just in time to see my old punt drift by with that old seal sitting up snarling over the gunwale and looking properly savage."

Dodd's adventure afloat on the east coast

'Here joyless roam a wild amphibious race,

sullen woe displayed on every face;

Who, far from civil arts and social fly,

And scowl at strangers with suspicious eye.'

George Crabbe 1754-1832.

To illustrate the commitment to wildfowling shown by the professionals we include here a true adventure that George Porter (nicknamed Dodd) from Manningtree experienced at the age of 19. Like so many longshore families he was following in his father's footsteps and even at this young age he had been taught the skills necessary to manage a gunning punt in tidal waters.

Manningtree is a small town at the head of the tidal section of the river Stour, Hamford Water being to the south. At the time there would have been a number of punts moored on 'the hard' and most would have been left with muzzle-loaders breeched on the punts. This particular morning Dodd's father woke him at 4.30 am and after a cup of tea he went down to the harbour and set off down river on the ebb tide. There was always plenty of competition but if you were 'first away' there was a fair chance of a shot as you went down the Stour channel to the mouth of the river. The channel is some ten miles in length and three miles down the north shore Dodd heard wigeon whistling and charming in the still morning air. The dawn light was breaking and Dodd held up and charged his muzzle-loader giving him the best possible chance of making a shot. As luck would have it he pushed slowly on and came upon a small sitting of wigeon, his shot was successful and he bagged nine.

After picking up and reloading he crossed to the south shore navigating a further two miles of the main channel. On approaching Woodfleet he observed a party of mallard on the move. By now he was half way down the river and the sun was rising when he spotted where the ducks had pitched in. They were clustered on a creek edge allowing Dodd to make his silent approach with the help of the now slowing ebb tide. His shot found the centre of the sitting and he picked up five birds.

Reloading again he rowed hard for Harwich in order to make the most of the last of the ebb for if he had met the flood he knew full well his task would be much harder. Once he reached the mouth of the Stour he turned south-west and followed the shoreline heading for Mill Bay and thence to Hamford Water. On entering at Crabknowe Spit, Dodd attempted to stalk some brent geese but they would not stand the stalk and rose wild. Not disheartened he pressed on and at Pewit Island, where the creek ran up to the old cottages, he spied some grey geese. Setting to them, it was not long before they sensed the threat from the punt and walked up the mud. Although it was a longish shot Dodd had confidence in his old muzzle-loader and took the shot, knocking over and picking up three fine birds.

By the time the pick-up was completed the flood tide was well underway and Dodd turned up Oakley Creek, branched west into Bramble Creek and, getting ahead of the tide, he approached the mud flats known as Cunnyfur. Ahead of the punt was a nice sitting of green plover which he stalked and once more brought his faithful gun into action. This resulted in seventeen lapwings being brought to hand. Now the tide covered the mudflats and it was time to head for his brother's house, so he rowed south west and with the help of the tide made his way up the winding channel to the little hamlet of Landermere at the head of Hamford Water. Dodd arrived around 5pm to be met by his brother who had watched him row the final mile up the channel.

His brother provided Dodd with some welcome refreshment and his tea. He was anxious to know how Dodd had fared as it was his job to take the bag to a shop in Clacton-on-Sea where they would be sold the following day. The punt and gun were securely moored and at this juncture you would have thought Dodd might have stayed the night with his brother but there was no chance of that. Dodd set off to walk the eleven miles back to Manningtree as there was work to be done in the morning. Eventually, he arrived home at 9 pm having travelled eighteen miles on the tidal water in his punt and walked eleven miles home, all in all a sixteen hour day.

This then was the life of the coastal gunner. Make no mistake the competition was ferocious and the reward for such effort was small but this is what men did to earn a living and many would not have changed it for the world.

Stanley Duncan gives us an insight into what a professional wildfowler might earn in a season. He knew of one south coast fowler who moved to the Humber estuary where he spent the winter fowling and in the summer months acted as a boatman at seaside pleasure resorts. Fowling on the Humber from September to February at the turn of the century, his very best season brought him an income of £90. His bag of geese was 190 which he sold for two shillings and sixpence each, an income of £23-15s in total. In addition there was the income derived from the sale of 850 ducks, plover and other waders. His expenses in powder and shot were £7-10s which left him £82-10s for six months work, roughly £3-6s per week. This may not seem a lot but in 1900 the agricultural labourer's wage was less than a pound per week.

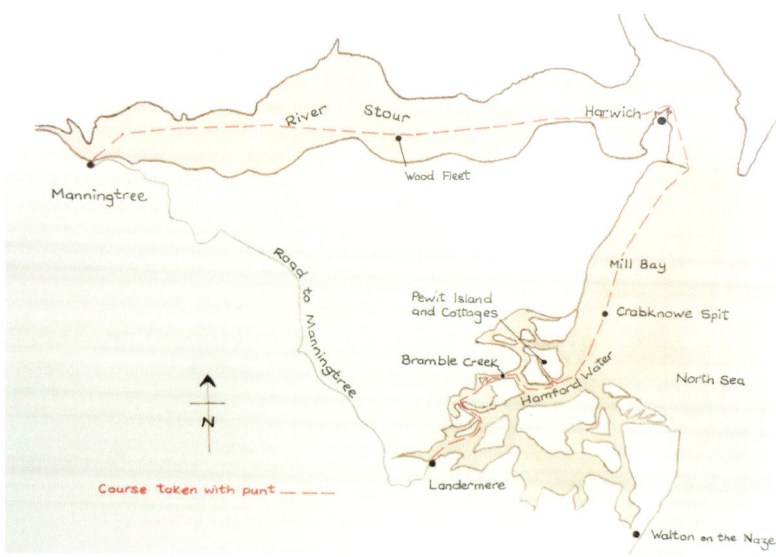

Dodd's adventure

3

The Victorian collectors

"Ye fowlers' manly strength your toil requires;

Defiance of the summer's burning sun

And winter's keenest blast, of hail or storm

Of ice or snow; nor must the marsh

That quivers to your step deter you."

Fowling – a poem 1808 John Vincent

Victorian Britain must have been a very exciting time for anyone passionate about birds. The coastal wildfowler was indeed passionate about wildfowl and waders and he was at the very forefront of studies of his quarry. Unwittingly the fowler became an expert ornithologist but he may only have regarded himself as a knowledgeable sportsman. Often what was hit really did become history and what was missed remained a mystery. Little was known about migration, less still about bird plumage and it was a time when, every year, undiscovered rare migrants were being identified. The very foundation of our knowledge about birds often lay in the hands of the fowler. A dead bird cannot lie and, throughout the land, museums and collectors were crying out for rare specimens; taxidermists' businesses flourished and a very useful shilling was turned by the fowler who bagged a rarity; and if it was not a rarity it was food.

Wandering bird watchers did of course exist, but they were at a decided disadvantage. Telescopes of the day were fairly primitive and better for watching ships than birds. Binoculars arrived towards the latter part of the nineteenth century but lens quality was poor. Cameras needed two people to carry them and travel was not easy until the railway network was widely established.

Today it seems unthinkable that a notable bird sighting might become a commission for the fowler; but how else could a rare sighting be verified? Some collectors were obsessive but thank goodness they were. Take Edward Thomas Booth (1840-1890), a wealthy Victorian eccentric who founded the Booth Museum in Brighton (1874). When he shot a bird he also collected

Edward Thomas Booth

specimens of the surrounding habitat adding meticulous detailed notes and sketches which were later recorded in three heavy folio volumes which he modestly called his 'Rough Notes'. Returning to his workshop, instructions were given to Savill, his taxidermist, to prepare a 'diorama' displaying the birds in their natural habitat. Savill never used perishable material or natural grasses when constructing the display cases, he made artificial tree-trunks and flowering plants and used papier-mache to make rocks, which is why to this day the display cabinets are so well preserved. The Booth Museum of Natural History flourishes under the management of the local authority and is well worth a visit. Booth's two punt guns are also on display with his punt.

The value and importance of collections may be hard to appreciate; take for example, Lieut.-Colonel Stonham's collection which, on his death was presented to his old school, the King's School Canterbury. This collection was reputed to be one of the finest in existence and comprised 200 cases all of which were collected before the First World War.

At the University Museum of Zoology, Cambridge you will find 450 specimens representing 210 species which were presented to the museum in 1950 by Clifford D. Borrer a naturalist and author who wrote using the name 'Sea Pie'. He was a well-known gunner on the East coast and many of the specimens he shot passed through the hands of Harry N. Pashley, the celebrated naturalist and bird stuffer who lived at Cley-next-the-Sea, Norfolk.

Starting with Hawker and looking back at the long history of books written by wildfowlers about wildfowling, you will invariably find that a large section of all these books is devoted to birds of the foreshore, their habits and distribution. Wildfowl and wader movement has always fascinated the fowler who gained an understanding of quarry species by noting seasonal changes, the influence of tides and wind that all helped to fill the bag. Observing birds in remote surroundings has always been a compelling element of the sport and our understanding of the habits of fowl today owes much to wildfowlers who exchanged, compared and recorded information. The end of the nineteenth and the beginning of the twentieth century was a particularly important time for previously undiscovered bird identification. That same fascination continues to this day. The letters we have uncovered show that there was regular and frequent correspondence between such eminent authors as Millias, Chapman, R. J. Ussher, Payne-Gallwey and Booth, all serving to illustrate the extraordinary drive the Victorians exhibited to unravel the mysteries of the birds of the foreshore. To emphasise this matter, at the turn of the nineteenth century, 'The Shooting Times and British Sportsman' advertised, 'The Shooting Times Field Club - Founded for the popularising of Natural History, more Particularly Ornithology and Zoology in the British Islands and Abroad.' Readers were invited to send accounts of birds observed and any interesting matters pertaining to the Natural History world. Dead game, birds and animals could all be sent to Mr W. A. Nicholson F.Z.A. (Scotland) and, providing they were properly packed, they were submitted for identification or analysis and thereafter often discussed within the content of the weekly publication. In fact, in almost every edition of the,' Shooting Times' before the First World War there was much discussion about ornithology and natural history.

4

Cometh the age of the railway

"Well may we pause to-day! May fortune smile

As kindly on each fowler's gen'rous toils

As she has done on ours!"

Anon

In 1850 the main rural transport of the day was the horse drawn carriage and dog cart. The isolated coastal villages and remote marsh lands were seldom visited by outsiders and sport remained the domain of the local fowler. Knowledge of the movement of wildfowl and waders was the key to their success and even this was closely guarded by the experienced fowlers. Good wildfowlers were proud of their reputation and this earned them much respect in their local community.

The building of the first public railway network was started in 1830 and by the middle of the 1840s many major towns had rail connections and sometimes they were served by as many as two or three lines. The result was that previously remote coastal wildfowling resorts gradually became increasingly accessible and were now in reach of town and city dwellers who were quick to recognise the opportunity to experience an exciting new form of free shooting that until then they had only read about. The coming of the railway network brought a less obvious effect on the lives of longshoremen. Hives of industry surrounding the hinterland of ports had hitherto been sustained by river traders transporting in and taking away goods and material by boat but now the railways provided an alternative method of transport and this slowly brought about a decline in the number of small smacks and working barges trading all around the coast. Longshoremen recognised that wildfowling and the chartering of their fishing smacks and small yachts could provide a valuable alternative source of income.

With the decline of river trade, it was not long before fewer resources were being devoted to managing the river channels. The old method of construction of headwater lagoons which were used to flush and scour the silt at low water were still in use but dredging, which was more expensive, was sometimes abandoned. This made navigation to the small ports more hazardous and many rivers leading to smaller ports became narrow silted channels with a trickle of water running between extensive mud banks. The result was a rapid decline in river trade and a corresponding decline in the opportunities for employment.

By 1850 wildfowling had begun to increase in popularity as a sport, undoubtedly due, as previously mentioned, to the publication of successive editions of Colonel Peter Hawker's book, 'Instructions to Young Sportsmen'. Those newly attracted to the sport often came from amongst the educated and better off and were inevitably referred to by the professionals as " fowl scaring toffs from Lunnon." We venture to suggest that they were attracted by a spirit of adventure which coastal wildfowling conjured up in an almost romantic way and, of course, with the added attraction that the sport was free.

'Marshman' recounts his adventure with Gaffer Gilson on an east coast estuary

Here is an account of sport written by 'Marshman' after he met Gaffer Gilson (GG), a professional wildfowler, whilst on holiday shouldergunning on the East coast. Imagine this conversation taking place around a roaring driftwood fire in a quayside tap room parlour where fowler and fisherman gather. The story of their day afloat follows;

"We sighted a wonderful gert pack o' wigeon on the banks s'marnin, an' I shall be after 'em well afore sun-up to-morrow. If so be as ye'd care to come along o'me you're welcome maister." Having delivered the foregoing unwanted flow of oratory, GG called somewhat boisterously for a "go of rum in water," charged and lighted a very short and over-ripe-looking clay pipe with a wooden spill, and seated himself in a highly polished and particularly uncomfortable Windsor chair.

Yes, of course, I would accompany the old big-gunner on the morrow, for although I had enjoyed some fairly good shore and flight shooting, never a shot had I fired from a gunning-punt during the fortnight's sojourn in the "one hoss" little town of H., which stands on the fringe of a vast expanse of marshes, overlooking a certain East Coast estuary, the sanctuary of legions of wildfowl in the winter months.

I was up betimes next morning, but ere I had finished my early breakfast I heard the clatter of GG's heavy sea-boots on the cobble-stones outside, and a minute later he entered the room with the news that, "wind and tide wor jest right for settin' to the fowl on the banks." He also expressed some little surprise at finding a keen big-gunner devouring breakfast when he should have been fully equipped and ready to embark. I did not keep the old chap waiting long, however, and taking my eight-bore from the corner of the apartment I accompanied him down the crooked, cobble-paved streets to a patch of shingly beach where a number of both double and single handed gunning-punts were hauled up high and dry, while a dozen or so antiquated but nevertheless serviceable, stanchion-guns reposed on a wooden rack, exposed to the weather and open to the ravages of the prowling thief. But neither wind nor weather can damage these ancient duck-guns, for their barrels are coated with grey paint, their muzzles plugged against rain, snow and salt spray, and their locks and breech parts clothed in waterproof canvas. Considering the pilfering fraternity, well old Gilson will tell you that a dishonest man may not be found in his native village. Let this be as it may, it would require an enterprising and Herculean thief to bear off one of these great fowling-pieces. The launching of the punt and loading and rigging of the stanchion-gun in the bows of the shallow craft did not occupy very much time, although the work was done by the feeble light of a much-battered hurricane lamp.

"We be the first gunners afloat s'marnin', an' they do say 'tis the y'urly bird as catches the wurrm," chuckled old Gilson as he shoved into the narrow winding gully, which with the rising tide would carry us to the great banks of sea-wrack-covered ooze, the favourite feeding-ground of thousands of wildfowl.

The first grey tokens which herald the approach of day were beginning to appear on the eastern horizon as we set out for the open estuary, my companion negotiating the sinuosities of the gully with the setting stick in that skilful manner born of life-long experience, which gives a professional punt-gunner such an immense advantage over the average amateur in the pursuit of fowl among the tortuous waterways that intersect the mud-flats. The tide was making rapidly, the gully running half bank high while the out-lying banks were well awash. Very soon the whistling of pinions and the merry "cackle" of a team of mallard passing overhead warned us that the flight of the fowl from their nocturnal feeding-grounds inland had already commenced and through the uncertain light we caught a momentary glimpse of their shadowy forms winging seaward. Then our ears were treated to the hoarse 'trumpeting' of a herd of pink-foot geese, which at the peep o'day deemed it wise to leave their favourite haunt on a treacherous sand-ridge and repair to the marshes and uplands.

"Drat they noisy ode varmints o'geese" growls Gilson, under his breath, "they kick up as much fuss as a pack of 'ounds, but nary pull can a big-gunner get into 'em. They allus favours the shore-poppers, and be damned to 'em."

Now, as to whether G's vituperation was hurled at the heads of the pink-feet or at the shore-shooter, whom he slightingly designates 'shore-poppers' I know not; but one thing is certain, by far the greater number of grey geese which are shot on our coasts during the winter months fall to the gun of flight-shooters. The heavens brighten perceptibly, and for our sport all too quickly. The broad belt of light cast by the pile lighthouse athwart the grey waters of the estuary waxes pale and sickly, and lights displayed by the fleet of smacks trawling out on the main as dimly as glow-worms in a hedgerow on a hazy summer night. But we are drawing very close to the middle banks, and ever and anon the far reaching "wheoh" of the wigeon or quacking of mallard is borne down to us on the light but piercingly cold north-easterly breeze, which as luck has it, is well-nigh dead ahead, and therefore we have the satisfaction of knowing that the keen scented fowl cannot possibly wind us.

"Do'ee yere they ode fowl a-talkin', maister? I doubt not there be a tidy lot under Cockle Bank, so keep a bright look-out," whispered my companion, as he dexterously and silently propelled the low-sided, shallow draft gunning craft nearer and nearer towards the sea-wrack-covered banks of slob.

Now the side of the gully nearest the banks was flanked by a high ridge of sand, locally known as Cockle Bank, and by hugging this we were well screened from the quick-sighted fowl and would, unless some unforeseen incident occurred to set them a-wing, be able to approach to well-nigh within range of the big stanchion-gun under cover of the ridge. Foot by foot and fathom by fathom crept the punt towards the still invisible fowl, until one could distinctly hear the curious slopping kind of noise which surface-feeding ducks and geese make in tearing up succulent grass-like weed which forms their staple food on the coast. A keen and ardent punt-gunner alone can imagine the intense excitement which takes possession of the wildfowler afloat when, after a long and difficult set to a company of fowl, he finds himself gradually but surely approaching within shot of his quarry. When through the uncertain light of the early morning I sighted right ahead an indistinct, but nevertheless unmistakable, close packed group upon a comparatively small patch of tide lapping slob, I tell you that the blood simply raced through my veins. I dared scarcely breathe or move an eyelid, and oh! how my tingling, frost-numbed fingers itched to tug at the trigger string and send a pound of shot pellets hurtling into the dense mass of feathered ranks.

"Don't pull until they rise from the slob," came the almost inaudible and quite unnecessary order from the old gunner. Hardly had the command been given, and while the birds were still out of range, to my utter surprise and unspeakable disgust a bright flash spurted out of a small gut which drained into the main gully at a point about one hundred and fifty yards above us. The flash was answered by a deep report of a punt gun which awakened the slumbering echoes of the morning and went booming across the vast expanse of tide and mud and salting. With a great to-do the fowl rose in a great cloud and headed towards the open estuary. A march had been stolen upon us and for a space of at least a minute and while the unknown gunner was busy picking up, Gilson and I stared blankly and sadly at each other. Then giving vent to a mighty curse, the old gunner shipped the sculls and pulled slowly and silently up a salting-fringed creek in the forlorn hope of picking up a stray duck or curlew with his shoulder gun.

Half-an-hour later a sprightly young wildfowler came poling along the creek in a light single-handed punt, the floor of which was richly decorated with wigeon, duck and teal. It was Gilson's youngest offspring, and roundly did the old man rate him as a, "pesky, undutiable son" for having spoilt for us the best chance of this season.

5

The increasing influence of the written word

"Then talk no more of future gloom;

Our joys shall always last;

For hope shall brighten days to come,

And memory gild the past."

Thomas Moore 1780-1852

The advent of a new magazine named, 'The Field,' first published in 1853, stimulated wider interest in wildfowling and in 1857 John Henry Walsh (Stonehenge) was editing the magazine. By 1858 he published his own book, 'The Shot-Gun and Sporting Rifle'. In the chapter headed ' Wildfowl Shooting' he acknowledges that it was the writings of Colonel Hawker that were responsible for introducing the sport of duck and wader shooting to wider public notice.

Articles written about wildfowling thereafter were regularly published in 'The Field'. A regular contributor was Henry Coleman Folkard, a barrister-at-law and author of the book, 'The Wild-Fowler,' published in 1859. Less well known are the excellent articles Folkard wrote, under the pen name Hoary Frost in 'The Sporting Magazine', headed, 'Days and Nights of Wild-Fowl Shooting.' Although Folkard's book was well written and comprehensive he has not gone down in history as a great authority on wildfowling. He was passionate about boats and author of another book in 1853 entitled, 'The Sailing Boat,' a treatise on English and foreign boats and yachts, one chapter being devoted to boats for wildfowl shooting. A further development of the post Hawker era was now emerging which embraced the use of the sailing boat and small yachts for wildfowl shooting at sea. The shooting yacht armed with a stanchion gun was attracting wealthy gentlemen to go in search of fowl beyond the fowling grounds where a gunning punt could safely navigate. The subject of sailing to fowl will be considered further in a later chapter.

Although 'The Field' magazine undoubtedly contributed to the growing interest in wildfowling, a new weekly magazine first published in 1882 was to change the course of wildfowling. 'The Wildfowler's Shooting Times and Kennel News' was edited by a flamboyant journalist named Mr

Sailing to brent geese

Lewis Clement who had formerly acted as reporter for all matters related to dogs and wildfowling for 'The Field.'

'Lew', as he was known, was now 38 and fanatical about the sport of wildfowling. He had earlier adopted the pen names 'Wildfowler' and 'Snapshot,' travelling throughout the Continent and visiting many of the coastal wildfowling resorts in Britain. His first book, published in two volumes, 'Shooting and Fishing Trips in England, France, Alsace, Belgium, Holland and Bavaria' described his travels to localities where wildfowl and other shooting could be obtained. The following year in 1877 two further volumes were published over the heading, 'Shooting, Yachting, Sea Fishing Trips at Home and on the Continent'. Two more books were added in 1880, one on loads for shoulder guns and punt guns, which is scarce, and 'Modern Wildfowling' which is now regarded as a wildfowling classic.

One further book was published in 1881 by Lewis Clement who was now living in the village of Framilode, on the banks of the Severn estuary in Gloucestershire, which brought about another major change to wildfowling as a sport. 'Public Shooting Quarters', subtitled as a descriptive list of localities where wildfowl and other shooting could be obtained, was another Field publication. This remarkable little book became a 'must read' for all budding wildfowlers and listed countless places where free shooting could take place. Consequently it rapidly became the talking point of every gunner.

Low water, Essex Smack with two punts astern

Sadly, Lewis Clement's journalistic career was to come to a rather abrupt and ignominious end when, in 1906, he was sent to jail for fraud, related to the sale of working dogs. Nevertheless through his books and articles he left an indelible mark on the sport of wildfowling and stimulated many of the aristocracy to become immersed in the romance of wildfowling.

The gun trade also flourished as a result of articles published about wildfowling. Newcomers to the sport were anxious to buy the latest guns for their new found pastime and understandably the gun trade was quick to respond. Amateur and aspiring fowlers increased in number and many gunmakers responded by developing new innovative punt and shoulder guns built to meet the demands of their new found clientele of well-heeled city dwellers. Hitherto, the muzzle-loading shotgun was the fowlers' choice but now the breech-loading action was the design that every sportsman was talking about. The new guns were widely advertised by such companies as Moore and Grey, W.W. Greener, J & W Tolley, Holland and Holland and Thomas Bland.

This was the beginning of what many regard as the zenith of wildfowling. Up until this time transport had been the limiting factor for the amateur fowler. Furthermore, until Lewis Clement's, Public Shooting Quarters book was published, few people knew where to go wildfowling and were wary of local regulations that might exist. With the coming of the railways and a 'Guide Book' of coastal resorts, gentlemen could now leave London and, in no time at all, visit the coast and spend a day or two exploring fowling grounds that, until then, had been the professional fowler's exclusive domain. The coastal resorts, particularly those of the east and south coasts, were the most popular. Hotels and inns advertised the services of personal guides for any gentlemen wishing to have a stroll along the shore with a gun. Guides were often the local fishermen fowlers, who could show the incomers the best places to shoot or fish. Local men had been quick to adapt, offering hospitality and a guide service for which they earned a welcome addition to their income. The visitors would often hire a punt and gun together with a puntsman to manage the craft. For the more adventurous, fishing smacks or yachts could be hired with a swivel gun mounted in the bows to pursue wildfowl and other seabirds on open water outside the sanctuary of the local harbour. All species were fair game, either for food or as specimens for the bird collectors who employed taxidermists to preserve their trophies.

By the latter part of the nineteenth century many of the famous estuaries and resorts for fowl around the coast of Britain were so disturbed that they were virtually devoid of birds with the amateur sportsmen 'popping off' all along the shore during the day and the professional fowlers punting at night.

Doubtless it was the indiscriminate shooting of everything that flew over the coastal foreshore, saltings and estuary waters that hastened the scrutiny of early legislation which made an attempt to give a degree of legal protection to birds. Ineffectual legislation dating from 1869 (The Sea-Birds Preservation Act) was eventually replaced by the Wild-Birds Protection Act which came into force in 1872. It divided birds into two groups, the scheduled and the unscheduled, which gave protection to wildfowl and waders from 15 March until 1 August (revised in January 1882 to 1 March until 1 August). It also gave County Councils the opportunity to use their discretion to defer locally the start of the closed season and alter when the season ended. Indiscriminate shooting which threatened the breeding success of birds certainly came under better control as a result of the Act but Stanley Duncan, writing much later in 1911, commented that the Act had become confused and complicated and there was underlying concern that it was depriving sportsmen of the privileges hitherto enjoyed. Writing his, 'Jottings for Wildfowlers' in the Shooting Times he states, "that unless steps are speedily taken to annul the progress of anti-cruelty faddists we (wildfowlers) shall soon be in a state of deadlock." Later chapters will show how right he proved to be.

6

Sport on board a shooting yacht

"And winter's eve, when our sport we leave

And on board so snugly lie,

How each one talks of the crashing shot

And the ducks that are to die."

Anon

The very rich were not concerned by the new legislation. They did not shoot wildfowl for a food source, nor did they sell them to provide income. It was sport that interested them and they were not confined to home waters. Shooting yachts were commissioned or built to an individual's preference. Live-aboard facilities and a full time crew enabled wealthy sportsmen to cruise all around the coasts of Britain, Ireland and beyond.

The following abridged version of an article written by H. C. Folkard in 1856 admirably describes wildfowling from a shooting yacht with mounted swivel gun.

"From punts and punt gun I launched into further extravagance; nor felt fully equipped until I had a shooting-yacht and swivel gun, and put to sea to try my luck at brent geese. This was by far the most expensive undertaking I had yet ventured on; but being naturally fond of water, and knowing the same yacht would answer every purpose of pleasure cruising, and fishing in summer, as well as the more formidable proceeding of wildfowl shooting in winter, I had beside another object in view. My poor old sporting boatman was getting too feeble to work his gunning punt; having observed on our last punting excursion, a visible lack of strength on his part, I feared the venerable old sportsman had well-nigh finished his sporting career.

I was therefore the more anxious for a shooting yacht, that my old friend Crimp might accompany me, and thus continue the enjoyment without fatigue of his favourite sport. I had made a companion of him because I knew no equal in the land. He had done everything in his power to instruct me in the secrets and mysteries of an art, of which he was assuredly a perfect master.

Yachtsmen of the present day who take their pleasure cruises in summer, dismantle their yachts of the sunny-sky canvas as soon as the season is over, and substitute smaller sails of stouter material, fit a chock and swivel on the bows and thus convert their vessel into a shooting-yacht.

Sailing to fowl at sea

It may be amusing for some readers to give a brief outline of a shooting-yacht and the cost of its equipment. For sea going purposes the yacht should be from fifteen to twenty tons, the cost of which is from three to five hundred pounds (only the very rich could afford such extravagance), it should be of easy draught of water; a fast but stiff burdensome vessel; a yawl, if a gun is to be worked from the cabin hatchway, but cutter rigged if the gun is to be worked over the bows from the forecastle hatchway. The cost of a sound gun carrying 1½ lbs. shot is with fittings, £50. Many gentlemen go to greater extravagance and spend £100 upon a swivel gun but this is not necessary. A yacht of this tonnage requires three hands to manage her. That is to say two men and a boy and this allows the yachtsman to devote his whole attention to the swivel gun.

The most difficult art a tyro has to learn is to judge distance. Small objects such as brent geese on the open sea are so deceptive to the eye that a good deal of practice is necessary before a man can correctly judge gun-shot range.

Black geese (brent) afford the finest sport of any of the wildfowl species for the yacht and swivel gun, in severe weather they come over from the Continent in immense flocks and are well worth powder and shot and are the finest flavour of all wildfowl that is brought to the table. When a flock of black geese is discovered at sea, it should first be considered whether they can be fetched to windward; for it is invariably found useless to attempt getting into range by running dead to leeward. The sportsman should bear away, or make two or three tacks in the contrary direction until he can find that he can fetch well to windward, then by reaching along at full sail the birds are on his lee bow and the sails of the yacht hide the deck from view so nothing can be seen stirring aboard. The moment the geese rise the helm should be put down to luff the yacht into the eye of the wind. Then is the time, if the birds are within range, to pull the trigger. Beware the danger of shooting away the yacht's rigging through over excitement.

Following pages: Sailing to brent geese

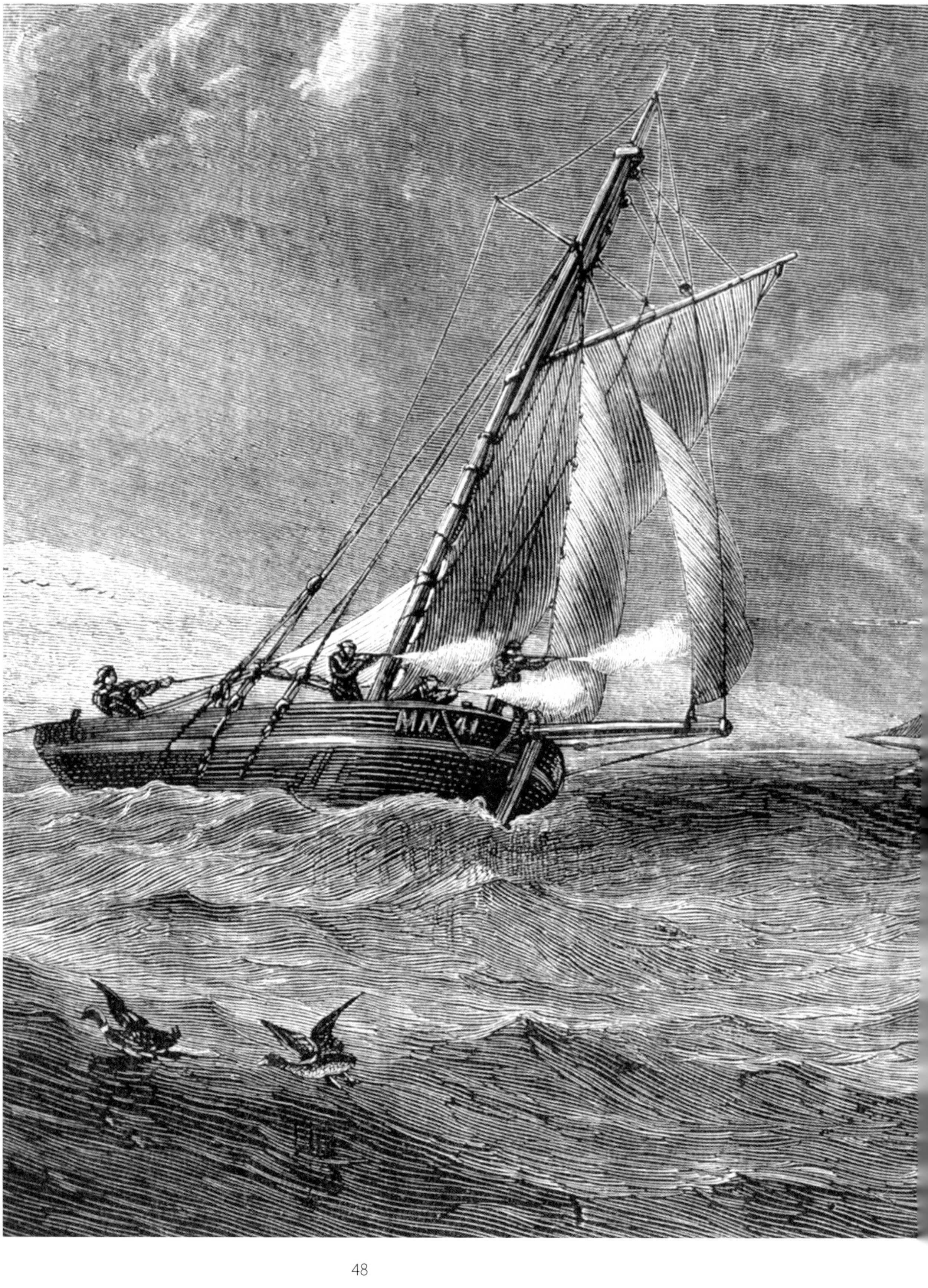
MN 41

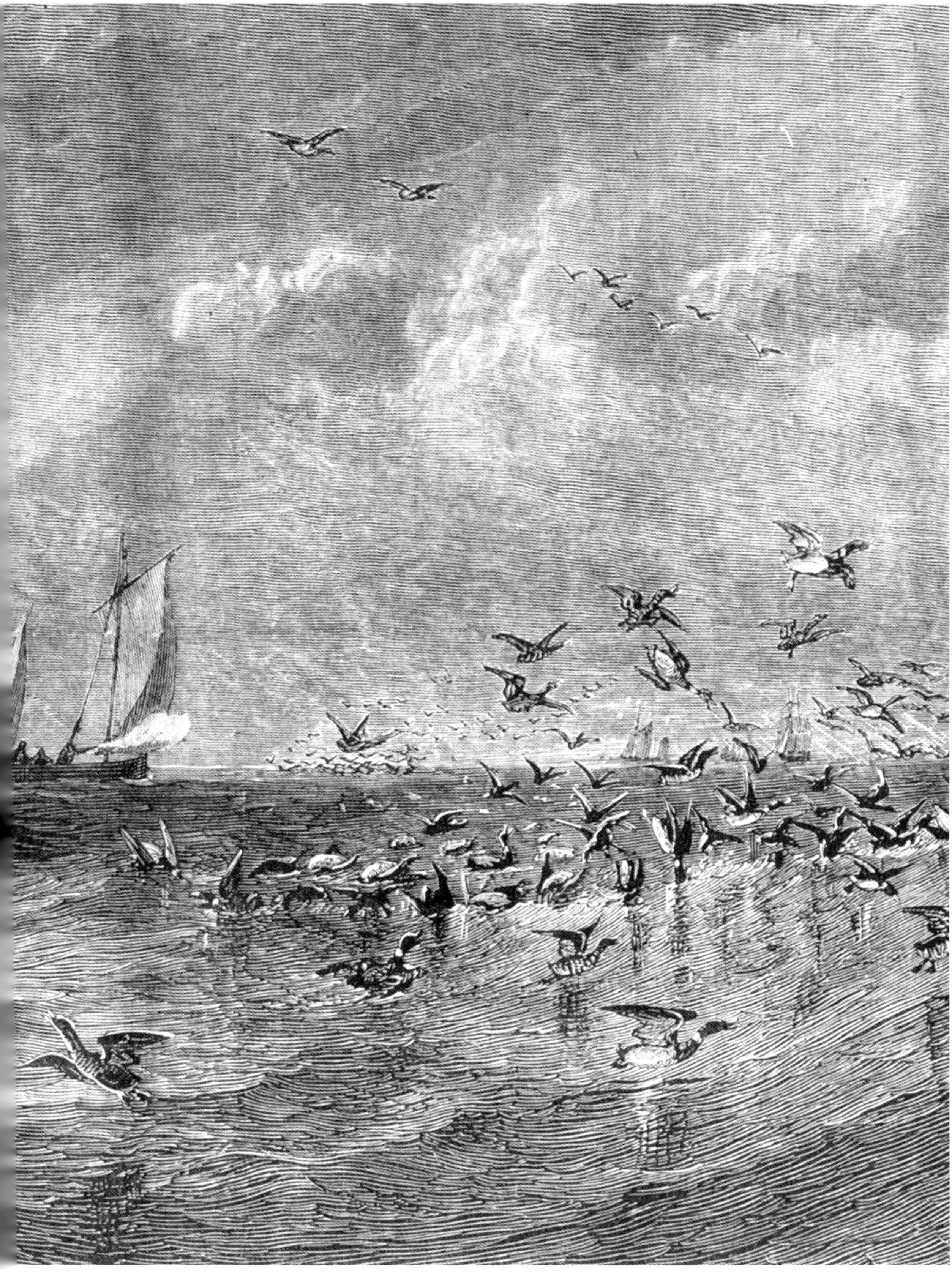

As there is generally a great deal of powder aboard a shooting-yacht, everyone should be cautious when lighting a pipe or cigar. The powder must be kept dry and should be in canisters and stored well away from the cabin fire as an accident would inevitably blow the yacht to atoms. It is usual to keep guns loaded aboard but never leave a gun or take it into the cabin without taking the caps off the nipples and placing a piece of tow over the touch hole.

Let no sudden surprise induce a man to forget he holds in his hand the most dangerous of all weapons and the slightest thoughtless action may cause a fatal accident. I can picture to myself no sharper sting of remorse than to have hurried a fellow man into eternity through a careless incaution.

Mild winters are unfavourable for wild goose shooting; for besides the scarcity, the birds are generally more wary in mild weather than in severe conditions. Sailing to fowl necessitates great skill in handing a sailing yacht and equal skill on the part of the gunner. The sport is exciting, healthy and invigorating to those whose constitution enables them to bear the cold without inconvenience, and cold enough it is at times but when success is achieved the sport remains unequalled by any other form of wildfowling."

Many gentlemen not only cruised the home shores but also visited the Dutch and German coastlines, where extensive fowling grounds provided exceptional sport in the autumn, when large numbers of ducks and geese were on migration. These yachts, some in excess of 60 feet long, were capable of carrying gunning punts and a following boat. The crew, with their gentlemen fowlers on board would often remain at sea for a month or more at a time following the fowl. Fowling on Continental waters is considered more extensively in later chapters.

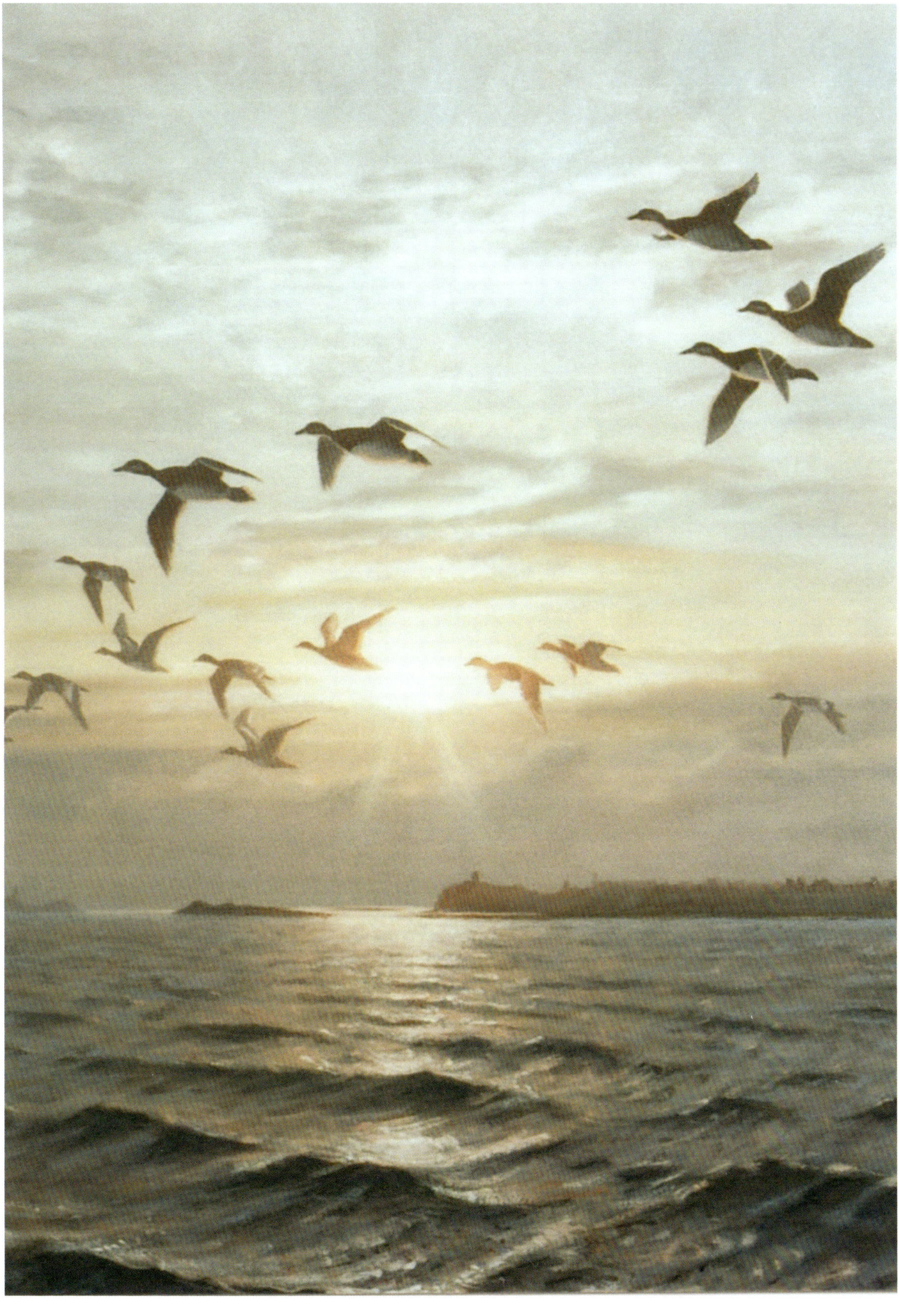

7

A TIME FOR INNOVATION

"Loud murmured the ocean with downward growl

The sea swam aloof, and the dark seafowl,

The pye-duck, sought the depth of the main,

And rose in the wheel of the wake again."

Reginald of Durham 12th century

THE ELECTRIC GUNNING PUNT

Challenging conditions on home estuaries did not deter some wildfowlers and they turned to innovative methods to get on terms with their quarry. In 1884 an electric gunning punt was made by Messrs. Gilbert Boyle and Co, Glasgow. The punt was fitted with Clark's patent electro motor and battery and intended for use in Balcary Bay, on the north Solway coast and the fjords of Norway. The first boat of this description was built for Mr John Mackie of Auchencairn, Castle Douglas, principally for duck shooting but also to be carried on his steam yacht, '*Gellert*.' Trials took place on 4 January 1884 when Mr Mackie, Mr Whitney and Mr Clark, the patentee, were present. According to a report on the trial, the punt was 23ft long by 4ft 6inch beam with a draught of 9inches. A two bladed propeller was driven at 500 revolutions per minute when two batteries were in use, giving a maximum speed of four knots. Four years later the same man was to develop his new idea of a semi-submersible punt.

A rather less successful idea was developed by Mr William Jeans from Christchurch. His new invention incorporated a 3ft. diameter wheel placed under the foredeck which was then connected by a shaft to a propeller, the wheel being cranked by the forward facing puntsman. Experiments with this punt proved disappointing as the speed of the forward momentum of the punt was slower than the speed at which the ducks could swim away on open water.

The development of the idea of an electric gunning punt, which was designed to carry Mr Mackie's thirteen stone punt gun, prompted an anonymous punt gunner to ask; "Will the next step be torpedoes?"

The steam propelled semi–submersible gunning punt

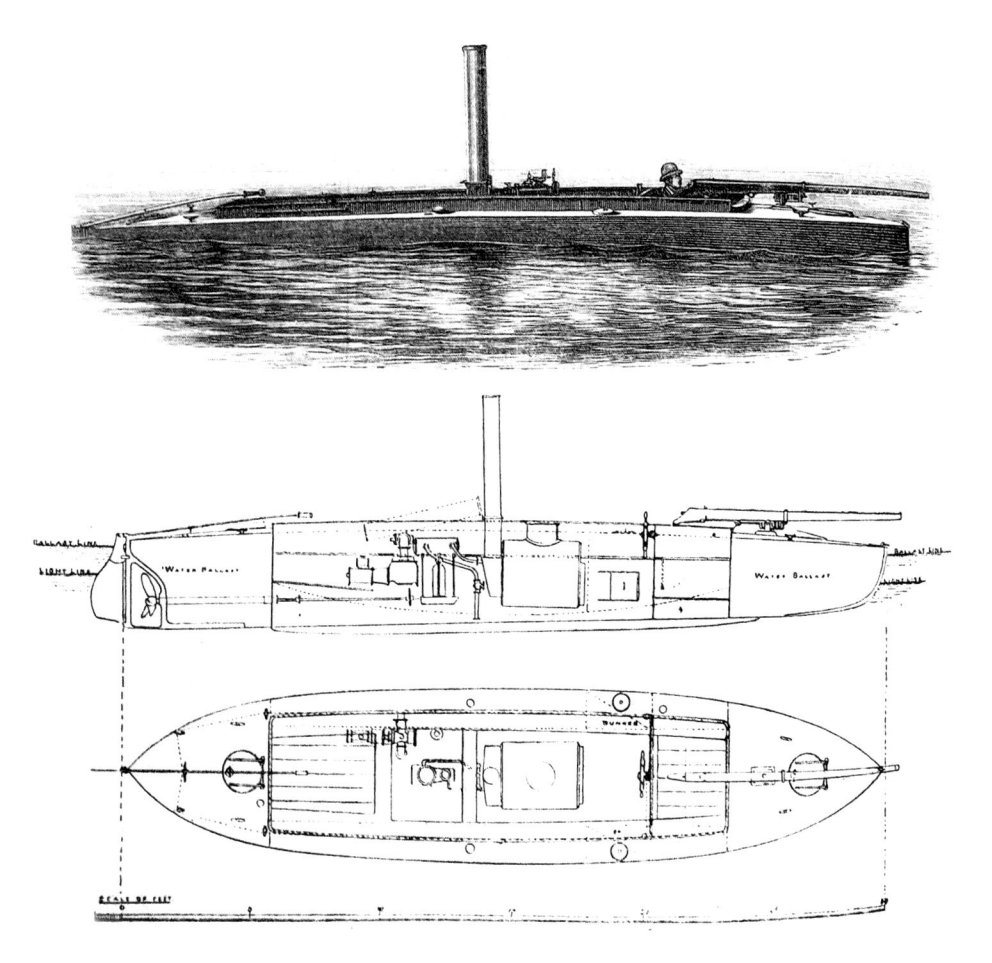

In 1888 Mr John Mackie, commissioned John Samuel White, of Cowes to build another unique punt in the form of a submersible steam launch. She was 30ft long with a 6ft. 6-inch beam and a draught of 3ft weighing an estimated six tons. This punt was made of galvanized steel with two separate watertight compartments fore and aft and tanks along each side. The compartments could be flooded using a Tangye pump which was capable of filling the compartments in five minutes. In so doing the punt took on the appearance of an ordinary duck punt. Reversing the situation, the tanks could be emptied in six minutes. Compound surface condensing engines provided 18 horse power to propel the punt and steerage was achieved through a stern rudder operated from the cockpit. Armament consisted of a 2 inch breech-loading Holland and Holland 'London' punt gun number 7305 originally breeched over the foredeck. The cost quoted was £335 in galvanised steel, but a cheaper wooden version was offered at £250. Mackie chose the galvanised build option.

There is no record of the wildfowling success achieved by John Mackie but we know that by 1890 the launch/punt was sold to Mr William Abdy Beauclerk (1859-1912), a London stockbroker. In the summer months he would sail competitively and in the winter he retained his friend and notable yachtsman Edward Sycamore (known as Syc) and together they went fowling on the east

The *Ironclad* at Brightlingsea after conversion

coast from the town of Brightlingsea. When he purchased Mackie's steel punt he christened her, *'Ironclad'*, most probably using at first his very successful racing yacht *'Babe'* as a fowling headquarters. At this point the armament section was re-planned due to it proving to be too wet at the bow and necessitating the extension of the foredeck to make it more seaworthy. The refit involved breeching two Holland and Holland guns in the centre of the punt and adding a 4 bore and an 8 bore to the arsenal. Beauclerk, writing about the severe winter of 1891-92, recounts how the punt achieved great success in pursuit of brent geese out on open water (the Main*) where they were feeding on the Zostera that had been torn out by the pack ice in the Blackwater and swept out to sea. The account of their adventures in the *'Ironclad'* and the various yachts they chartered including *'Alpha Beata'*, in the winter of 1892/93, *'Sapphire'* in 1894/95 and *'Manica'* (Nettle) in 1896/97, serves as a testimony to how popular wildfowling was at the time.

'The Ironclad' remained in Beauclerk's ownership until 1907 then, by 1908 Lloyds records, her owner was Mr F.W. Leith who lived on the houseboat *'Evandra'* at West Mersea.

Sadly history tells that Abdy Beauclerk shot himself in the mouth with a revolver at his office on 12 December 1912. He was only 53. His old pal and faithful companion Syc was at the head of the coffin when he was buried in New Southgate Cemetery a few days later.

*A term used to describe the sea off the Essex coast

Cometh the steam launch

With the advent of the steam launch it was not long before they were converted to carry punt guns. One such example was the *'Bacchante'* specially built for wildfowling and sailing out of Brightlingsea, on the Essex coast. She was 32ft long with a beam of 6ft 6inches and drawing 2ft 6 inches, she could achieve a speed of 10 knots per hour and carried two punt-guns. One gun was 9 ft. long with 1½ inch bore, weighing 170lbs and fired 1½ lbs of shot. A smaller gun was also mounted and breeched alongside. This gun was 7 ft. 6 inches in length, 1¼ inch bore weighing 75 lbs and loaded with ¾ lb of shot. These steam launches were well designed so that when approaching fowl the steam and smoke could be turned under water instead of up the funnel. Smokeless coal was frequently used and on some launches the funnel could even be dropped to make the launch less conspicuous to fowl. It was not unusual for the charted launches to stay at sea for several days. The experienced crew would watch for fowl and call the gentleman gunners topside when the opportunity for a shot arose.

Footnote: Shooting from mechanically propelled boats and pursuing wildfowl from such a boat is now prohibted.

LEWIS CLEMENT RECOUNTS A STEAM LAUNCH ADVENTURE ON THE SOUTH COAST

"What swarms of fowl have been shot over the last pipe.

And when accompanied by grog it is simply slaughter."

Anon

The following account gives a wonderful insight into wildfowling aboard a steam launch. "It had been blowing exceedingly hard for three days when we started from Cowes, on our trip in the good steam launch *'Swallow'*, (old style). Joking apart, she is as good and as trim a little craft as any man could wish and we spent two happy days in her, steaming up and down the Solent and Southampton Water.

The *'Bacchanté'* (steam launch) in pursuit of wild swans off the Essex coast

The crew consisted of two men and the owner, James H and myself were the only passengers. From long experience we had both found out that more than two guns on any craft is a mistake. It does not conduce to one's peace of mind to know, for instance, that behind you whilst you are squatting in the bows watching for fowl, maybe some young fellow is fingering the trigger of a four bore loaded with ten or twelve drams and three ounces of shot! No it does not! Not by any means. Therefore, as we had both gone more than once through the momentary expectation of getting the said load raking us fore and aft, or rather aft and fore, on sundry previous trips, we had now come to the startlingly unanimous conclusion that we would get on much better by ourselves, and we laid plans accordingly in solemn conclave. With no less startling unanimity our crew endorsed our plan most heartily, and it seems they had good reason for it, for Jimmy told me that last season his cousin Georgie had actually fired a barrel of the cripple stopper 12 bore through the floor of the launch, within a foot of the Captain's legs. Small wonder then that this worthy fought shy of too many guns aboard.

"Yes," he said to me when explaining the affair, "Mr George he was a lingering of 'ere gun behind me, and I say to him, better be careful says I, when bang goes the lot into the planking! If it had not been that our lead and iron ballast stopped it there is no knowing but what we might have gone to the bottom too. Thank you sir, I like it warm please."

Well, then James and I were to be the only gunners. We took a single handed punt with us and had got her lashed on deck, bottom upwards, because we intended going on shallows and up the creeks whenever we could see any fowl or big shore birds about and of course the launch could not get near those gentry there on account of her draught.

We started at 4 am on Monday it was bitterly cold, and snow was topping the cliff by Netley. Just the sort of weather to get on, in fact, but the cabin fire was truly welcome after one had been on deck for an hour or so with the wind in his teeth. We had slept aboard so as to be ready for a start and the first notion I had of being underway was when we cleared fairly out of the harbour and headed for the Needles. There we met a chopping sea, which nearly pitched me from my berth on the cushions on to the floor, so I thought I had better get up which I did and went on deck. I found the launch hissing along through the sea at a fine rate and Jim forward, was rigging my punt gun over her bows. "Either of us", said he standing in the fore hatchway, "will have a good chance of scoring without being seen." "Just so" I replied, I will get the cartridges handy below, on the cushions, out of the spray.

Meanwhile one of the men was forward preparing our breakfast, to which we subsequently did honour and then thoroughly ready for the fray, just at daybreak, we took our stations, my friend in the hatchway with the punt gun loaded with S.S.G. shot as we expected to fall in with geese and I sitting on the cabin with my Dolland binoculars and two single four bores, one hammerless by Messrs Tolley and the other a hammer gun by Messrs Bland. For cripple work Jim had got hold of a double 8 bore Tolley. Of course I am aware that punters per se will deprecate steaming to fowl;' Twas ever thus! But let them grumble, we were ready to do battle. The only drawback was the noise of the engine and this had to be considered when we worked up to birds. To achieve this we had always to head to wind so as to avoid the birds hearing us from any distance, and the dodge moreover was to go full steam ahead until we got to within 300 yards of them , then she was eased and glided on to them noiselessly with her own impetus as though a thing of life. That is the way to do it.

We got our first shot off Lymington Creek. There were seventeen ducks, all bobbing on the tide heading up the breeze and our engineer to whom I handed my glass took their bearing so well that we went slap bang into them in a most masterly style. By preconcert arrangement I was to fire first so as to put them up, then the punt gun (whose load had been altered for duck) would sweep in their rising ranks. So on we went, the birds were on the starboard, and I had got hold of a 4 bore, loaded with BB shot. Forward was James in the hatchway, with his left hand on the pistol stock and his right with the trigger-thong coiled around it and he was looking very grim and making himself as small as he could, peering over the gun'ale . Behind me on my left were the men crouching by the engine which was now eased. On we go gliding almost imperceptibly, but swiftly all the same. The birds began to, 'smell a rat' and look rather dubiously at the advancing monster. At 150 yards they are looking up, at 120 yards they crowd a bit, at 100 yards I am clutching the 4 bore and Jim is squinting over his murderous barrel. 80 yards they are paddling, up I get, 'Bang', I kill outright one bird and another is hard hit, the rest are up and going. Boom goes the 14 oz. of shot into the flock and as the leaden hail whacks through them we see wings turning up in the smoke. All cleared we find nine fowl on the water with their paddles turned to the sky.

Our captain who has ("heye like a 'awk") presently says, extending his horney finger three points over the port quarter, "there be another burd settled yonder sir, I can take you right on to him when we have picked up these 'ere ones." The whole lot are picked up and then the captain heads for the fowl he has marked down. James shot the dropper at 50 yards with the cripple stopper and he was soon on board.

We then fell in with a fishing smack whose skipper called out that he had seen 200 or 300 geese off Keyhaven. "Hurrah!" said we, so we steamed along-side and handed him a glass of whisky, and he of course supplemented then his information, "they are near the flats" he said, "so you'll have to use yon punt of yours." And we parted.

The day had turned out very fine and most bitterly cold and we were glad to go below a bit, until our men called down that the geese were ahead. There was no one in sight so we augured well for our success. We at once got the punt ready and the sea being tolerably smooth, we launched her and riggered the big gun on her swivel and Jim went aboard. We then towed him above the birds and cast him off to enable him to row vigorously towards the shore.

It was a lovely scene we could now observe. Right behind the punt we could see on the horizon the New Forest; on the shore two little villages, in the distance Lymington, and Keyhaven. There on the green sea was my chum in the little boat forging ahead with a will, whilst the unconcerned geese were preening themselves and half a dozen of them were dozing peacefully with their heads under their wings. James was then 300yards from them. He shipped the oars, removed his seat, laid down flat, cocked the gun, placed the cripple stopper handy near his right hand and seizing the sculling oar, he began plying it with all his might.

The excitement aboard the steam launch mounted as we watched as the nearest birds shifted uneasily, the others however were unconcerned. I was looking at them with my glass when suddenly, all got up; about a dozen tumbled down. I looked at James and saw the punt gun smoking, and then came her roar on the wings of the breeze.

"Well done sir! Bravo!" Shouted the two men enthusiastically, and putting steam on we went as near my friend as we could. He soon came aboard with his spoils; we aligned fourteen geese in a row. Together we drank a 'bumper' of Geisler dry to celebrate whilst the men spliced the main brace with a drop of Irish cold.

We took home nearly forty birds in our two days and two nights .They consisted of geese , ducks wigeon, two divers, a grebe, five razor bills and a couple of cormorants for stuffing purposes, and three curlews. I forgot two woodpigeons which happened to fly overhead when we were at Keyhaven. That we enjoyed ourselves immensely goes without saying.

Footnote: The cost of hiring a smack and punt together with a skipper and another sailor's service was £1 per day in 1883. Lewis Clement found it difficult to secure the services of a man and a smack as they could earn £3 or £4 from the sale of birds if they went punting at night.

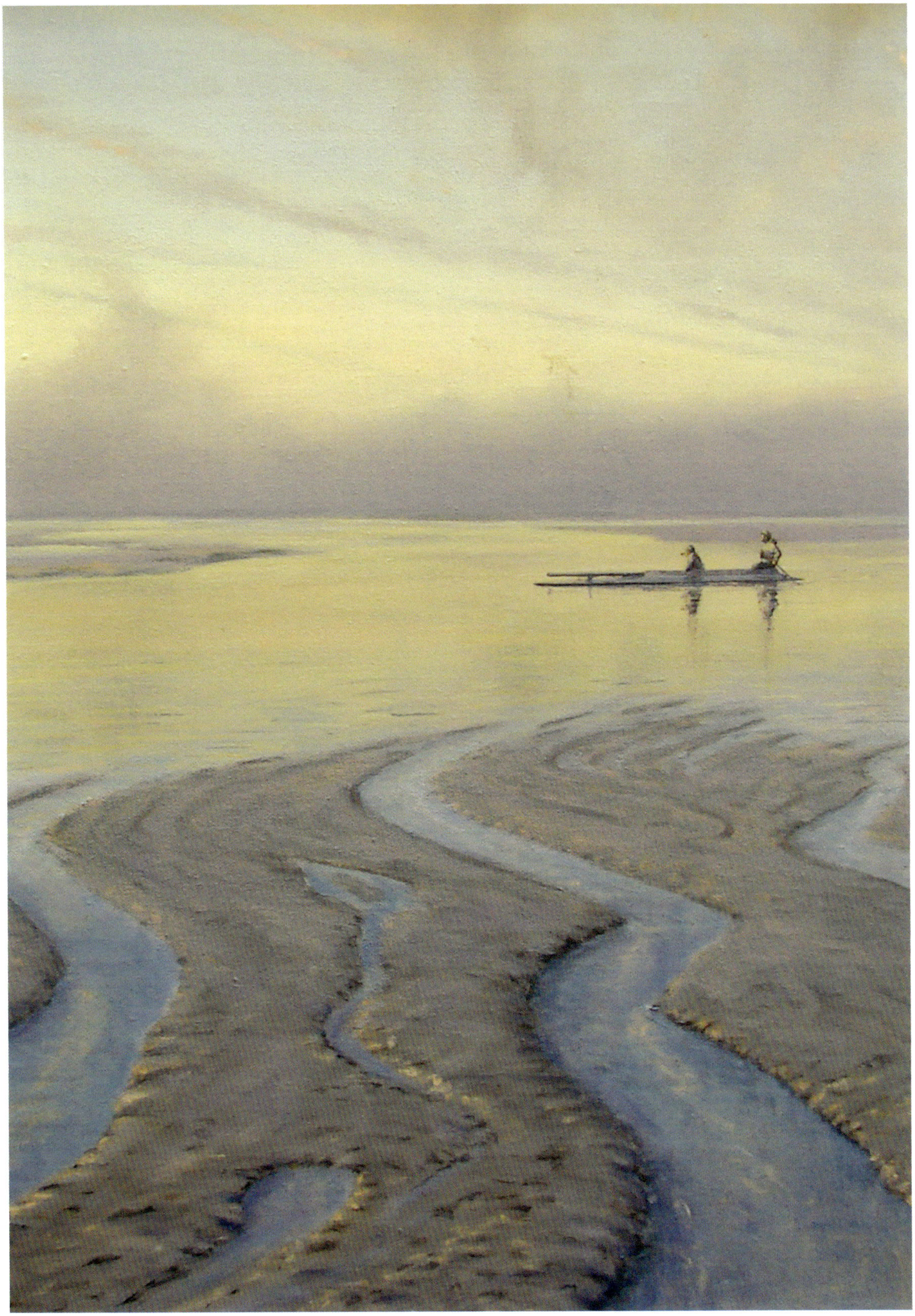

8

Legendary amateur gentlemen wildfowlers on the Essex coast

"The vanishing flocks, expelled from northern shores,

In varied forms pursue their trackless way,

Courting the genial aspect of the south,

Whilst iron Winter holds his despot sway. "

T. Hughes

Colonel Champion Russell punted the Blackwater. He commented on the growing intensity of fowling along the Essex coast; "Our coast is more disturbed than ever, people have taken to hunting the fowl in steam launches. Every bird that swims is driven away, even such rubbish as scoters, except the brent geese which keep well out of the way of boats, but will not however leave the country. I think they will soon cease to visit us. The disturbance is getting worse and worse and the feed failing more and more. The Zostera is gradually disappearing everywhere on the Essex coast and in the rivers. The geese have less and less feeding ground every year. There is hardly a place where they can sit at low water and feed far enough from the edge not to be liable to be disturbed. Yet the geese of late years come more regularly than thirty or forty years ago."

In 1881/82 the Colonel noted that brent geese came quite early considering the mildness of the weather. He records that there were about 300 in early autumn and numbers slowly built up to 1000 between the Blackwater and the Crouch Estuary. In 1883 he was on the Dutch coast aboard his 20 ton yacht *'Sheldrake'* and noted there were no young either in Holland or on the Main.

It was two decades earlier during the severe winter of 1860 that the Colonel commanded a flotilla of 32 punts that advanced upon a grand gathering of brent geese out on St Peter's Flats off Bradwell. On his signal all fired their punt guns bagging what has been recorded as Britain's largest punt gun shot of 704 Brent geese (an average of 22 birds per gunner).

Saturday, March 28th 1903. Colonel R.P. Davis pictured at the controls of his 10 horse power touring car. Beside him is his game keeper, 'Spider' Eaton. The brent geese are a result of a recent trip afloat in the *Tyche*. Eleven of the geese can be identified as juveniles; so the Summer of 1902 must have been a good breeding year for the brent in the Arctic. Standing is Bill Hammond a local punt gunner. Bill was known as the Skipper and with his brother Tom owned a fishing smack named *Madeleine* on which was mounted an 1¼ inch muzzle loading punt gun. They took out gentlemen fowlers including Clifford Borrer who wrote under the name of 'Sea Pie'. He referred to Bill and Tom as the Walton Brothers.

The most notorious amateur in the Walton Backwaters was Colonel R.P. Davis of New House Farm, Walton. He was High Sheriff for Essex, a Justice of the Peace and represented the Walton division of Essex on the County Council. Colonel Davis had been a punt gunner since he was a young man but, with advancing years, he decided to explore the possibilities of using a steam launch to pursue the fowl that seemed to be becoming more and more difficult to stalk successfully with his double punt. In 1894 he commissioned Forrests of Wivenhoe to build him a new steam launch. The launch was designed by Joseph Edwin Wilkens who had previously owned the Forrests' boat building yard up until its sale in 1888. Wilkens was a talented naval architect and his design work was in much demand until he was declared bankrupt in 1894.

The Colonel's new steam launch was to be 30 feet long and named '*Tyche*'. On delivery he employed Captain Griggs, who came from Brightlingsea, to skipper the launch. Griggs was also a professional fowler so he was a good hand to help the Colonel. '*Tyche*' had a hinged funnel that could

'Tyche'

be lowered when approaching fowl. Mounted in the bows were two swivel guns consisting of a fine 2 inch Moore and Grey breech-loader firing two pounds of shot and alongside was mounted a 1¼ inch muzzle-loader firing a pound of shot. Once the Colonel became accustomed to going afloat he put his gamekeeper Charles Eaton in charge of the launch. Eaton was known by all who knew him as 'Spider', this was on account of his arms being so long that his hands were nearly level with his knees!

A typical day out in *'Tyche'* would see the Colonel and friends cruising the Backwaters with Spider Eaton on the helm. This usually took place on a rising tide as the launch drew a fair draught and going aground on the mud flats was not the Colonel's idea of fun. An account of a November foray shows that the bags were not large: four shots resulted in four brent geese, two ducks (mallard), two teal and a goldeneye. A second goldeneye got away into the shallows and as the tide had turned the Colonel chose not to follow in case he went aground.

As the winter weather became harder shooting pressure grew and the fowl sought the sanctuary of the open sea. This is where the brent geese and wigeon liked to rest and would normally be beyond the reach of even the bravest double handed punt gunners. The attraction for the fowl was not only the security of the open sea but the abundance of floating Zostera carried out by the tide. There were a number of reasons why the Zostera drifted seaward on the ebb tide. It was torn up by wind and waves, by fowl that fed on it, especially swans and brent geese, who ripped it up by the roots and always left more than they ate floating in the water. The largest amounts left floating were during hard weather. Snow falling on the Zostera beds would freeze and with the rising tide the eel grass was torn out as it was embedded in the ice, and then washed out with the ebb. The largest Zostera beds were in the Blackwater estuary, a few miles south of Walton. The ebb brought abundant amounts of grass floating north east along the

Walter Linnett

coast, the direction of the ebbing tide, and the fowl knew exactly where to find this plentiful food supply.

It is hard to imagine today how vast the Zostera beds used to be a century ago. Today the mud is bare but back then it was even difficult to row a punt through the floating blades of eel grass. Imagine a rough sea, driven by an east wind calmed to a gentle swell when it reached the Zostera beds!

Walter Linnett the famous professional fowler from Bradwell, whose house was on the seaward side of the seawall facing the North Sea observed that some winters, due to constant persecution, the brent geese remained 'out on the Main' and did not come within sight of land all winter. Walter detected their presence by their calls carried by the onshore wind as they fed on floating Zostera.

Colonel Davis knew that fowl would not expect to be assaulted far out on the sea. Boats frequently passed the great rafts of ducks and geese but, as we have heard from Folkard, fowl are forever wary as vigilance is essential to ensure their survival. Great skill is needed to achieve success under sail.

An equal amount of skill was needed to achieve success under steam. Once again any attempt to approach birds directly was bound to fail. The tactic adopted was to cruise the launch, funnel down and all persons hidden from view in an ever decreasing circle. This gave the impression that the launch was just passing and was not a threat to the fowl. Slowly the gun boat would get within range of the birds. At this point the skipper would put about the boat. As the gun crossed the line of the birds this was the moment to fire the muzzle-loader at fowl on the water and then discharge the larger breech-loader as they rose. The panicked fowl would tend to flare up and sometimes pass close to the launch, especially if caught by the wind, the crew would then bring the double four bores into action. The shooting over, it was time to retrieve the birds and any wounded would be quickly dealt with using a 12 bore and a landing net to scoop the dead birds from the water.

Colonel Davis kept 'Tyche' moored in the Twizzle, a large creek off the main Walton channel, which was adjacent to his salting and farmland. To enable the Colonel to come and go at any state of the tide he constructed a walkway down the soft muddy slope of the creek side. This was achieved by placing two parallel lines of elm boards to retain stone that formed the hard pathway. One hundred years later the remains of the Colonel's 'Hard' can still be seen, the rotten elm boards and stone pathway being a reminder of times past. The tide still works hard twice a day to wash away the last relics into the Twizzle Creek. Remarkably, a faded lichen encrusted sign high on the saltings states that this place is the Colonel's Hard, a private place and landing is forbidden.

Colonel's Hard and the signpost "This Hard is private property"

Bargemen and watermen had a reputation for poaching and to set foot on the Colonel's preserve would evoke certain retribution but, the Colonel's bark was perhaps greater than his bite. His hospitality often extended to fellow watermen and a jolly time was enjoyed by those that he invited to New House Farm. The challenge was always getting home after such an evening in the Colonel's company. The story goes that all merry makers were always warned to beware the pond on the drive! To navigate it successfully it was necessary to keep the gate post 'on' with a certain tree. On one occasion accompanying and acting as a pilot for his departing guests a certain amount of jostling and prevaricating resulted in the Colonel landing in his own pond, upon which he was heard to say; "Why, I'm a fine pilot I'm in the pond myself."

'*Havoc*' a sister to '*Tyche*'

A sister launch to '*Tyche*' was built in 1894 by James Husk Jnr. of Wivenhoe for Mr Henry William-Jones of Plum Hall, Colchester, and his brother in law Mr A.S.C. Doyle (known as Kit). Once again Joseph Edwin Wilkins was employed to design this steam launch which was a copy of '*Tyche*' being made of wood 31ft 4inches in length, beam 7ft and a draught of 3ft 4inches. Propulsion was by means of a compound inverted engine supplied by Mumford of Colchester. Lloyds register describers her as a 'Screw Lugger.' On launching, William-Jones and Kit Doyle named her '*Havoc*'. From all accounts '*Havoc*' was afloat and in action most winters between 1894 and 1922. She was sold to Lt. Colonel G.C.O. Ryan, of Ryde, Isle of Wight in 1902 and later bought back in 1907 by William-Jones.

Remarkably some records and photographs have survived to give a vivid insight into what it was really like to be in pursuit of fowl on board one of these steam launches. '*Havoc*' was moored at Brightlingsea and used on the river Colne, the Blackwater and out on the Main.

'*Havoc*' under steam

Aboard '*Havoc*', Cyril Gordon-Jones (centre), Kit Doyle on the right.

In the bows of '*Havoc*'. The gun is a Holland and Holland 1½ inch breech-loader 'London' gun.

Records of the steam launch - '*Havoc*.'

1909	12 December	3 brent geese.
	15 December	0
1910	27 January	2 brent geese, 4 duck (mallard)
	30 January	2 brent geese.
	5 February	1 brent geese.
	13 March	0
1910	4 December	2 brent geese.
	18 December	2 brent geese, 1 mallard. (bad weather)
	31 December	2 brent geese. (bad weather)
1911	5 January	3 brent geese, 1 wigeon (foggy)
	17 January	0 Henry William-Jones (alone) 4 shots, (foggy)
	29 January	5 brent geese, 2 wigeon, 2 duck. (very foggy) HWJ & Cyril Gordon - Jones
	26 February	Gale of wind could not go out.
	5 March	3 brent geese, 2 teal, 1 mallard, H W J & C G -J
	12 March	0 C G-J alone. Blew and could not get to Leeward.
1912	20 January	13 brent geese. Very foggy and fine.
	4 February	2 pochard, 2 duck, 1 brent, 1 merganser (cold, windy)
	11 February	4 brent, 2 duck. (hot and fine–birds wild)
	18 February	1 duck, 1 wigeon. (hot and fine–birds wild)
	3 March	0 Pyefleet, Gut in afternoon; west wind, very rough.
1912	9 November	12 brent Dull and windy, geese all in river Colne
	23 November	1 brent, 1 duck. Too much wind, went up Geetons mid-day
	? February	0 Too much wind G.J Smith & G.J.
	? February	2 brent. G.J Smith & G. J.
1913	30 November	1 duck, No geese seen, too much wind on the main.
	13 December	5 duck. Geetons and Pyefleet. Too windy, shot badly.
	20 December	1 brent. Birds very wild, fine.
	4 January	0 Too much wind, Geetons and Pyefleet in afternoon.
	1 January	2 wigeon, 1 teal. Too much wind, fresh E. One shot in Geetons.
	25 January	1 wigeon, 1 goldeneye. Too much wind. (G.J.S. & H.W. J.)
	13 March	0 No shot. Wind and rain, birds wild. (H.W.J & C.G-J.)

Summary: Five seasons 1909 to 1914. 31 days afloat (including attempted days). Total bag 96 head. An average of just 3 birds per day.

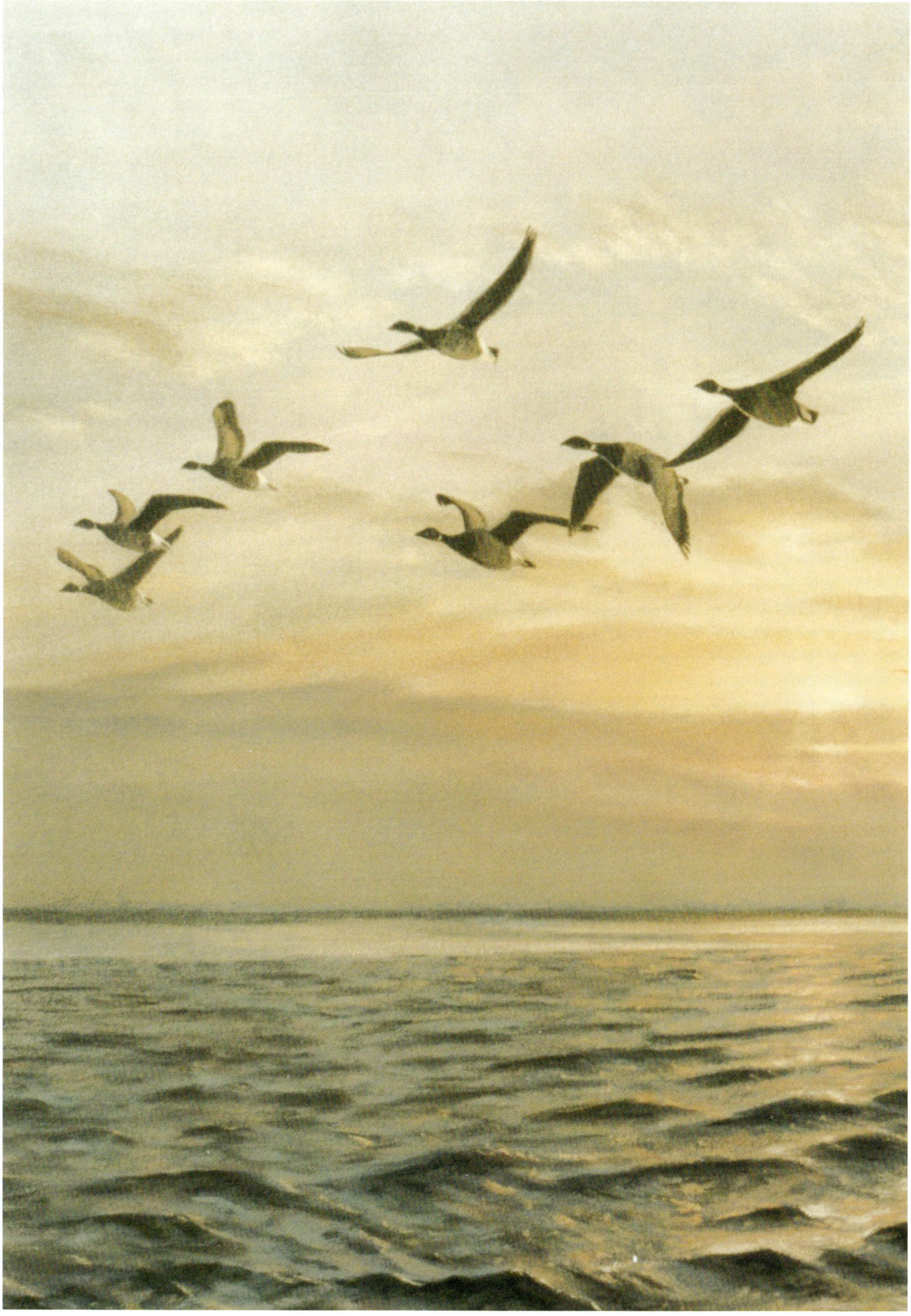

9

GUNNING PUNT DESIGNS

"As now the season comes, the fowler marks,

Sagacious every change, and feeds his hope

With signs predictive."

HAWKER'S PUNT DESIGN

As we have shown in a previous chapter, alteration to gunning punt design soon led to trials of new methods of punt propulsion; steam, petrol engines and electric motors were all tried but did not meet with success. Duncan's fear of the common use of motor gunning punts never materialised and with the passing of 'The Protection of Birds Act' in 1954 all these innovative designs came to an abrupt end. The Act stated that mechanically propelled vehicles and boats were forbidden for the purpose of driving and killing a wild bird.

However, Hawker's basic punt design did continue and anyone who is prepared to research the subject will find useful information in a number of books. Payne-Gallwey gave very precise details on the construction and measurements of punts, both singles and doubles. Look no further than, 'The Fowler in Ireland' 1882, The Badminton Library 'Moor and Marsh' 1889 , Part 3 of his 'Letters to Young Shooters' 1896, or Duncan and Thorne's book, 'The Complete Wildfowler Ashore and Afloat' 1911 and 1950; the latter two books perhaps giving readers the most comprehensive data. Duncan's designs for single and double punts have become most popular and are now commonly used as a basis to build punts. To this day enthusiasts organise an annual Norfolk punt race. The only difference today is that a new punt is unlikely to be constructed using well-seasoned broad widths of yellow pine or larch as these have become increasingly difficult to source. The preferred material appears now to be marine ply. However, all the original dimensions are still followed using the traditional skills of the boat builder.

The professional fowlers often built their own single punts and followed local designs. These evolved through the fowlers' experience of the harshest winter conditions, taking into consideration the effects of wind and tide on the estuaries where they went afloat. The punts were usually narrow and slab-sided out of necessity, to enable the fowler to lie prone and to use

C.G. Jones poles his Blackwater punt in 1913. It was built by Wyatts of West Mersea and identifiable as Wyatts by the Y shaped stern

hand paddles over both sides. Their punts were either partially decked or undecked, depending upon whether the punting grounds were exposed or in sheltered waters. The professional longshoremen often used their punts for a variety of fishing. Eels, flounders and shellfish were harvested and the punts could easily be pushed over mudflats or across the shallows, loaded with nets and the fruits of their efforts.

It is interesting how punt design varied from one estuary to the next. As an example, in Hamford Water single punts were generally seventeen feet in length, decked fore and aft with fairly low sides constructed from a single plank. On the adjacent river Stour punts were constructed with high sides, clinker built with two overlapping planks. On the upper reaches at Manningtree the punts had oak 'ice boards' fixed along the sides at the waterline for about four or more feet from the bow. The reason was simple; there was always more fresh water here that was prone to turn to ice. The ice boards protected the sides from damage particularly when the flow and ebb of successive tides turned to pack ice which could cut through the side timber of even the strongest punt. This was in contrast to Hamford Water where there was little fresh water and ice was not a great hazard. Further down the coast on the river Blackwater there was yet more variation with design, punts often being open and high sided and such variation even existed between punts used around Mersea Island and those in service on the upper reaches of the river at Maldon.

It is not hard to understand why different designs gradually evolved. In some instances, unseaworthy punts even led to the loss of life, but, punting had to continue as it was a source of income. On open estuaries, such as Morecambe Bay and the Solway, the rise and fall of the Spring tides spelt danger to anyone who dared to go afloat in anything other than the most seaworthy of punts. A few wildfowlers worked the tides on both sides of the country punting the Solway and then visiting Holy Island on the East coast. Their punts were often 24ft in length with a beam in excess of 4ft, high wash boards and massively flared sides. They sat low in the water making them barely visible but with the added flare they were, in addition, very seaworthy.

Here are some wise words written by Stanley Duncan in 1918; "I personally built and had built no less than seven punts before I realised, to the full, the words of Colonel Hawker when he wrote, 'copy them you can't.' It is only after severe training and long acquaintance with designing

and construction of these things that one begins to note how little you know, when you thought you knew so much; besides the magnitude of the much, there is yet more to learn. When we consider what a duck punt has to do we will see, compared with other floating craft, the importance of correct shape and construction. In the first place it must be light and manageable, quick in action to a touch, yet strong to withstand the recoil strain of the gun heavier perhaps than the boat and function as a recoil apparatus in itself. It must above all be shallow in draft, slightly affected by wind, inconspicuous yet seaworthy to the extent of a semi-submarine. What other boat has so many things to perform? Then, more important than anything, "she must punt." Now the last phrase holds only what can be understood by wildfowlers of experience, for, save this great and important feature, slight defects in gun balance, general trim, weightiness to way, and other small drawbacks can certainly be endured, but never if she will not answer the setting pole, scull, oars or paddles. Speaking of things and having practical knowledge of them are two different matters. To describe what punting is can only, therefore, be intelligible to those who can punt. But, providing a man can punt, (an art that is not learnt in the time it takes to ride a bike) then give him a punt that is correct in every detail and he will be a happy man able to work his craft in a wonderful way."

Punts are complex boats to build and anyone who has ever gone afloat in a punt has their own opinion about design. In the end it is about having a punt that will get you home with, or more often than not without, some ducks on board. A wildfowler can readily appreciate a good punt if he is lucky enough to secure one. But, all too often punts have been commissioned without experience and as a result prove to be a costly waste of time and money, and totally useless.

Our pal James Dorrington was talking to a punt gunner who proudly announced he had just completed the construction of his new punt which was, he felt, near perfection. James listened intently to the description of the punt. He then reached into his pocket and pulled out a box of Swan Vestas. He shook the matches under the nose of the punt gunner and announced, "burn it, it will be useless." As it turned out James was right; it was a useless punt.

A MOTOR-DRIVEN PUNT DESIGN

Stanley Duncan, Honorary Secretary to the Wildfowlers' Association of Great Britain and Ireland (WAGBI) writing in 1911 gave a detailed plan for a motor punt of traditional design, powered by a 6 hp. petrol or oil inboard motor. A motor assisted punt to be handled in shallow water by a prone punt gunner was, undoubtedly an engineering challenge. At the time such a craft had not been constructed due, not least, to the problems of overcoming noise from the motor and the feathering of the drive in shallow waters. However, Duncan was confident the difficulties would be overcome and even went as far as stating, "I have not the least hesitation in saying that the day is not far distant when we will see the motor gunning-punt top of all, and the only ones which will be able to secure fowl."

A gunning punt designed to carry 120 lbs. gun, heavy man and 4 h.p. to 6 h.p. petrol or oil motor

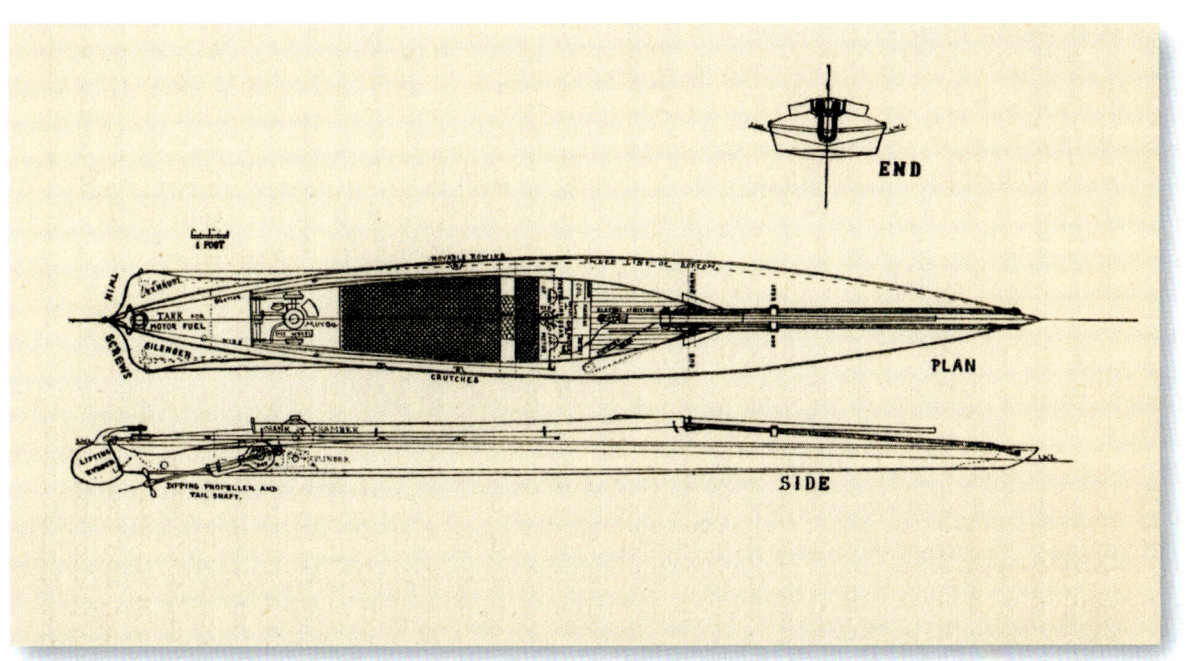

71

10

The gentlemen head for sport abroad

"Behold his punt now ride the restless wave,

A little speck, scarce scanned from off the shore.

Hear the proud thunder floating on the tide

Mark the dread flight of the death-winged shower"

T. Hughes

By the 1860s the constant disturbance and competition along the British and Irish coastline led the wealthier gentlemen gunners to seek sport in more distant lands, their destination now focused on Continental waters. It was well known that the main wildfowl migration route in the autumn was predominantly along the North Sea coasts of Denmark, Germany, Holland and France and some fowl wintered as far south as the west coast of Africa.

The Continental coast had professional gunners but as the area was vast and with a relatively small population, there was plenty of room for visiting fowlers from Britain. The main attraction was the immense numbers of wildfowl found at certain times of the year all along the coast and it did not take long for the visiting fowlers to find out when exactly was the best time to arrange their visit.

Typically, professionally crewed yachts sailed from London or other ports on the east coast carrying all supplies together with punts and guns stored either on deck or side davits. They often sailed to the Dutch coast calling at Flushing, to take on a local pilot experienced in navigating the channels that dissected the vast low water mud flats and who was well aware of where a yacht could be safely anchored to take advantage of the best low water wildfowl roosts. It was not unusual for fowlers visiting Continental waters to remain on the fowling grounds for several months during the winter, sometimes following the passage of migratory ducks and geese along the foreign coastlines.

Gentlemen sportsmen regularly went abroad. Between 1877 and 1907 Captain George Gould was wildfowling off the German, Dutch and French coasts. We will look more closely at his

THE GENTLEMEN HEAD FOR SPORT ABROAD

After a heavy snow fall. Dutch Skokker at Middleshaven Sluice, South Holland. Note gunning punt on deck.

The crew of *'Merganser'*

73

adventures later in the book when he was accompanied by Sir Ralph Payne-Gallwey.

Captain Frank Dowler regularly punted the German coast, using his single punt and a gun firing fourteen ounces of shot. One day he succeeded in bagging 264 wigeon, mallard and teal; when all were stowed in his punt there was barely enough freeboard to see him safely home.

Lewis Clements, writing as 'Wildfowler', in his book 'Shooting and Fishing trips in England and France', published in 1878, gives a wonderful account of how he accompanied a Mr Elmore to the Dutch coast on board a 40 ton yacht with two punts stowed on deck. The sport they enjoyed is vividly described giving the reader an excellent insight into life and sport in Continental waters.

At about the same time the brothers H.J. and T.M. Pike punted for 18 years and held a lease from the Dutch government which allowed them to shoot on the Veere Gat, South Holland. Tom Pike had a steam ship named *Bulldog.*. Hugh Leyborne-Popham (1864-1943) was a wealthy gentleman who had inherited Hunstrete House estate in Somerset from the Popham family. He was an avid wildfowler and in the winter also used Veere as a base. His yacht with its crew of five was called *'Merganser'*. In later years he operated from a large steam yacht called *'Toso'*.

'Merganser' moored in Veere

From "THE FIELD," January 20th, 1894.

"Mr. Walter Crawshay had good sport during the late frost, shooting with a double-barrelled "Payne Gallwey," by Holland.

January 1st.— One shot   15 mallard.
,,   2nd.— Four shots   38   ,,
,,   3rd.— Two shots   45   ,,   flying.
,,   4th.— One shot   7   ,,

WALTER CRAWSHAY, Esq., writes, March 2nd, 1895.

"I run my score of ducks to-day up to 365, and 4 wild geese. My gun is a wonder. I never miss now, but always kill more than I expect."

Prices of Double Punt Guns,
From 120 guineas.

Estimates given for building Punts of the latest designs suited for the various kinds of Punt Guns made by us.

The Holland and Holland sales catalogue of 1897 advertised Holland and Holland double Payne-Gallwey punt guns at the price of 120 guineas. The advertisement includes an endorsement of these guns written by Mr. Walter Crawshay,

On the French coast Mr Walter Pope, a wealthy solicitor from Biggleswade, punted each winter for ten consecutive years in an area known as the Gulf of Morbihan. He chose the splendid Chateau de Truscat as his wildfowling headquarters positioned overlooking the Bay of Sarzeau, the main feeding grounds for thousands of wigeon and brent geese. The Chateau was a summer residence for the Francheville family and was not used by them in the winter. Access to the foreshore was within walking distance of the great house and the double punt would have been moored 200 yards from the house, in a sheltered creek that gave access to the main low water channel. The whole expanse of water was studded with islands and, as the tide ebbed, vast Zostera beds were exposed. George Gould was invited to stay at the Chateau and punt with Pope in 1893 and 1894, where they enjoyed excellent wildfowling together. We will look again at Gould's adventures with Walter Pope later in the book.

In January 1894 a report appeared in 'The Field' magazine stating that on the French rivers Loire and Allier, Mr Walter Crawshay (partner in Youngs Crawshay and Youngs, brewers of Norwich) together with his son-in-law Captain St Clair had enjoyed some fine sport afloat with their new double barrelled Holland and Holland punt gun. The main species encountered in this region seems to have been mallard and on New Year's day, they bagged 15 with a double shot. The following day, four double shots resulted in 38 mallard and then on 3 January they had two double shots resulting in 45 mallard.

Baron de Jaubert (1864-1935) was a celebrity who shot clay pigeons for France in the 1900 and 1912 summer Olympics. He was also a keen wildfowler and visited the Loire region where

Steam Yacht '*Toso*' at Brouwershaven. Note punts on deck

he went punting. He records bagging 70 mallard in three days, with one excellent shot that accounted for 31 with a breech-loading Holland and Holland firing 18 ozs. of shot.

Records show that the gentlemen gunners had been sailing to the Continental coastal fowling grounds since 1850. One of the earliest records we found was the travels of Arthur Mac Murrough Kavanagh, who was related to the Kings of Leinster living in County Carlow in southern Ireland. He was a remarkable man born only with the rudiments of arms and legs but with indomitable resolution he triumphed over his physical disability becoming an expert angler, riding to hounds and writing a delightful book about his sporting adventures. 'The Cruise of the 'R.Y.S. Eva' written in 1865 includes an excellent account of cruising in this 130 ton schooner off the coast of Albania. He carried on board a gunning punt breeched with Colonel Hawker's punt gun known as 'Brown Bess', the same gun that was exhibited at the Great Exhibition. His book gives a full account of the sport he experienced and makes fascinating reading.

Fine sport was undoubtedly the main motivation for visiting the foreign estuaries, but the wildfowl that were shot were in great demand with yacht crew costs and living expenses being offset by the sale of fowl. Dutch game dealers would sail out to the visiting yachts, anchored off shore, to purchase the wildfowl and waders. Records from 1880 show that they were prepared to pay the Dutch equivalent of one shilling per bird (for ducks) which was a considerable amount of money for ducks at that time. Game dealers then made a tidy profit from the sale of the spoils to the local population who lived close to the rivers and canals.

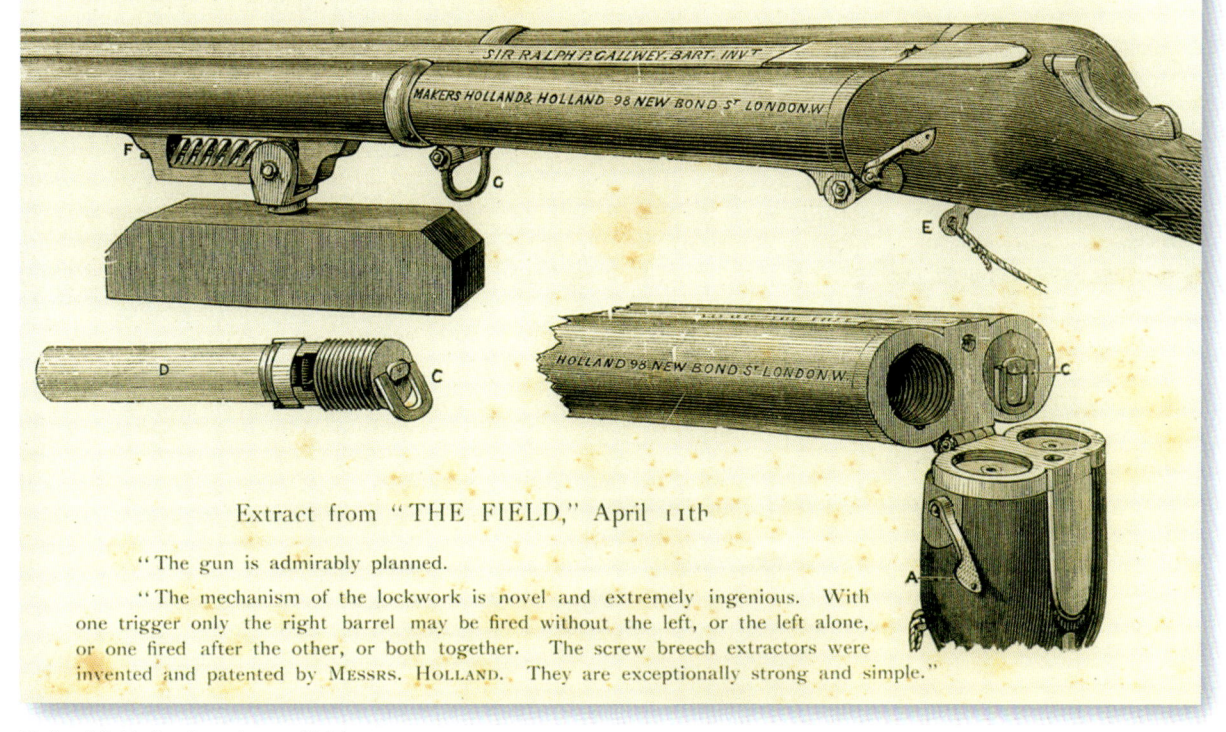

Holland & Holland catalogue, 1897

11

The effect of duck decoys at home and abroad

"The decoymans dog- the piper

Tho' gay and winning in my gait,

I'm deadly as a viper:

Follow me and sure as fate,

you'll have to pay the piper."

Henry Folkard

The visiting British fowling yachts did not go unnoticed and before long friction towards their presence began to stir. This animosity was mainly amongst the decoymen and decoy owners who made a good living by catching up wildfowl from their decoy pools. The word decoy is derived from the Dutch word 'eende-kooi' which means 'duck-cage.' Each pool had a combination of curved ditches covered in netting which are refered to as decoy pipes, into which the ducks were lured by a 'piper dog' which often resembled a fox, the ducks are then trapped at the head of the pipe where they were dispatched by the decoyman.

By this time the value of duck decoys were well recognised, many having been constructed in the early part of the nineteenth century. There were numerous commercial decoys close to the estuaries and wildfowl haunts in southern Denmark, Germany and Holland. The decoys were very profitable and their owners did not take kindly to foreigners moored off shore, disturbing and shooting what they considered to be their ducks.

Nowadays it is hard to imagine the impact of coastal duck decoys but to give an example; in 1883, off the German coast of Schleswig Holstein, the islands of Fohr, Nordstrand and Sylt each had a number of decoys. On Fohr there were five which regularly took 60-70,000 teal each season. On the island of Sylt beside Blidsel Bay was sited a very successful decoy. Records show that in the season of 1841 it took 25,064 teal. This decoy was constructed in 1809 and until it ceased working in 1921 had accounted for 695,957 wildfowl, mainly mallard, wigeon and teal.

Nacton decoy

Remarkably it was only the size of a double tennis court. Another successful decoy on the island of Amrum took 1,500 pintail in a single day.

The Dutch have used decoys for more than six centuries; their working has always been shrouded in secrecy and the wildfowl they sold was concealed from enquiries. It would be pure speculation to put an annual figure on the total number of wildfowl harvested by decoy owners. History tells us that the decoys were important to the local economy and at times the wildfowl were exported to markets in France and London. We know that the owners of the decoys were well organised and a respected influential group. In Germany they started to put pressure on the government arguing that visiting wildfowling yachts with their punts were affecting their livelihood. Such was their influence, that by 1884 they succeeded in stopping all punt gunning on German coastal waters even to the exclusion of local wildfowlers.

It was not long before the Dutch government was under similar pressure from decoy owners in Holland. A so called 'Inquiry' was held in 1899 and the Government banned punt gunners from Dutch public waters. Punt gunning was wilfully misrepresented during the Inquiry with accusations that visiting gunners from England were disturbing and shooting far more ducks than in reality was the case. Of even more concern was that for every visiting English fowler the Dutch government chose to ignore the interests of the many local gunners who relied on gleaning a meagre living from fowling during the winter months. The inquiry evidence suggested that only

Duck decoy pipe at Ellemeet, Schouwen Island, Holland, 1900

80,000 fowl were taken by all the decoys and a figure of 4,000 fowl by the gunners. The misrepresentation was, of course, the low figure taken by the decoys.

Secrecy shrouded the real facts and it was not until a report was published in 1941 that a more realistic picture emerged. Two years prior to 1941 The International Committee for Bird Preservation had set up a Wildfowl Inquiry Sub-Committee under the chairmanship of Percy Lowe O.B.E. to look at the factors affecting the general status of wild geese and wild ducks in the British Isles and elsewhere. Chapter 4 of the report was devoted to British decoys which by this time were very much in decline .The report estimated that on average 11,767 ducks per annum had been taken by the last remaining 10 working decoys in Britain over the previous ten years. It was also noted that Denmark and Southern Ireland had already prohibited their commercial use. But what of duck decoys in Holland? The report said, "no foreigner could hope to obtain information as to the Dutch decoy trade." A powerful vested interest maintained a firm grip on the publicised numbers of ducks which were taken each year by the decoys in Holland. In 1939 it was estimated that there were still 150 commercial decoys working in Holland. In 1888 there were an estimated 170 active decoys and in 1838 it was as high as 220 working decoys. Decoy owners would not submit numbers of duck caught in the decoys, but it was thought that each decoy would have to catch and sell at least 3,000 ducks to cover the annual running costs. The decoys were not run for philanthropic reasons such as ringing stations or as wildfowl reserves. They were worked purely for their owners profit motives and it was even thought that the government taxed each decoy 1,000 guilders per annum so they also benefitted financially. Despite the lack of hard facts the Inquiry concluded in 1941 that the Dutch Decoys were harvesting close on one and a half million ducks each season. No doubt the figure would have been higher at the turn of the century when the figure given was 80,000, at a time when there were far more working decoys.

With the coming of the ban on punt gunning on continental waters, many of the gentlemen fowlers decided to look elsewhere for their sport, but, by this time, many had given up punting through advancing years. Others might have thought they had enjoyed the very best of sport abroad and had no desire to return to the overcrowded home waters. To them 'the zenith of fowling' had been reached and was now passed. It had lasted for less than 50 years and with the coming of the First World War in August 1914 all was to change. It was effectively the end of an era when punt gunners had the freedom to go and shoot without restrictions wherever they wished and wherever the fowl took them.

The decoyman with his dog. In his left hand he holds a sack and a piece of burning peat. This was traditionally used by all decoymen to disguise their scent

12

Sir Ralph Payne-Gallwey Bart and Captain George Gould

"When 'Time', who steals our hours away,

Shall steal our pleasures too,

The memory of the past will stay,

And oft our joys renew."

Thomas Moore. 1780-1852

Sir Ralph Payne-Gallwey was born in 1848, the eldest son of Sir William Payne-Gallwey and the grandson of General Sir William Payne-Gallwey who commanded the heavy Cavalry at Talavera in 1809. His mother was Dame Emily Payne-Frankland and her father was Sir Robert Frankland-Russell MP, the seventh Baronet of Thirkleby whose predecessors had occupied their Yorkshire lands for three centuries.

Payne-Gallwey's primary education commenced at North Stanley School, Ripon and he entered Eton at the age of thirteen. On leaving Eton there followed a period of private tutoring, in order to enter the army as an officer. His first tutor was the Rev. Digby Legard, son of Digby Legard and Frances Creyke; of the line of Legard of Ganton, a baronetcy established in 1660, Rector of Whitwell near Malton, East Yorkshire. Thereafter tutoring followed under the guidance of the Rev. Edward Hawley, Rector of Shireoaks, near Worksop, Nottinghamshire. Here in the grounds of Shireoak Hall the young Payne-Gallwey learnt the art of fly fishing and the seeds were planted of an enduring fascination for the countryside and field sports which was to last a lifetime.

Following the long family tradition of, 'Serving One's Country,' RPG entered and passed the army entrance examination at Greenwich in 1867 and in 1868 he joined his first regiment, the 4th Battalion Rifle Brigade at Chester Barracks. In 1870 he exchanged into the 92nd Gordon Highlanders and served with this regiment in the Punjab, India which exchange he records as, 'mainly for sporting'. In 1872 he records being invalided home, with no further details of his ailment. A period of recuperation followed necessitating a winter in the Mediterranean sunshine aboard his father's yacht, *'Ballerina.'*

With health restored it was back to army life and a further exchange of regiment, this time to the 15th East Yorks, based in Dublin. From Dublin he went with the regiment to Cork and it was here that he met Edith Alice Usborne who was to become his wife. RPG's army career was now coming to an end but not before he spent a year on the Isle of Alderney remarking that, "the rabbit shooting was exceptional." It was then back to Aldershot whence Captain Gallwey left the Army in 1874.

Life in Southern Ireland appealed to RPG. He had spent time there when on leave from serving in India. He had firm family friends there and he was in love! A combination of romance and the attraction of excellent fishing and shooting now inspired him to return to the Emerald Isle. There followed three years of what, we suspect, were some of the happiest years of his life, culminating in marriage to Edith at St. Andrews, Westminster on 25th April 1877. They spent the year following their marriage in various parts of Ireland, moving first to Glenmore, Queenstown Harbour, County Cork. A year later they moved to a shooting lodge called The Grove at Rushbrook, County Cork and from The Grove they went to Castle Widenham, near Mallow. In 1881 they moved to Cowling Hall, Bedale, Yorkshire and finally they took up residence at Thirkleby where they managed the family estate until RPG's death in November 1916.

Sir Ralph Payne-Gallwey Bart

Captain George Gould

RPG's wildfowling diaries reveal that many of his most successful adventures were spent in the company of Captain Thomas Ingelheim George Gould. It is appropriate at this stage of the book to try and trace the history of this remarkable gentleman/wildfowler in order to gain an insight into how this close friendship might have evolved.

George Gould was born George Jackson on 7 February 1845 in Italy. His mother was Henrietta Amelia (Donaldelli) Jackson and his father was Captain Hamilton Llewellyn Jackson, an officer in

Thirkleby Hall

the Austrian army. As a result of his father succeeding to the Gould estates of Upwey, Dorset he changed his name by royal licence to Hamilton Llewellyn Gould in April 1871. Young George Jackson was to follow his father's example, changing his surname to Gould later that year.

George Jackson's early education is unclear but we know he entered the Royal Military Academy at Woolwich and on passing out as Lieutenant G. I. Jackson on 17 April 1866, joined the Royal Engineers. Thereafter he served in Bermuda and it was on his return from this posting in 1871 that he was permitted to change his name to Gould. He was then stationed in Devonport in 1872, in Gibraltar from 1873 until 1877 and in 1878 was sent to Camden Fort, Crosshaven, Cork Harbour, Ireland. Promotion followed and by 1881 he was in command of the 18th company of the Royal Engineers stationed at Cork Harbour. It comes as a surprise that by December 1881 he decided to retire from his regiment. He received a gratuity and gained permission to retain his rank and wear the prescribed uniform. He was listed as a reserve until 1885.

He was financially secure as, in addition to the Upwey Estate, his father had inherited the land and buildings around the almost derelict sixteenth century castle of Fanningstown in County Limerick.. George knew that, on his father's death, the responsibility for the whole estate would fall to him and he would be Lord of the Manor of Upwey (Tithings of Waybayard). The Gould family were very much respected in the Parish of Upwey, his ancestors having been the manorial lords since the fifteenth century. Perhaps this influenced his decision to leave the army at the early age of 36. However there may have been another reason, for on June 29th 1880 he married Ellen Louise O'Grady who hailed from Cork and they were shortly to be blessed with the first of their four children.

Now we can only speculate that Miss Ellen O'Grady might have known Miss Edith Usborne for they both lived in Cork and would most probably have mixed in similar social circles. Consider also the two officers Captain Gallwey and Captain Gould whom we venture to suggest met each other in their respective Officers' messes. Was this the start of their friendship and did RPG tell Gould of the visits he made to Derry Castle, a place where he had learnt all about wildfowling?

We know from RPG's diary that Gould had certainly joined him on board the cutter 'Gipsy' by the winter of 1880 but we cannot say exactly when they first went wildfowling together. The precise date is irrelevant as from 1877 they became firm friends. Thereafter when they started wildfowling they spent many winters together with common fanatical interests in wildfowl, sailing and in particular punt gunning.

RPG records details of George Gould's considerable wildfowling success over a span 30 seasons and although we have been unable to trace Gould's wildfowling diaries, several extracts are reproduced in the Badminton Library ' Shooting, Moor and Marsh'(1886) and 'Wild-fowl' in the Fur, Feather and Fin series (1905). We will refer to them later in this book together with letters that have been traced, many of which were addressed to RPG.

After leaving the army much of Gould's time was spent in Ireland where he established a home for his family at 19, Stradbrook, Monkstown in Dublin and later moved to Stradbrook Hall, Blackrock, Dublin. His last recorded wildfowling season was in 1907 (aged 62) and thereafter he travelled extensively in his car and was a member of The Royal Automobile Club, Pall Mall. He is also known to have spent much of his time in Morocco but in later life he returned to Upwey living at Island Cottage. The last four years of his life he lived and was cared for at the Gloucester Hotel in Weymouth until his death on 22 February 1934 at the age of 89.

Captain George Gould is standing with both hands in his pockets aboard his dutch Skokker 'Watergeus.' Sir Ralph Payne-Gallwey stands in the punt and their puntsman Steven Shuttler in the stern. This is the only photograph of George Gould that we know exists.

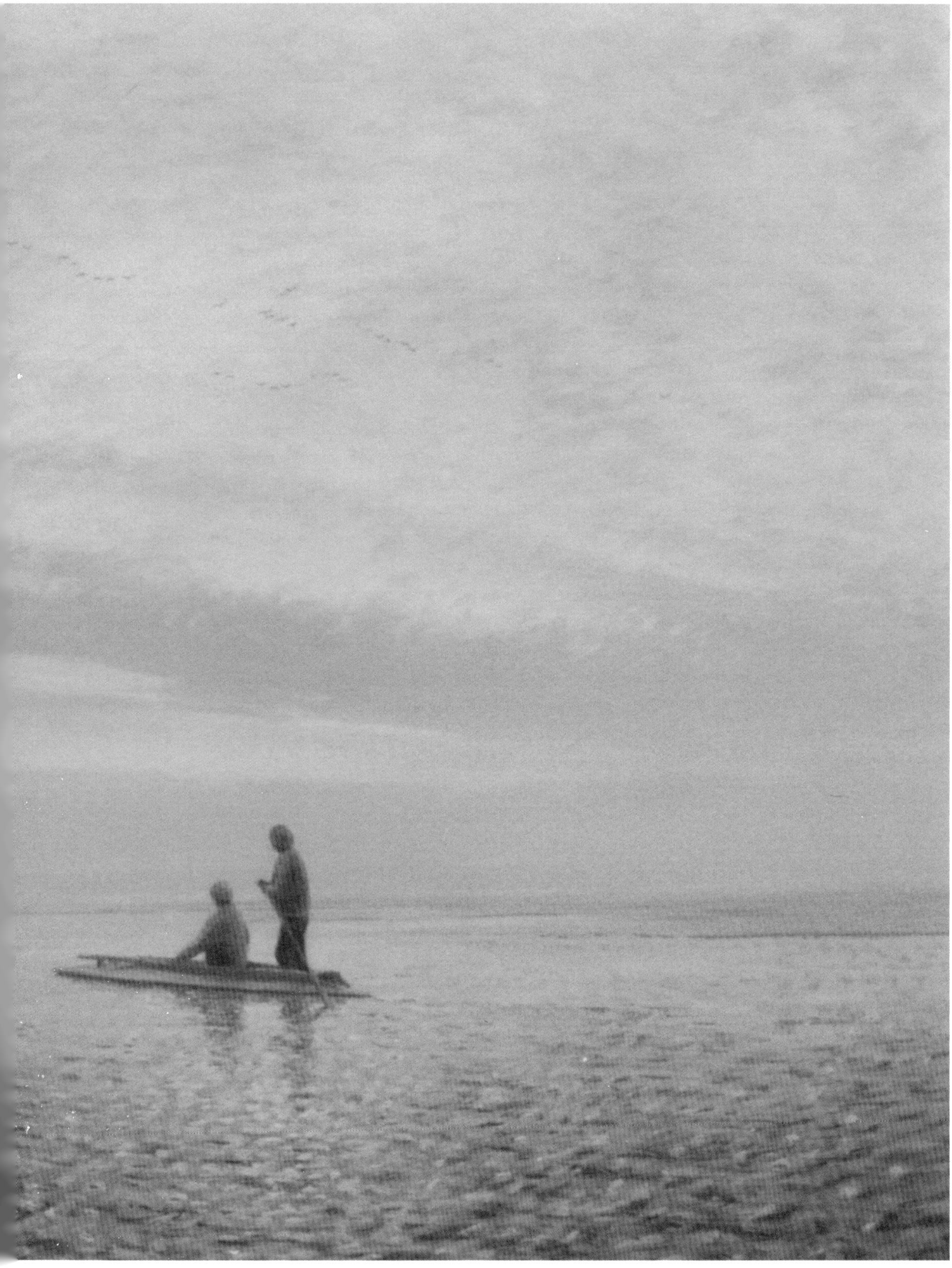

13

The Wildfowling Diary of Sir Ralph Payne-Gallwey Bart. 1874-1916.

"A fowler's life is made up of hope. He hopes for fine weather- rough weather- wind - calm - frost and snow, for North, South, East or West winds or for no wind at all! He hopes the birds will sit, will fly, will swim; he hopes for dawn, for dusk, for sun, for moon, for stars. He hopes for high water, or for low water, there is no variation of time or tide or weather or light that he does not hope for according as his chances of sport are served there bye, or hindered. His one predominant hope is that someday he may make a really good shot. His lifelong regret would be that he either missed or his gun misfired when the one magnificent opportunity of his whole shooting career was before him. In his mind it would always be his best shot he never made."

Sir Ralph Payne-Gallwey Bart

The following chapter traces RPG's wildfowling adventures spanning a period of forty years. All the details are entirely factual and have been obtained from RPG's hitherto unseen Wildfowl Shooting Diary documenting events written down by him the same day that they occurred.

Southern Ireland the formative years

Sir Ralph Payne-Gallwey (RPG) started wildfowling at the age of 19. Through his Irish connections, he went to stay with William Speight, a dear family friend, who owned Derry Castle, situated 30 miles inland from the mouth of the Shannon estuary on Lough Derg. Visits to the castle would have taken place when he was on leave from serving with the 92nd Gordon Highlanders in India. It was here, under the guidance of William Speight's puntsman Mike Considine, that Payne-Gallwey would have had his first experience of punt gunning. There are no records of those early wildfowling adventures from Derry Castle on Lough Derg. He does however record that Mike Considine had lost one leg but frequently went punting with a wooden stump.

William Speight of Derry Castle

Sir Ralph Payne-Gallwey and the puntsman Joss Fletcher

Derry Castle was the perfect place to stimulate a young officer's interest in the countryside and field sports. He writes, " At Derry we had a 30 ton steam yacht for cruising and all kinds of fishing boats for summer and shooting punts and swivel guns for winter, all lying ready for use close to the house."

Payne-Gallwey returned from India in 1872 to convalesce and shortly afterwards joined the 15th East Yorks. Regiment based in Dublin. He must have looked forward to returning to Derry Castle but sadly the main house was burnt to the ground the year before he arrived home. Following the fire the house was never rebuilt but the outbuildings were converted to a comfortable house which still stands to this day.

In 1874 he left the army and settled in Southern Ireland where he devoted much of his life to country sports. It was at this time that he started to keep more detailed records of his wildfowling adventures.

In spite of the loss of his 'fowling headquarters at Derry Castle, Payne-Gallwey returned to Lough Derg in the Autumn of 1876, staying in the small village of Mount Shannon north of Killaloe and almost opposite the site of Derry Castle. There are no records of the number of shots he made with punt and gun although we do know he was using a single barrel 1½ inch Tolley breech loading gun which he said was loaded with 2 lbs of shot. In view of the gun's weight of 120 lbs the recoil must have been a little harsh! We know also that he used a double handed punt as it was here that he met and employed Joss Fletcher whose portrait is in the frontispiece of RPG's first book 'The Fowler in Ireland.' Joss Fletcher "an admirable assistant with a wonderful eye and hand for duck", acted as RPG's puntsman until February 1884, when he was eventually dismissed for "having turned into a drunken blackguard".

On returning to Ireland in 1878 RPG comments briefly about the 1877 season, which was interrupted by his marriage He mentions in his diary returning to the same 'fowling grounds as the previous year, "I lost a good part of the winter in consequence of having to go and be married. A nice hard season too, with frost!" Some 15 years later he made a note to the margin of this entry which read, "To the best and sweetest of wife's(sic) any man could wish for, and well worth giving up the most famous of wildfowl seasons to secure." And then an additional note written in April 1912, "Confirmed a hundred times over after 35 years of married life!" One wonders if he might have been concerned that Edith would read his diary?

In the autumn of 1878 RPG hired Glenmore Lodge near Queenstown Harbour. He had purchased a muzzle-loading 1½ inch swivel gun made by Truelock and Harris weighing 80lbs, handling a service load of 16oz of shot. He described the gun as, "a capital little weapon." Armed with his punt and gun he spent three and a half months at Glenmore wildfowling around the extensive marshlands and saltings near Queenstown. His interest in fowling equipment was developing and during the winter he commissioned, and had built, a steam launch to enable new fowling grounds to be explored in safety. The steam launch was never breeched with a punt gun but would have been used to tow the punt and as a following boat.

Interest in larger punt guns began in the spring of 1880 when RPG commissioned a new 1⅞ inch muzzle-loader from Bentley and Playfair of Birmingham (which he frequently referred to as a 2 inch gun). The gun weighed 180lbs, had a barrel length of 9ft 6 inches, with a service load of 8ozs of powder and 36ozs of shot. During most of the 1879/80 season he was based at a new fowling headquarters known as 'The Grove.' He continued to use the Truelock and Harris but clearly this was not enough gun for the ambitious duo of RPG and Joss Fletcher (puntsman). Throughout the season they continued fowling around Queenstown Harbour but there is no record of either their success or failure.

Writing in 'The Field' on 18 January 1879 RPG entered into the discussion regarding punt guns; "In the much vexed question of breech versus muzzle-loaders I can only say I should be delighted to buy or borrow one of the former if I thought it equal in power of shooting to my muzzle-loader." The Field editor rebuffed him; he thought RPG was altogether behind the times suggesting that he had no practical experience of modern breech-loaders.

The ever thoughtful RPG was certainly not behind the times: he was already drafting his classic wildfowling book 'The Fowler in Ireland' which was to be published in 1882. The book looked in detail at the arguments for and against breech-loaders and muzzle-loaders. The design of breech-loaders was evolving, but many were complex and even regarded as unsafe by RPG. Quietly RPG was assessing the design and merits of the new breech-loading punt guns and a clue to the direction of his thoughts is given on page 392 of his new book which was shortly to be published where he writes as a footnote; "Mr Holland of 98, New Bond Street is, to my mind far in advance of all other gun makers in the manufacture of punt guns. To anyone who can give the price I recommend the above maker's guns should they desire to purchase a breech-loader. They are beautifully made and safe."

The attraction of living on board a boat appealed to RPG and in December of 1880 he writes of hiring a small cutter named '*Gipsy*'. He was accompanied by Captain George Gould and his puntsman Shanahan. They went afloat on the tidal Shannon estuary below Limerick around Tarbert and Kilrush, changing anchorage to take advantage of opportunities for sport as they arose.

A clearer indication of his fowling success now begins to emerge. The Limerick Chronicle reported on 'Shooting on the Shannon'. "The shooting season on the Shannon which has just closed has been one of the most successful which has been enjoyed for many years. As an instance of the immense number of birds which have been killed it may be mentioned that Mr Ralph Gallwey, Rushbrook, Queenstown, shot 600 wild fowl including duck (mallard), wigeon teal and geese. Mr Gallwey has the advantage of possessing the finest gun which was used on the Shannon, and it is worthy of note that it was manufactured at the firm of Mr H. Moreton and Son, Old George Street, Cork. Messrs. Patrick Grimes (puntsman) and Mr Richard Bourke, of Thornfield, Limerick shot from 700 to 800 birds."

Patrick Grimes' son Michael later became puntsman to Gould and RPG and lived at 14, Upper Denmark Street, Limerick.

The reference in The Limerick Chronicle to Mr H.Moreton as a punt gun manufacturer is questionable as RPG was using the Bentley and Playfair. Perhaps Moreton had undertaken some work on the gun. There has always been mystery surrounding the forging and boring of punt gun barrels. Specialist equipment is needed which would most likely be available only in Birmingham, a city that had the reputation of being at the heart of the gun trade. In 1881 there is an interesting reference to a gentleman visiting the gunmaker Mr W.W. Greener at St. Mary's works Birmingham. He describes seeing a pair of barrels being manufactured 9 feet in length and estimated to weigh 230 lbs without breeching apparatus. This raises the question, was Greener making all the punt gun barrels for the trade?

In the autumn of 1880 RPG was afloat, punting from his yacht '*Gipsy*' for three and a half months. Having spent some time around Tralee Bay, he then crossed the Kerry Mountains, travelling by road and taking all his wildfowling belongings, to attack the wildfowl on Dingle Bay. The yacht was sailed into Dingle Bay and anchored at Rossbegh where he experienced some exceptional sport.

Here is his account of a typical day aboard the yacht in January of 1881; "Just come on board the yacht for breakfast. Been out all night and since three yesterday afternoon. Grand weather and sport; fowl on all sides in great numbers. Cold, bitter, but most intense just before dawn, paddles, oars, movables, frozen tight to each other or to what they rested on. The only chance of thawing my trigger hand was now and then to shove it under the wing of a fresh killed bird or between a couple. Fired four shots."

On one occasion whilst staying in a small cottage on the shores of Tralee Bay RPG had a narrow escape; "Feeling cold one evening I lighted the fire by means of old newspaper and bits of an old chair in my bedroom (in which I could write my name in the damp with my finger). In a few seconds the fire grate was blown out, all the panes of glass in the window broken and the room one mass of smoke, dirt, and burning embers of peat wood and coal!"

It transpired that the little bare footed drab of a girl who attended to the rooms of the cottage had a sweetheart fond of shooting (i.e. poaching) with an old muzzle-loader that he owned, "He, having no powder or money had persuaded his lass to purloin a pound of my punting powder, and she had temporarily concealed it at the back of the fire grate of the bedroom, never anticipating that any one would ever again light the fire." There is no mention of what happened to the young girl!

The wildfowling season of 1881 was sadly interrupted by the death of RPG's father Sir William, on the 19 December. In a letter to Mr Ussher, a well-known Irish ornithologist, he describes how his father had died at the age of 76 as a result of an unfortunate shooting accident when he fell across his gun and died of internal injuries. As a result of the death RPG inherited the family seat, Thirkleby Hall, a baronetcy and a considerable fortune.

1882 RPG and Captain George Gould aboard '*Crescent*'

In the autumn of 1882 RPG was joined by Captain George Gould who now resided in Dublin. Both young men, Gould aged 37 and RPG aged 34, were by now fanatical wildfowlers. They each appeared to have limitless funds and time enough to devote to their sport. One can imagine they took great pleasure from each other's company.

RPG joined George Gould aboard '*Crescent*', a 60 ton Yawl, shortly after Christmas of 1882. This winter they had returned to the River Shannon, near Paradise House, a delightful sheltered anchorage close to the island of Inishmore on the north side of the Fergus estuary. We know little about their success but RPG recounts an interesting incident. Stepping from the following boat into the punt he missed his footing and went overboard into deep water feet first. His telescope went overboard with him and sank like a stone. Lost for ever! Well not so! In March 1900 the telescope was returned to him after an interval of 18 years. It appears that sometime after the telescope was lost a fisherman found it on the sand that was uncovered by an unusually low spring tide and he kept it all those years, not knowing to whom it belonged. Quite by chance he told the story to Gould's puntsman, Grimes, who was in company with RPG when he went overboard. Remarkably and much to the delight of RPG the telescope was returned in working order.

In December 1882 the Clare Advertiser indicated that visiting fowlers were not always welcome, and a letter was published under the heading, "Indignation Meeting held at Kilrush! Those attending the meeting protested against, "the facade of a money making Englishman from Yorkshire coming over here and killing, destroying and frightening our ducks!" It was politely suggested by local fowlers that RPG should, "make himself scarce" and "take good care when visiting Clonderalaw Bay!"

On board the yacht '*Crescent*' conversation would have ranged freely with discussion on wildfowl, punt design and punt guns. Both Gould and RPG had been punting for many years by now and they would have been keen to exchange ideas. On this trip they would have used RPG's equip-

'Crescent'

ment, including the big Bentley and Playfair muzzle-loader. However, Gould was already in discussion with Henry Holland, and had commissioned the London gunmaker Holland and Holland to build him a new 2inch breech-loading punt gun with a service load of 30ozs of shot and 5ozs of Col. Hawker's powder. The gun was to be ready for the following season.

RPG was not yet convinced that the design of screw breech punt guns had been perfected and he wrote extensively on this subject in 'The Fowler in Ireland.' However, he would have listened intently as Gould told him about the design of the action for his new gun. The early Holland and Holland punt guns were not to RPG's liking. They employed a push in breech plug system, secured by two round or square ' Clayton' bars through the plugs. This system was never patented by Holland and Holland as Clayton, another gunmaker, had already used the system much earlier. From 1860, Holland and Holland marketed this gun as the 'London' punt gun.

George Gould would have been well aware of the shortcomings of the early London guns as we know he owned and used one, a 2 inch gun. The breech design resulted in the recoil being exerted on the bars which secured the breech plug and Gould was concerned that this was not a safe system so he waited until the design had been improved before placing an order for a new gun. This punt gun incorporated the very latest patented screw breech which ensured that the recoil was taken by the barrel itself and, in so doing, the troublesome Clayton bars were dispensed with. He would have paid about 65 guineas for his gun and the Holland and Holland Numbers Books indicate that it was gun number 7634 completed on 27 June 1883, just in time to be shipped to Husum for the 1883/84 season. Gun number 7634 is recorded in the Holland

Holland and Holland breech. Stock and breech plug are one piece.

and Holland numbers book as 1⅞ inch. A letter written to RPG by Walter Pope stated that the gun had the breech plug and action all in one piece. This was an intermediate design before the separate screw in breech plug was patented by H&H. Gould commissioned Holland and Holland to build a similar 1¼ inch gun in the same year.

Fowling on continental waters

Husum is a small seaport on the coast of Schleswig Holstein, Northern Germany, about 60 miles north of the Elbe. George Gould asked RPG to join him aboard his yacht '*Crescent*' and he arrived on 19 September 1883 via Hamburg. '*Crescent*' was moored one third of a mile off the island of Nordstrand. George was already aboard with all his fowling equipment and his new Holland and Holland breech-loader. The weather was fine and he had been busy trying out his new gun and had already shot a total of 91 wildfowl, his best shot being 27 wigeon.

RPG was impressed by the new punting grounds and commented, "Though I have in other places seen larger numbers of wildfowl I certainly never saw birds pack so beautifully for the big gun as they did here. They crowd in dense companies on the smooth sand and generally on the verge of small creeks at low water."

Gould and RPG were aware that punt gunners who visited the area were not welcomed by the owners of traditional duck decoys situated close to the coast as they thought punt gun shots disturbed the ducks excessively. The German Government were being urged to ban the use of swivel guns and Gould feared this would be his last fowling trip to this area. He and RPG agreed that if this was going to be their last trip it was going to be a memorable one. And it proved to be the case.

In eight days punting, 480 ducks and geese were shot using the new 2 inch Holland and Holland. George Gould must have been delighted and probably amply rewarded his puntsman, Steven Shuttler, who came from Lymington. Shuttler had a strong punting pedigree as he came from a family of longshore folk and his father, 'Old Shuttler', had acted as puntsman to Colonel Peter Hawker (referred to in Hawker's Diary in 1852).

After RPG departed for England on 10 October, Gould remained and before the end of the season had brought the season's total bag up to 1,351. By now it may well have been going through RPG's mind that these new breech-loading Holland and Holland punt guns were the finest guns that had ever been made.

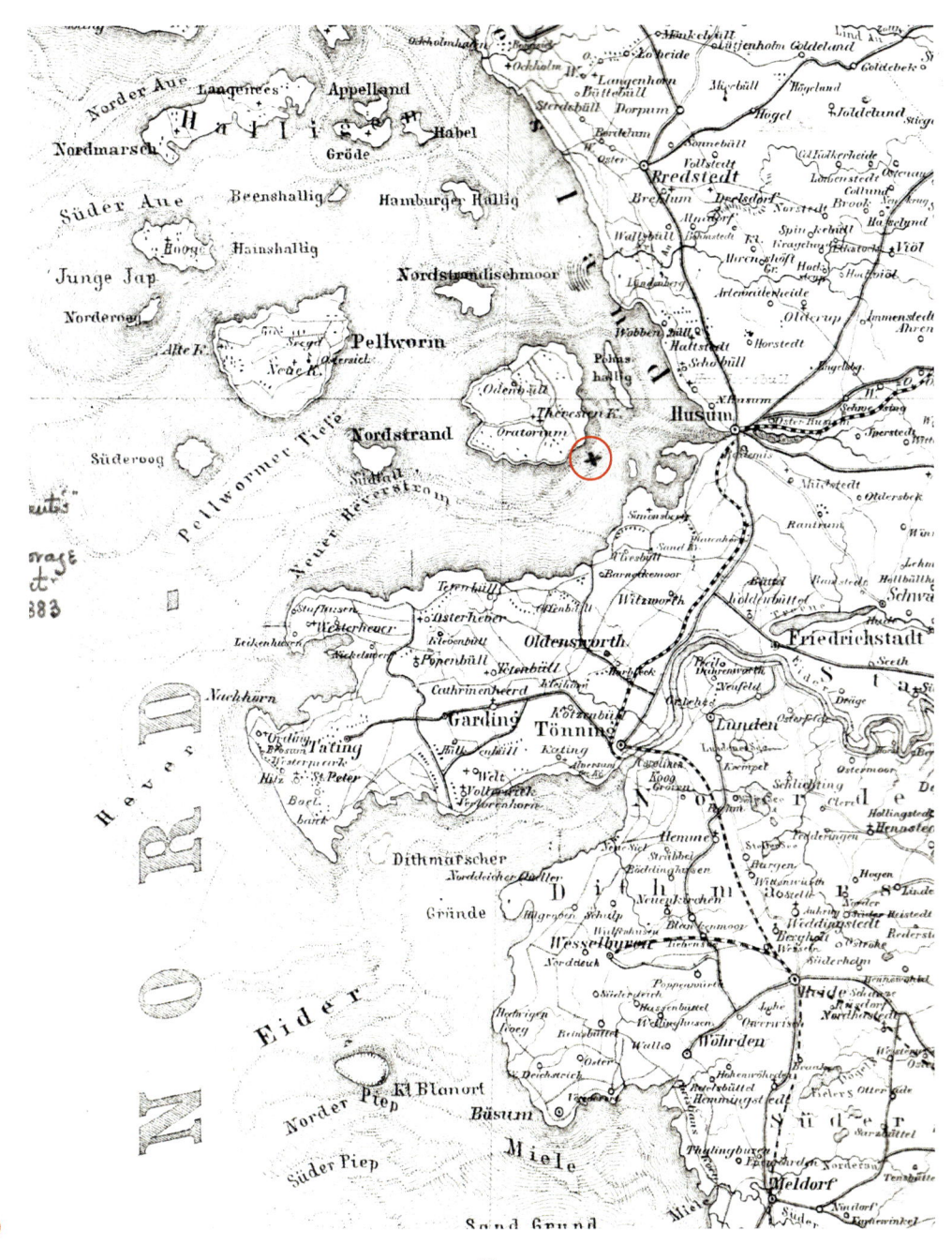

Fowling grounds off the island of Nordstrand. 'Crescent' moored here ⊗

RPG's vision of a breech-loading double punt gun

RPG writes in a short footnote in 'The Fowler in Ireland' p386 (1882), "I have recently tried to get a large double (punt gun) built in Birmingham and offered to send a wooden model to work from; but no factory will undertake the job. The gun makers say special and costly tools would have to be made and they decline the order with thanks. The fact is nothing will pay in the gun trade that is not made by the hundred. Even small swivel gun barrels are forged half a dozen at a time and afterwards converted into breech or muzzle-loaders as required. Messrs. Osborne of Whittal Street, celebrated makers of big tubes turned out the last double swivel guns (a pair) made in Birmingham for Clayton (now Patstone) of Southampton; and this firm still possess the model from which they forged Colonel Hawker's splendid weapon."

Exactly when RPG went to see Henry Holland, and his father Harris, to discuss this subject is not clear but we suspect it was shortly after returning from Germany. Evidence suggests that he had been thinking about a double barrelled breech-loader for some time, but reading RPG's notes it is easy to see why the trade were not inclined to undertake a commission. The model gun he had at first presented to the gun trade incorporated two barrels with the muzzles parallel to the water but with oval bores. His theory was to send a lateral spread of shot into the company of fowl. Evidently this idea was scrapped and the more conventional Hawker round barrel configuration was adopted. This compromise may have paved the way to fulfil RPG's dream of designing and having built a breech-loading double punt gun to rival Hawker's masterpiece.

RPG had experienced the reliability and effectiveness of George Gould's gun. The problems which he had previously perceived and written about at length related to safety but now, with a redesigned breech plug, Holland and Holland had resolved the problem he may have felt that, with a little input of his own expertise, a gun could be manufactured to his complete satisfaction. The way was now clear to make the perfect double breech-loading punt gun.

His plan was to ask Holland and Holland to build a double barrelled 1½ inch breech-loading punt gun. RPG had a very clear idea of what he wanted to achieve in the design of this gun. He and Gould had discussed every aspect of design and of course the 2 inch single Holland and Holland that Gould had commissioned was a working example of the Holland breech-loading system.

RPG was still unsure whether Holland and Holland could be persuaded to take on his commission. Meetings would have taken place in the hallowed boardroom at 98, New Bond Street. Mr Harris Holland was now aged 77 and his son Henry was very much in the driving seat of the company; he was only 37 but was known for his hugely inventive mind and the project would understandably have appealed to him. The factory manager William Froome would certainly be paying a keen interest in the project as he would have the responsibility of regulating the double barrelled gun should the order be placed.

RPG would have been living at 30, Eaton Square, his London home and it is here that he would have formulated his final design proposals to discuss with London's foremost master gun makers. It is not clear if George Gould accompanied him but he may well have done.

There remained some minor problems related to Gould's gun, but this was largely due to the design of the screw breech plug. Later Henry Holland was to further modify the design used on Gould's gun. The revised breech plug design ensured that the claws that held the cartridge did not rotate when unscrewing or screwing in the cartridge case. Holland and Holland then took out a Patent on this clever design.

In 1884 RPG had another major decision to make: should he choose to have the barrels made from iron using the traditional 'skelp twist' technique? At this time Gould favoured 'skelp twist' for his single barrel gun and this would have influenced his decision. Perhaps they both admired the craftsmanship that went into Hawker's gun, or simply because they thought the barrels would be better balanced, stronger and perhaps more fitting for the design they had in mind. In any event they both settled for forged iron "skelp twist" barrels. RPG's new double was designed with nine feet barrels, chamberless and both bored full choke.

Other aspects of the gun were discussed and incorporated. RPG admired the Hawker spring recoil apparatus which consisted of a spiral spring working in a slot fixed beneath the barrel, giving the gun perfect balance when the stanchion was mounted correctly in a sliding block. The mechanism of the lock work was to be complex but ingenious. With one trigger only, the right barrel could be fired without the left, or the left alone, or one after the other, or both practically together. The stock, which held the locks, was short and robust, hinged at the bottom of the barrels and, when closed, fastened in position by a half screw bolt. All exposed parts were to be nickel plated and left dull. Best quality walnut to be used for stocking.

Holland and Holland accepted RPG's commission on or around 28 May 1884, giving the company about 10 months to manufacture the gun. We know that on 2 March 1885 he was called to try out the new gun at Kensal Rise, Holland and Holland's Shooting Ground, but more on this subject in due course. In accepting the commission Holland and Holland may have decided to put more than one double gun into their production schedule as at least five similar guns were eventually completed but there appears some question about the fifth gun as the Holland and Holland records are unclear. Batch making was a common policy in the gun trade, giving production flexibility should something go wrong, but also adding the economies of scale, assuming more orders would follow from the successful production of the first gun which Holland and Holland marketed as the 'The Gallwey' double punt gun. There was no question of the guns being completed at the same time.

Holland & Holland breech plug. Patent number 152 obtained on 5th January 1885 and first used on RPG's double gun

A letter in 'The Field' magazine, on 22nd Dec 1988, describes a double gun made for Edmund St. Clare and used on the coast of Orkney earlier in February 1888. This must have been the second gun completed by Holland and Holland but there appears to be no record of this punt gun in the Numbers Book. In another letter in 'The Field' on 29 December 1888 there is an account of a double shot producing 26 mallard using the same gun on the Loire in France. The gun was fired by Mr Walter Crawshay who was Edmund St Clare's father-in-law.

Because of the importance of the gun one would also expect the order entry to include a clear specification, setting out every detail of the gun. In fact there appears to be no detail, the guns carry no identification number, and clients are not shown. This leads to the question of why this might be? One can only speculate on this subject but could it have been that Holland and Holland accepted the commission but found it necessary, or perhaps more convenient, to instruct trade outworkers with the necessary skills to, at the very least, make many of the components that went into making this important punt gun?

Would Holland and Holland really want to make the barrels which followed Hawker's design originally made by William Fullerd in 1824? After all they did not have their factory at 527, Harrow Road up and running until early in 1893. Prior to that, work was confined to a small workshop at 98, New Bond Street. Skelp twist barrel making of this quality was a complicated and complex process. Fullerd had died and the finest barrel makers for punt guns were now in Birmingham. This would suggest that the barrels might have been made by Charles Osborne

Table of "The Gallwey" double punt guns

1. Number 8155 1½" bore double punt gun tested 2 March 1885 (RPG's gun *)

2. Not recorded in Holland's record book. Edmund St Clare describes in 'The Field' magazine of December 1888 using his own H&H 1½" breech loading double puntgun on Orkney the previous February.

3. Number 12883 1½" double punt gun completed 27 August 1890

4. Number 14275 1½" double punt gun completed 1891

5. Number 17218 1½" double punt gun tested 7 November 1893

* Strangely no reference is made to RPG as the client.

Evan Lloyd, puntsman, with the double H&H punt gun owned by Geroge Long and now owned by Peregrine Armstrong Jones.

and Co. Ltd. trading from 12-13 Whittal Street, Birmingham. Osborne was also trading from 3, Broad Street Building, Broad Street, London and then at 7, Whithall Place in 1885, so Mr Froome, factory manager at H&H would not have had to visit Birmingham when checking the progress of the barrels. We have already mentioned the note, in 'The Fowler in Ireland' here RPG records that Osborne possessed the model from which William Fullerd forged Hawker's barrels.

We know for certain some components were made by trade outworkers. The locks were made by Edwin Chilton trading from Lowe Street and 41, Newhampton Road West, Wolverhampton. Edwin was also proprietor of Joseph Brazier and Son, the maker of Hawker's double punt gun locks. We know Holland and Holland were trying to perfect the design of their screw breech plugs and this is really where the engineering skills were far in advance of any other punt gun manufacturers at this time. It therefore seems likely that they would have taken on the job of machining the breech threads and fitting the plugs. The quality of the walnut stock and lock work fitting show all the signs of work completed by Holland and Holland. All this work would again have been undertaken under the supervision of Mr Froome.

All this may be logical but it remains pure conjecture on the part of the authors and just when one idea emerges so another possibility arises. In 1888 the rib on the double gun lifted resulting in the need for re-jointing and re-setting of the barrels. Why did RPG send the gun to W.W. Greener to undertake the work? Could Greener have been supplying punt gun barrels for Osborne? After all, two of the other double H&H punt guns completed in 1890 and 1891 both had steel barrels and Greener was well placed to bore steel tubes of this length.

The final cost of the gun on delivery was £150. To put this in perspective, at that time a Holland and Holland Royal hammerless sidelock ejector cost 65 guineas, so equating this price with the cost of a similar gun today you would expect to pay a minimum of £65,000 for a best quality Royal. The Payne-Gallwey punt gun might therefore cost around £150,000 if commissioned today. When compared with the cost of Colonel Peter Hawker's flint and percussion double barrelled punt gun made in 1824, the price was really quite reasonable. Hawker entered into a protracted dispute with his gunmaker and ended up paying the massive sum of £210! Today that price might be as much as £200,000.

1884. Exploring the Humber Estuary

We will return to the story of the H&H double gun when it was completed in March 1885. In the meantime RPG decided to explore the punting grounds on the Humber estuary.

On 3 January 1884 RPG went to stay at the Lifeboat Inn, close to Spurn Head, East Yorkshire. He arrived by rail at Patrington railway station and made his way to the Inn, some 14 miles away. En route he stayed at Ottringham in what he described as a miserable inn, full of drunken and quarrelsome horse dealers. The following day he was joined by Joss Fletcher who had brought a double handed gunning punt and the 2 inch Bentley and Playfair gun all the way from Ireland. RPG had heard that there were a good many wildfowl on the Humber and Spurn Point might be productive. For the next week he was plagued with bad weather and commented in his diary that he saw many fowl, but time and time again he was forced to retreat to safe ground and he could never get close enough for a shot.

Returning to Spurn in early February he tried to get on terms with the ducks but, frustrated by bad weather, he returned home commenting, "Spurn is a grand lonely desolate spot and in a gale, an exciting one from which to observe the shipping pass the point. It is a wonderful place for woodcock; when a flight is on in migrating times, as many as 50 have been killed here in a day."

Apart from his disappointment RPG, records one interesting incident. He found a dead dunlin or purre (*Tringa alpine* now *Calidris alpina*) which had met its death in rather an unusual manner. The bird had been feeding on the shoreline picking up molluscs and had attempted to feed on one mollusc with open valves. The latter had closed upon the bill of the bird so tightly that it prevented the bird from feeding and in consequence it had starved to death. On this occasion the vitality of the cockle proved to be greater than that of the bird!

1884. RPG joins George Gould in Holland and then returns to Spurn Point

As anticipated, the German government stopped all punt gunning in 1884 but George Gould was not deterred and he moved his operation over the border to the Waddenzee in North Holland. The yacht he had been using as a fowling headquarters was found to draw too much water for the new shallow punting grounds and Gould decided to purchase a new Dutch yacht named '*Watergeus*', a Dutch Skokker of 50 tons, 55ft long, 16 foot beam with a draft of 3 feet 10 inches. The yacht was most suited for work in shallow water and was anchored off Holwerd, Friesland.

Translating the name '*Watergeus*', it could mean a watergoose (brent) but our research shows this was a term given to 'sea beggars' a special heroic name given to a confederation of the Calvinist Protestant nobles against the Spanish catholic hegemony. They adopted, as a badge of honour, the derogatory name 'geuzen' given by the Spanish. The 'sea beggars' revolted against the Spanish during the 80 year war of the Dutch against Spain (1572). A special licence for piracy was issued by the Republic of the Netherlands permitting a man to fight under the 'letters of Marque' against the Spaniards.

On 9 October 1884 RPG was on his way from London to Antwerp via the Port of Dover and onwards on 11 October from Antwerp to Groningen, eventually arriving at Reidor Polder a farm house on the shores of the Dollart estuary, where he had arranged to meet Gould, who had arrived some days before with his punt and gun. Bad weather prevailed but not before a shot of 16 teal had been made and they had observed large numbers of avocets. In view of the weather they decided to travel to Zoutkamp, a small town at the mouth of the Groningen canal where it runs into the Lauwers Zee. They then visited a duck decoy just outside the town of Zoutkamp and thereafter to Dokumer Zyl along the coast where they observed, "vast numbers of wigeon on the flats."

RPG had to return home on 19 October and did not go wildfowling again until 1 December. Gould remained in Holland until 7 November accounting for 464 duck most of which were wigeon. There is no record of the number of shots he had.

RPG's punt and gun were still at Spurn Point and, against his better judgement, he returned there in the hope of making a good shot. He took with him Alex Sutherland who had been his gillie on the River Thurso. After spending Christmas at home he returned again in late December, remaining there until 15 January.

A diary note sums up RPG's opinion of Spurn; "May I never see this wretched disappointing place again, on which I have wasted much money, time and temper. It took me 8 hours to reach Spurn from home, including a drive of 14 miles from Patrington and then a desperately heavy walk of 4½ miles to finish with the grand total for a best forgotten season of 16 teal and 6 wigeon."

Testing Payne-Gallwey's double gun at Kensal Green 2 March 1885. Present are Henry Holland, Ralph Payne-Gallwey, William Froome (factory manager) and an employee to pull the trigger.

Mr Froom, manager at the shooting ground

2nd March 1885 Holland & Holland shooting ground at Kensal Hill. Test firing the Payne-Gallwey double breech loading puntgun.

1885. Trials with the new double Holland and Holland punt gun

1885 was an exciting year for RPG. Ten months had passed since he had commissioned his new punt gun and numerous visits to 98, Bond Street had taken up much of his time. The gun had been made to his design following the drawings he had made, with only small improvements being added, as suggested by William Froome as construction progressed. The new barrels had passed proof successfully using the improved breech plugs and the gun appeared to have been made to perfection. The entire gun weighed 230 lbs. including the recoil spring apparatus. The time had come to put the gun to test at The Holland and Holland shooting ground.

Holland and Holland described their Shooting Grounds at Kensal Rise in their period catalogue. "Our Shooting Grounds are probably the largest (about 30 acres) and most complete in England. Not only have we the necessary appliances and try guns for ensuring the perfect fitting of guns to our customers, and for shooting and regulating of guns and rifles. A spacious and well fitted pavilion has been erected for the convenience of our clients and their friends. Thirty minutes from Bond Street."

The great day arrived, 2 March 1885, and the assembled group would have most likely consisted of Henry Holland, William Froome, RPG and a young man to pull the lanyard and another to reload the gun before RPG fired a few shots. RPG also mentions, 'friends' and one wonders if George Gould might also have been present.

RPG provides his own account of the day in his diary;

> "I personally shot the gun on trial at Messrs Holland's ground at Kensal Green. It worked admirably in every respect. I fired many shots both double and single with the gun from a recoil frame built on the principle of a fowling punt. It consisted of a 14 inch square log of wood on 6 inch wheels. A platform of boards was fixed on the log behind the gun to enable me to lie down and fire it. This is the first breech-loading double gun ever made. Colonel Hawker's famous double gun was much the same size and shape, although slightly smaller and was a muzzle-loader. I intend this gun for foreign shooting where fowl are more plentiful than at home. The theory and indeed practice of a double punt gun is as follows. The barrels are placed parallel, the centre of each barrel being the same distance apart at both the breech and muzzle from each other. If both barrels are fired simultaneously at a bull's eye the result is two circles that overlap about one third of their diameter at from 60 to 70 yards. Take instead of a bull's eye the thickest part of a company of wildfowl. They will, therefore, get the extra amount of shot, where the birds are closest caused by the two circles eclipsing one another. Being side by side the two circles also make a longer or more drawn out pattern and one that suits in its shape a line of birds on the ground or water, or when springing up off either. It must also be remembered that where the circles overlap, twice as many pellets are put into the fowl where they are thickest. Another thing; the locks of the double gun I have so arranged that they cannot even with the quickest pull of the one trigger be fired absolutely together. There is a small though appreciable difference. The effect of this is that the first barrel wipes the bird on the ground or water and the second cuts them down the moment they extend their wings and spring at the just previous shock of flash and rattle of shot. The way Colonel Hawker managed this feat was by having one barrel of his gun ignited

by flint and the other by a percussion detonator and pulling off both of the barrels together, the two ignitions therefore differing in rapidity. The way I have succeeded is by making one hammer as it reaches the cap of its cartridge, loose off the other lock. With both hammers at full cock I can fire with my one trigger one barrel by itself, one after the other, as quick as thought, though not, for reasons that I have shown, really simultaneously. Else I can fire one barrel at a small number of birds; and if I find there are more fowl than I thought or some were hidden, or others spring up near, or they offer a fair shot then I can send the other charge after them as soon as I like. To do this I would require a stiff breeze to clear away the smoke from the first shot."

Having described the gun, RPG goes on to describe the shooting trial;

"Not having shot the gun before, I had to learn as I went on, how it acted as to its elevation. I found that it shot high (a very good thing in all punt guns) when aimed point blank. Had I known this at first I could have averaged another 100 to 200 pellets on the target for several of my single barrel shots. I used as my bull's eye an exact outline in size and shape of a wigeon, cut out of cardboard; all shots were fired at 70 yards measured. Right barrel-20 oz No.1 shot (82 to the oz.) 4 oz of Colonel Hawker's coarse grain powder. Average 500 pellets in 6ft by 6ft target; 50 pellets in a 20 inch diameter circle. The result was the wigeon in the centre of the target was hit by 5 pellets. Left barrel - same charge. Average : 532 in 6ft by 6ft target; 43 in 20 inch circle and 8 pellets in the centre wigeon. Right barrel - same charge only single (75 to the oz.) Average 509 in 6ft by 6ft. target; 33 in 20 inch circle and 5 in the wigeon. Left barrel - same charge as last. Average: 515 in 6ft by 6ft target; 52 in 20 inch circle and 6 pellets in each of the wigeon."

RPG was delighted with the result and was pleased that it shot such a regular pattern. On studying the spent shot he found that it had been flattened thinner than paper or splashed into fragments.

Double shots followed at a target now increased in size to 18ft. long and 6ft. high. On the target were stuck eighteen card wigeon 2 feet apart, in two lines. The lower line one foot above the lower edge of the target, the upper line one foot above them. Charge 4 oz. of powder and 20 oz. of No.1 shot in each barrel, distance as before 70 yards.

RPG observed, " in the centre of the pattern plate, in a space 6ft. by 6ft. were 1353 pellets. Every wigeon was struck all along the line. The six centre birds were struck by 11, 19, 12, 11, 9, 8, pellets respectively."

Twenty double shots were carried out without damage to the recoil apparatus. The recoil carriage ran back only 18 inches when both barrels were fired and this was without a check rope. When one barrel was fired the recoil was as little as 8 inches. The gun also proved to be very well balanced and had it not been for cattle in an adjoining field RPG would have been tempted to try a flying shot at a single pigeon released from one of the shooting ground traps. His chance to try the gun on quarry species was to come when he visited Southern Ireland later in the year.

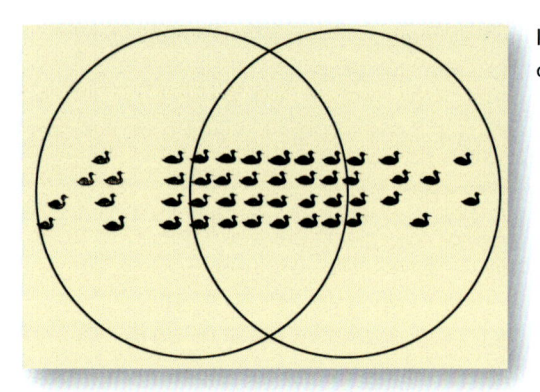

Illustrations from 'The Field' depicting shooting trials targets.

1885. THE INTERNATIONAL INVENTIONS EXHIBITION

Following the successful field trial the gun was dispatched to the International Inventions Exhibition held at South Kensington, London commencing in March 1885. RPG's gun joined the display on Messrs' Holland and Holland's stand. The exhibition must have been impressive as the gun was mounted on his new double handed gunning punt, showing how the gun was breeched together with all the equipment that a fowler would be expected to have for a successful day afloat. RPG had on display a new Game Register for shooters that he had recently invented. The full range of Holland and Holland guns were also displayed and the Stand received an Exhibition Gold medal. All the Medals awarded were listed in the Morning Post on Thursday 13 August 1885.

Within the halls and corridors of the Exhibition were magnificent displays of machinery, sections on musical instruments, jewellery, dress and furniture. This was truly a time of great invention and the Exhibition attracted Oriental, French and American entrepreneurs. Holland and Holland were not the only gunmaker to exhibit their inventiveness; Messrs' Lancaster, Watson and Hancock, Kynoch & C. Turner & Co., together with Armstrong guns and the Nordenfelt Co. also exhibited. The magnificent exhibition was set in gardens tastefully illuminated at night by incandescent lamps. During the day bands played in the grounds to the crowds that flocked to the show on the newly opened subway to South Kensington Station.

Holland and Holland also exhibited their breech-loading punt guns at the Sportsman's Exhibition held at the Agricultural Hall, Islington. This shows the importance that Holland and Holland attached to the sale of punt guns. The factory Numbers Book indicates that most orders taken for punt guns were in 1881 (12) and 1882 (11).

The 1885/86 wildfowling season

RPG now arranged for his new punt and double H&H punt gun to be transported to Southern Ireland. His intention was to visit the Humber in late November and then travel to Ireland to try out the new outfit on familiar punting grounds around Queenstown Harbour.

RPG had his old punt and 2 inch muzzle-loading Bentley and Playfair gun at his disposal and all his punting equipment was dispatched to Paull, near Hedon on the Yorkshire side of the Humber about six miles East of Hull. Arriving at Paull on the 23 November 1885 he went afloat every day until the 27 November when he returned home. It was another disappointing trip and he remarks that he saw thousands of plover but no wildfowl. He notes also that he had no trained puntsman and employed Walter Arnes, a fisherman to assist him. Sutherland, whom he had high hopes of, had gone to Holland with Gould. Shortly afterwards he heard from Gould that Sutherland was useless and had to be sent home as he could not stand the cold!

RPG reached Eastgrove, Southern Ireland on 15 December 1885, renting a house belonging to Mr Bagwell whom he describes as an old friend. The house, Eastgrove, was situated close to Queenstown Harbour and was perfectly placed overlooking the estuary. He lost no time in hiring a steam launch which was anchored close by in sheltered water. Mike Grimes, Gould's puntsman from the Shannon joined him and, once settled in, they went afloat on 18 December for the first time with the new outfit. Clearly RPG was intent in making the very best of this, his first adventure with his new gun. Mike Grimes was a professional puntsman and there was no better man in Ireland capable of getting RPG a good shot at fowl. Success did not come easily, the birds were scarce and the weather was mild. He records that day a bag of 4 wigeon, 1 teal and a plover but it is unclear if any of the birds were shot with the Holland and Holland. On 19 December they experienced their first chance of a decent shot and they knocked down, with a single barrel of the H & H, 28 curlew! A day or two later they had two shots, one of 8 wigeon and then 15 golden plover bagged on Christmas Eve. There followed a series of small shots with success coming on 4 January with a single shot of 11 duck (10 wigeon and 1 mallard); this was the day before Gould joined them at Eastgrove. He had been in Holland aboard '*Watergeus*' until 2 December and reported a bag of 274 duck, mostly wigeon.

That evening RPG told Gould an amusing story that had happened some years before when he was invited to dinner at Eastgrove where they were staying, "I arrived at the door with other neighbours (he lived close by at the time), to be met by the Irish butler who was so tipsy that when we arrived he handed us bedroom candlesticks, to light us up to bed instead of showing us into the drawing room!"

A remarkable day occurred on 8 January 1886 and it all happened by chance, just when RPG was getting depressed about how things had changed since he was last there, remembering that was the 1878/79 season.

"I this morning made a splendid shot with my new big double duck gun firing both barrels together, (2½ lbs of BB). I knocked down and counted directly after the shot 51 and bagged 46. This is far the finest shot ever made in Queenstown Harbour or ever likely to be made. It was rare luck. I came round a point and just caught some 300 wigeon packed close together beautifully

Queenstown Harbour

Shooting Lodges
1. 1885/6 Eastgrove
2. 1878 Glenmore
3. 1880 The Grove.

⊙ 46 wigeon shot here in January 1886

placed for a rake on the ooze. In another minute the birds would have left the harbour for their usual haunt far away at sea."

At this moment RPG must have felt amply rewarded for the time spent designing and building 'The Gallwey' double gun. His euphoria can be sensed from the entry in his diary;

"I never ever saw nearly so many fowl in these parts before tho' I have shot here for three winters now, my average best shot hitherto rarely exceeding a dozen birds and never 14 or 15. This was truly a wonderful shot and I am now quite satisfied if I do not obtain another shot here."

Sport continued until 13 January, but by now there were very few wildfowl about. RPG commented that the harbour was now overrun with steamboats and sailing boats, and the shore was traversed by rail roads. On this account Gould and RPG decided to move their punt and gun plus all the shooting equipment to Foynes on the tidal Shannon, it was here that they had such great sport in January of 1881. They arrived on 20 January taking with them Mike Grimes whom RPG now referred to as, "my puntsman." He bought a following boat at Limerick and then engaged another man to assist Grimes. His enthusiasm and high spirits were evident.

Between 20 January and 5 February RPG and Captain Gould were afloat together. When Mike Grimes was not acting as puntsman, he would manage the 'following boat' and help pick up after a shot. They had good sport with shots of 24, 25 and 34 wigeon. Gould's shot of 25 wigeon was particularly spectacular as it was a flying shot and he dropped 24 birds dead, at a measured distance of 120 yards.

Once again they were frustrated by wild, wet, warm weather. RPG's entry in his diary reads, " I never saw such magnificent chances day after day of killing 80 to 100

Eastgrove Queenstown

wigeon in one shot. That is to say if we could have approached 100 yards closer than they would ever allow. Apart from the mild wet weather we had to endure the stupid jealous behaviour of some idle dirty ruffians who made the fowl doubly wild by continually endeavouring to kill them with a shoulder gun at long range. I can hardly reflect with common patience on the glorious shots these bunglers drove from us."

Before leaving Ireland RPG returned to Derry Castle to visit his dear friend William Speight. Following the fire which destroyed the Castle in 1871 the stables had been converted into a comfortable lodge, six of the stalls making the dining room! No doubt he would also have called to see the now elderly Mike Considine, the puntsman who first instructed him in the art of punt gunning. He would have delighted in recounting all the fishing and fowling adventures he had since enjoyed. After all it was Considine who had inspired him to first go wildfowling on Lough Derg when aged 19.

Following the end of the season the double gun was returned to London where it went on display at Holland and Holland's London Gunroom. RPG wrote in 'The Field' a glowing description about the successes he had had with his new gun and invited people to call at Holland and Holland's premises to inspect it.

'*Watergeus*' moored at Antwerp 1885

In October 1886 George Gould extended another invitation to RPG to join him, this time in North Holland. RPG was to remain with Gould for ten days. He reports seeing thousands of wildfowl but never having the luck of obtaining a good shot. Perhaps this was because Gould had already made a very good shot of 57 before he arrived! In Holland they would have used Gould's punt and 2 inch single Holland and Holland gun.

A Dutch newspaper article appeared about this time which translated reads; "Holwerd October 1886. Since a few days ago the English yacht, about which we reported last year, is again in the Waddensea to hunt for wildfowl which is brought in full loads to the mainland. People say that also the decoy men fare well, because the birds, disturbed by the noise of the hunters, flee to the duck decoys, refuges that are even more dangerous for the birds. Also, the shopkeepers fare well because the foreigners purchase all they need in our village."

George Gould records his own score of 420 fowl bagged before returning to Ireland at the end of October 1886.

RPG returned home to Thirkleby Hall. There followed twenty days game shooting including an outstanding day at Cley Hall, Swaffham, Norfolk. The four guns: RPG, Sir Herbert Lewis, John Penn and General A. Hawksy shot 842 pheasants, 7 partridges, 51 hares, 40 rabbits, 3 woodcock and 4 various making a total of 947.

1887. Exploring Holy Island, Northumberland

In January 1887 RPG established a new wildfowling headquarters at Fenham le Mill, renting a cottage located on the west side of the Fenham Flats. Looking east, Holy Island could be seen and to the south the Farne Islands and Bamburgh Castle.

Wildfowling on the Holy Island flats had long been the preserve of local fowlers and one famous visiting author. In 1896 Abel Chapman wrote 'First Letters in the Art of Wildfowling', and was a regular 'gentleman punt gunner' there accompanying Selby Allison a professional Holy Islander fisherman/fowler.

Abel Chapman was born at Silkworth Hall, County Durham on 4 October 1851, the eldest of six sons to Edward and Jane Chapman. He was an accomplished field naturalist, wildfowler and author. His delight was studying his quarry, writing about them and illustrating them in their wild surroundings. He was a talented naturalist of the old school and the author of ten books. Many of his trophies and specimens can be found in Sunderland Museum, the Natural History Museum and the Great North Museum in Newcastle.

In later life he moved to Houxty in Northumberland where he created his own nature reserve. Chapman was a shy man known worldwide as a great naturalist; perhaps one of the greatest. He remained unmarried and died on 23 January 1929.

An account by Abel Chapman when he was amongst the brent geese on the Holy Island slakes

The following wildfowl tale is written by Abel Chapman using the pen name 'Boanerges.'

"The morning broke with one of those surprises to which in our 'temperate' clime we are more or less accustomed. A sudden and heavy snowfall had occurred during the night. While men slept all the familiar features of the landscape had disappeared, buried under the wintry mantle. Moreover, the feathery particles still continued to fall heavily, and with that steady persistency which bodes a 'breeding storm.' How differently is such a phenomenon regarded! To the writer it is ever welcome, as presaging new campaigns among the wild fowl and fresh successes in the wild sports of the coast. The morning's post brought an invitation for a couple of days' covert shooting to wind up the season (it was the middle of January), but this in the altered condition of things could not now be entertained for a moment. It is strange what an overpowering fascination the pursuit of wild fowl has for its devotees. No other sport is so precarious, yet no one who has ever entered into its spirit, or been smitten by its enthusiasm, would dream of exchanging the chances of going afloat in a gunning punt, with all its risks, hardships, and uncertainties, for even the most abundant game shooting which the season might offer. With that thought I travelled down to an out-of-the-world corner of the country, more to prospect and arrange for further campaigns than in great hopes of sport afloat. On arrival the reports of fowl were satisfactory. Several hundred geese had appeared within the last few days, and the evening was spent in discussions piscatorial and ancipial.

The object of the expedition being chiefly the geese, which would then be snugly roosting on the rolling waves a mile or two outside the bar. Nothing could be done that night or until the tide commenced to flow about six in the morning. At that hour the morning proved fine; the moon only a few days past the full, shone brightly in the western heavens, and by her light we could dimly discern the desolate features of the broad estuary, extending far away inland, a dreary succession of dusky sandbanks and oozes, backed by the snowy outline of distant hills. The tide being now low, we had to launch the punt over some two hundred yards of sand and shingle, no easy matter with a craft some twenty-one feet long and so heavy as to require our full strength (myself and puntsman) to lift her on to the launching carriage. Moreover, the sand was soft and the wheels sank in places up to the axles and, ever and anon, ran against a half-hidden boulder. However, the morning was intensely cold, snow lying a foot deep down to the high-water mark, so the hard work was not unwelcome, for it set the blood tingling through our veins. There is a certain spirit of strange weirdness about these dark hours just before dawn which is peculiarly impressive on the coast. The wind moans with melancholy cadence, there are dreary periods while clouds cross the moon, and the murmur of the dark wavelets on the shore has an 'eerie' monotony. Of all Nature's creatures man or rather that amphibious variety, or 'sub-species,' of our race which dwells on or lives by the sea, is perhaps the hardest working, and has the keenest struggle for existence. Already, at this early hour, the brown sails of the fishing fleet are disappearing in the gloom to seaward. They will be back with the produce of their 'long lines' before noon, to get their fish to market that day, and the results will perhaps appear on the tables of the piscivorous, possibly hundreds of miles away, before night.

That hoarse 'clank clank' resounding across the dark water is also human; it proceeds from the small schooner which put in for shelter last night, and is now hauling taut her cable preparatory to getting away on her voyage by daylight. The only other sign of life is the weak little pipe of king dotterels, running along the shore close to us in search of breakfast.

Our destination is the wide stretch of ooze where Zostera Marina and Samphire grow, and whither the geese resort at daybreak, some three miles up the estuary. Our course at first lies across the harbour channel, where the tide sheer knocks up a nasty sea, some icy cold sprays breaking on board of us. Just as daylight begins to break my man decries some duck ahead, but not being myself endowed with crepuscular vision I fail to make them out. However, 'faith' is still the essence of my creed so we flatten on our chests, and after cautiously setting for some distance in the direction indicated they become visible. Six teal on the point of a sand spit. Unluckily we had forgotten to remove the handful of tow placed in the muzzle of the big gun to prevent her 'drowning' as we crossed the rough water, and I didn't quite fancy the risk of firing thirty-two drams of powder with so solid an obstruction in the barrel. However, teal are the simplest of wild fowl, and as they sat well together a shot from the large shoulder gun stopped four out of the six, all drakes; lovely objects, with their exquisitely pencilled plumage and bright contrasted colours. This was a good beginning, and a mile or so further up the estuary we observed a couple of geese sitting on a dry sandbank. They were evidently 'pensioners' or pricked birds, so we decided to wait till the flowing tide should take us to them, when I killed the pair, right and left with the 'cripple stopper,' as they rose off the sea within 40 yards. This last acquisition, however, had cost us a considerable delay, over an hour, and during that time the main bodies of geese had been passing in from the sea, filing off in long, black, gaggling skeins to the salt grasses ahead. And on our arrival on the edge of their feeding grounds, we truly have good reasons for abusing that unlucky pair of pensioners, and our own folly in wasting a precious hour in securing them. For there, all congregated on the wide stretching flat of slobby ooze, sat some thousand geese, greedily guzzling on the succulent salt grass, while two creeks in the level mud, which appeared to converge on their position, were each occupied by a rival gunner.

How we anathematized our 'ill luck' (as bad judgement or carelessness is usually called) needs not to be told. Regrets and posthumous wisdom were alike of no avail, and nothing remained to us but lie flat and watch the course of events. Gradually, foot by foot, as the flowing tide rose in the creeks, we watched our rivals pushing nearer and nearer to the black and clamorous phalanx before them. Presently they lay within a gunshot and a half, and their success appeared but a matter of moments.

But a sudden change took place in the tide of fortune. All at once and for no visible reason, the thousand pairs of dark pinions were spread, and with a sonorous roar the anserine host rose on the wing. Directly towards us they shape their flight: close over the three prostrate punters passed their loudly gaggling columns, apparently quite unconscious of threatening danger, for in the open water just outside our unseen craft they splash down with wheeling flight and graceful evolution, describing in their descent a thousand eddying, opposing circles, concentric, eccentric, and elliptic. The position of the rival gunners was now reversed, for while the two 'early birds' had to extricate themselves, stern first from the creeks, we were in a position for immediate action. Luck had stepped in to help us where foresight failed. The geese sat very scatteredly, so much so that while occupying acres of water they did not offer at any single point a dense mass on which to direct the stanchion gun. In a few minutes we were close on their flank and already among the rearmost stragglers, and within range of the main line, when they again rose suddenly and spontaneously as before. A shot as they rose would probably have secured four or five; but I prudently refrained, for they were only shifting their quarters, and almost immediately pitched again on the mud edge, within a quarter of a mile. Once more we set in towards them: again we reached the fatal range, and ere they rise the big muzzle yarns within 200 yards of their dense ranks. Then the clamorous roar of their departure resounded: they had just risen clear of the mud, when the thunder of the stanchion gun booms over the watery waste. Back rebounds the punt, and through the cloud of smoke we see the deadly result. Their line is broken, and the wide gap cut by 10 oz. of B.B. is strewn with the spoils. Ten geese fall at once on the mud, another, hard hit, slants obliquely downwards, while from their retreating host a pair more of 'droppers' turn over, and fall dead on the sea. Now follows a lively quarter of an hour, and just as all are secured down comes the snow again. Thick and fast it comes in blinding sheets, blotting out the sight of sea and sky, of geese and gunners. But the tide is now over; we have had enough; so with a fresh breeze, and the ebb in our favour, we set sail and spin away homewards."

Tension between Abel Chapman and RPG

In 1886 it is not hard to detect a sense of growing tension between a young Abel Chapman and RPG. In that year the book, 'Shooting, Moor and Marsh' was published in the prestigious Badminton Library Series. RPG co-authored the book with Lord Walsingham and wildfowl, waders, and methods of shooting were all described in detail by RPG.

Surprisingly Abel Chapman, when asked to review the book wrote;

"Do not let me appear to write disparagingly of the Badminton Series, to one section of which (Big Game Shooting) I am to be a humble contributor. It is only in comparison with the high standards of the rest of that excellent work that I venture to regard the wildfowling section as inadequate, scarcely worthy either of the theme or of the Badminton Series. The technical details as to measurements of punts, punt guns with the descriptions of ordinary coastal fowling are all right, but as to the rest, well stick to Hawker".

On reading the foregoing RPG rallied his supporters and it was not long before letters appeared in 'The Field' condemning Abel Chapman's comments. Edward Sharp and Leonard Brook wrote letters complimenting RPG on the content of the wildfowling section.

But why did Abel Chapman write so disparagingly about RPG's wildfowling section? Here is a likely explanation. In 1886 Abel Chapman had written a series of articles on, "Wildfowl of the North-East Coast" which appeared in 'The Field' magazine. Shortly after publication he had received a letter from RPG. We reproduce this as it appeared in Chapman's book.

> *"Sir, please pardon a stranger troubling you. I know you are an accomplished wildfowler and may be inclined to give me some advice. I am anxious to have a few days' punting now and again within reach of here. I go abroad every year for wildfowling, but am rather in want of an odd day now and again nearer home. I may say that I have no notion whatever in the smallest degree of putting my punt on other folks' water, and might only come for a week in the entire season I want more to collect specimens than to get heavy shots."*

Abel Chapman with his puntsman Selby Allison.

The feud between Chapman and RPG had arisen because Chapman had punted at Holy Island for many years and in 1887 RPG intended to set up his Wildfowling Headquarters at Fenham, on the mainland opposite Holy Island. Here he would have access to the same punting grounds that Chapman and island punts frequented every winter, moreover RPG seemed intent on spending a considerable amount of time there.

Sometime later Abel Chapman reflected on the correspondence he had with RPG

> *"On the faith of these (unsought) assurances, and their writer's name, I gave such local information as lay in my power, offered the use of my boat and gun &c. with the following result. Almost immediately afterwards this gentlemen not only placed his own punt, with one of the largest guns, on the very water where I and others were already established, but proceeded to install thereon a professional puntsman, in his own pay, to shoot all day and every day from the start of the season till its close! Not content with this, this gentleman-poulterer and wildfowl shooter by proxy caused nets to be stretched across the mudflats calculated to catch the flights of small waders &c, by wholesale; and also endeavoured to establish a decoy on private ground adjoining, so as far as possible to deprive the local gunners of any sport; and this on open waters, for which neither he nor they paid rent, or enjoy any preferential claim , and where from time immemorial the shooting had been free for all."*

There is no doubt that the gentleman-poulterer referred to by Abel Chapman was RPG and Chapman was deeply offended by this behaviour.

RPG's Diary continued

1887. RPG's new wildfowling headquarters at Fenham le Mill

RPG comments about Fenham le Mill and the cottage he had rented ," this is a perfect place for me in many ways, it is within four hours by rail of Thirkleby, near a station (within two miles) and a telegraph office, daily post,- a comfortable house, the walls of which are washed by the sea, a good cook (my landlady) and a safe and easy launching place for fowling punts, the shooting all to myself, where it is worth going afloat, and thousands of wildfowl if only I can get to 'em!"

He arrived at his new fowling headquarters on 24 January 1887. His punt and double gun would have been transported by rail to Beal station and dispatched on a horse drawn carriage to Fenham le Mill. At the end of the week he laments, "I had no regular puntsman at Fenham which was much against my success.". One can only speculate who he had with him; perhaps someone from his estate or a local man?

The cottage at Fenham-le-Mill.

The map shows the position of punting grounds at Holy Island 1887. RPG's fowling HQ. is circled in red.

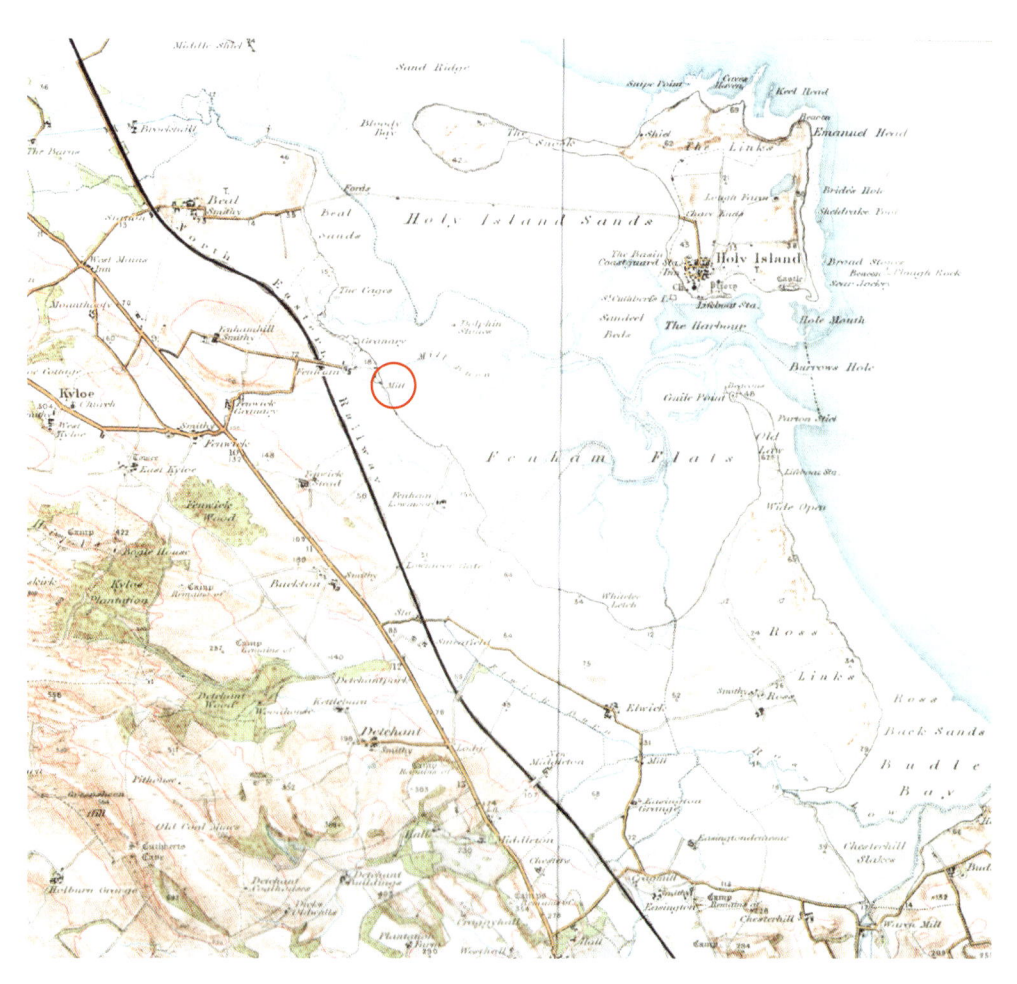

Several small shots of brent geese were made, the largest being 8 on 25 January. Returning home on the 28 January RPG rejoiced that, despite there being a number of other punts working the Fenham Flats, they all launched from close to the harbour on Holy Island where a number of punt sheds had been erected. He observed that from his position on the mainland at Fenham Mill he had the advantage over the island punts as when the wind blew from north to south they were unable to go afloat, but he would be able to venture out. RPG was once again excited at the prospect of great sport. Optimistic as ever, his diary reads, "I have frequently seen geese on Fenham Flats just round my house, so closely packed that could I come well within shot of them I could kill over 100 birds!" In fact, rather amusingly he was to return on 15 February, staying for three days, and records he was "blown off". "No sport!" Perhaps the wind was from the east and this would have favoured the Island punts. Such was punt gunning.

1887. RPG visits Friesland, Northern Holland

In October 1887 RPG travelled from Thirkleby to Leeuwarden in Northern Holland, again to join Gould on board *Watergeus* lying off Holwerd, Friesland. He arrived on 8 October after a journey that took two days. Gould was already on board and the pair spent the next day preparing to go afloat and assessing where their best chance of a decent shot might be achieved. Below decks, in the evening, the talk would have been of sport; RPG had just enjoyed fourteen days of good partridge shooting since the beginning of September and before that, a couple of days grouse at Swinton Park, Yorkshire producing over 400 brace on each occasion. Interestingly George Gould seldom features as a guest of RPG's at Thirkleby Hall. He did not seem to have a great interest in shooting what he referred to as 'poultry'. His focus always appears to be wildfowling.

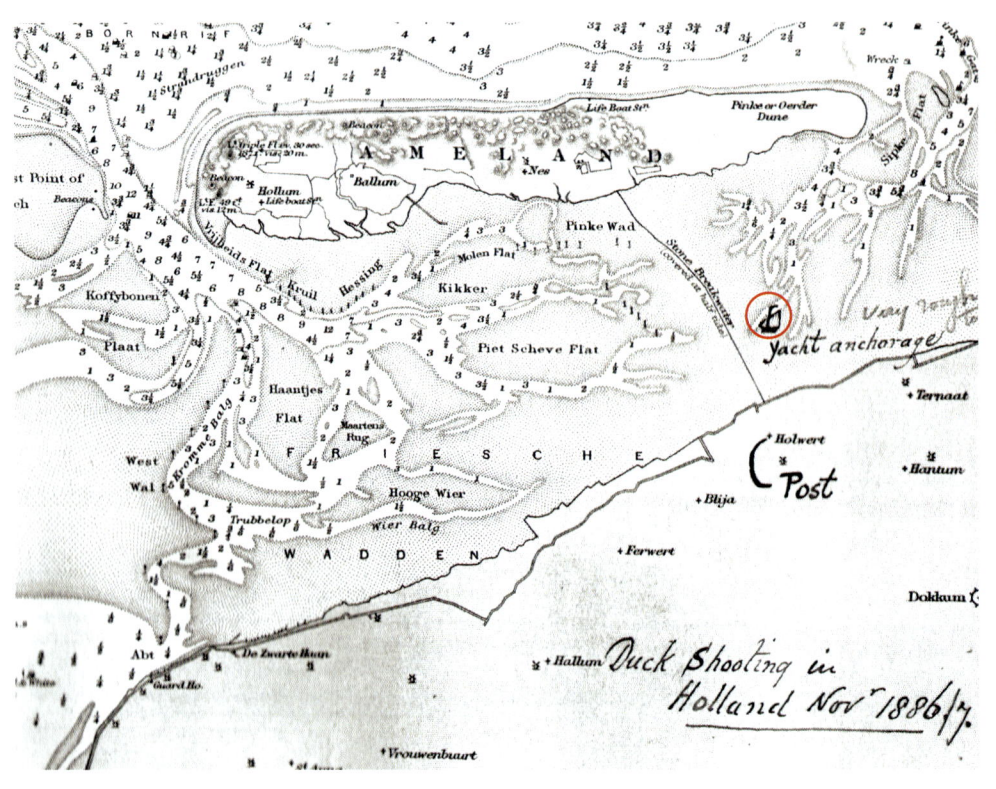

North Holland the punting grounds and RPG marked the anchorage of *'Watergeus'* in November 1886/87

Their first day afloat was very productive, using Gould's 2 inch Holland and Holland the total bag for the day was 53 wigeon and 2 pintail. There is no record of the number of shots taken, but there most certainly would have been several. Gould would have watched from the following boat as RPG and Grimes stalked the wigeon and when a shot was taken he was always close by to help with the pickup. The gunners would then change places and it would be RPG's turn to enjoy the spectacle of his friend trying for the next shot. A hurricane blew the following day and such was its force that two vessels were lost on the coast not far from where they were moored. As is often the case, sport was good on the days after a storm with RPG getting a shot of 45 wigeon and 1 pintail and another excellent shot of 30 wigeon, 1 teal and 1 pintail. They then endured four days when it was simply too rough to go afloat. Further small shots were made by each of them on 18 and 19 October and then it was time for RPG to return home. Gould stayed on and records a bag of 742 duck for the season (probably mainly wigeon).

RPG summarised the trip, "We saw countless numbers of wildfowl on the flats off the shore near Holwerd; but never could manage a good shot, as the birds constantly frequented the centre of inaccessible banks, and the banks being very flat, by the time we could work up to the ducks, they were all afloat and scattered. If fowl would only frequent the channels more than they do, we might have grand sport."

1888/89. Holy Island revisited

RPG returned to Fenham on 16 January 1888. Steven Shuttler had travelled up from Lymington to make everything ready for his arrival. RPG had been impressed by Shuttler's skill in working a double punt to fowl when he had punted with him in Husum in 1883. Now he had a competent puntsman and the prospect of some good fowling lay ahead. As so often the case with wildfowling, not everything went to plan: the first week produced very little; 8 Brent geese and a small number of wigeon. Interestingly he left out of his Wildfowling Diary a shot on 19 January of 52 dunlin and grey plover which was recorded elsewhere! Sport must have been poor as he went back to Thirkleby to shoot pigeons for a couple of days. February was equally unrewarding although a fine flying shot of 10 brent geese was made on 14 February. RPG's season finished on 16 February but Shuttler stayed on until 1 March adding another 27 head including a wild swan, 19 brent geese, 6 wigeon and a mallard.

RPG summarised the season, "I had very bad luck at Fenham. I was constantly on the verge of obtaining several splendid shots at both geese and wigeon but always failed. There were about 2000 wigeon and 4000 brent geese about the flats but the weather being calm, warm and fine, the birds usually kept out of reach on the open sea and when they did come in to feed were almost unapproachable."

In the autumn of 1888 there was no trip to Holland as Gould was not punting abroad that season. RPG's wildfowling did not start until 4 February 1889 when he went to stay at Fenham Mill, joining Shuttler who had already bagged 75 head, including 19 brent geese, 16 wigeon and a number of mallard. A new single punt had been built for Shuttler's use and he used this punt with the 2 inch Bentley and Playfair when RPG was not at Fenham.

On RPG's arrival the double punt was put into service breeched with the double gun. First the weather was mild and then the wind went north and hopes were high but the next day a hurricane of wind and snow made punting difficult. A number of small shots of ducks and geese were made; perhaps the most notable being 7 brent geese on 7 February. Gould then came to stay but sport was poor and as luck would have it, the day he left RPG made a 'capital shot' of 13 wigeon. He describes the shot, "I killed the wigeon in one shot. If only I could have approached 50 yards nearer to them I should have killed 50. Though the birds were splendidly packed, and many of them, it was blowing so hard we could scarce work the punt and the water being so rough I could not lay the gun true!"

The season closed for RPG on 23 February and he noted that it had proved to be a poor season at Fenham.

We digress to recount a short story RPG tells in his diary. One night RPG was flighting wigeon under the moon, close to Fenham Mill, when he saw a large black object far out on the sandbanks. He was unable to fathom out what it was. He thought at first it was a bear! At length he made it out to be a large dog which appeared more dead than alive, soaked to the skin and covered in sea weed. The story goes that RPG fed it some biscuits and even offered it a swig of brandy which it rejected. The weather had been stormy and he concluded the dog had been washed overboard, from a wrecked steamer or a passing vessel and then swam to the sandbank. The dog followed RPG back to Fenham and the next day he gave it to the Captain of a small coaster. It thereafter lived a happy life cruising the Northumberland coastline. The dog turned out to be a Newfoundland water dog!

RPG and Steven Shuttler beside the double punt on which is mounted the double breech-loading puntgun. His HQ is the cottage on the shore at Fenham-le-Mill.

Footnote1: In March 1889 RPG received news that his old friend and mentor William Speight had died at the age of 76. There is no record of whether RPG attended the funeral.

Footnote 2: In July 1889 RPG went to Foster's sale room in Pall Mall and purchased Col. Peter Hawker's double Flint (Right lock) and Percussion (left lock) punt gun (built in 1824 and first fired in 1825 at Starlings). The price he paid was £12 (another quoted figure was £15 but this may have been after commission).

Autumn 1889. Remarkable sport off the coast of Holland

RPG left London on 20 October 1889 crossing to Holland and arriving at Leeuwarden and thereafter onward to Holwerd, Friesland, where he joined George Gould on 21 October aboard '*Watergeus*'. This was his third visit to Holwerd and it turned out to be a remarkable fortnight of fowling.

RPG notes that Gould had joined his yacht a week earlier on 13 October and had already enjoyed some excellent sport. His two best shots being 67 wigeon and 50 wigeon; and with other shots a total of 319 fowl brought to hand. It must have crossed RPG's mind that he had, so to speak, missed the boat.

Gould, always the gentleman, got RPG into the punt as soon as the weather allowed. It was 12 o'clock when they set off from the yacht and by 3 o'clock he had fired four shots! In RPG's words, "I killed in these four shots no less than 132 wigeon. Each shot was as follows 33-14-40-45. The third shot was without exception the best one I ever fired and had I aimed properly I must have bagged 80 to 100! There were many hundreds, covering half an acre, sitting so close that it would have been hard to put a pin between them. I approached within 50 yards of the birds as they sat huddled together on a level spit of smooth sand. As it was (as badly as I managed it) this was the best day's sport I ever saw or even heard of in so short a time. In three shots I killed 118 wigeon! The second shot appears an insignificant one, but the fact is I dropped 25 or 30 birds. I did not delay to gather them because of the magnificent shot number 3 that suddenly appeared within a quarter of a mile to windward. I knew also that Gould was coming up in the following boat to pick up the birds. Then, by the time I had finished off the 3rd shot yet another grand shot was to be seen within a few hundred yards. Re-loading, I went at once to the 4th shot and bagged 45. By the time I could return to the scene of the former shots many birds had drifted away on the flood tide. Magnificent sport, and a curious mixture of ecstasy and slavery and a predominant feeling that I ought to have (with the glorious chances thrown my way) surely bagged many more fowl than I did."

There followed a spell of wild wet weather giving time aboard '*Watergeus*' to reflect on the sport that both men had enjoyed. They had experienced a period of strong easterly wind, and they concluded that this was what had brought large numbers of migrating fowl to their shore.

Weather conditions made punting difficult but they got afloat on 24 October. RPG was again on the gun and made another splendid shot, this time he laid the gun well and although not expecting to pick up more than 20 birds, the shot was well placed and the bag was 60 wigeon and 2 pintail.

Thereafter the weather deteriorated and the east winds strengthened to gale force. It was time to trade the spoils of their sport, in the small port of Leeuwarden and collect provisions. The storm abated and they found by 28 October that many of the fowl had moved south. They picked up several small shots of wigeon and brent but by 31 October decided to seek pastures new.

Gould sailed the yacht to Zoutkamp, some 20 miles to the north and RPG went by road, via Groningen, a town he wished to see and where he had business to do.

'*Watergeus*' anchored in Zoutkamp Sunday 3rd November 1889. The results of the previous days three shots are displayed.

The Wildfowling Diary of Sir Ralph Payne-Gallwey Bart. 1874-1916.

Gould made good passage to Zoutkamp, anchoring en route to lower the punt and make three shots; another 39 wigeon and 7 pintail coming to hand! In the meantime RPG remarks that his trip had not been much fun as it had involved a 4 hour boat trip on the Groningen Canal, resulting in him arriving very late in the evening of 1 November. They were now together and there was once again the prospect of good sport. Their new fowling grounds were undisturbed and Gould knew that, 'Babbler's Creek' had every prospect of providing them with the opportunity of a good shot. It was here that he had seen enormous numbers of wigeon, noting that, as they rose, their wings, "sounded like thunder!" So it was that on 2 November both men made successful shots. RPG took the first shot, picking up 47 wigeon and later Gould made a similar shot of 44, and another of 30. RPG comments that it was, "another glorious day". In fact, had Gould been luckier he would have accounted for 100 birds.

The 3 November was a Sunday and as they did not go afloat, there was time enough to pose for a photograph (see page 120/21). Thereafter for the next three days they punted together taking it in turns to go with Steven Shuttler in the punt as opportunities arose. They had the yacht moored close by with crew members on board so, in the event of poor weather, they always had a safe haven. Their day would have been spent 'glassing' with telescopes for fowl from the 24ft following boat and then, one going to stalk fowl while the other watched from a distance. Immediately after a shot was taken the crew of the following boat would have come to assist with the pick-up.

On the 4th they picked up 33 wigeon and 2 pintail. The following day 23 wigeon and 1 pintail. Finally on 6th, although going afloat from six in the morning, they only added 7 more wigeon and 10 brent geese. The weather had changed; it was now calm and warm and the fowl became 'wild as hawks' which ended any chance of another shot.

In seventeen days of fowling they had shot together 802 ducks and geese. Their two best days were 132 and 121. RPG writes, "The first day all to my gun. My heaviest shots 67-47-46-40. Gould's heaviest shots 67-50-44. I also twice bagged 33 at a shot, and Gould once 33 and again 32."

On 7 November RPG departed Zoutkamp and returned to England.

1890. An account by Thomas Mayer Pike; punting in severe weather conditions, Veere Gat, South Holland

"A wet sheet and a howling sea,

A wind that follows fast,

And fills the white and rustling sails,

And bends the gallant mast."

Cunningham

George Gould concentrated his punting operation in North Holland, while in the big estuaries of South Holland, the East and West Schelds, Thomas Pike presided. This is a record of a few days afloat giving a wonderfully descriptive account of what it was like going afloat on Continental waters.

"Following the mildest January for 50 years something like seasonable weather made its appearance towards the end of February in 1890 which reminds us of the old saying, "a green Christmas and a full church yard." Strong easterly winds and night frost had lasted for over a week when on the 27 February I decided to try some of the big estuaries for a short cruise. It was a beautiful morning with a light north east wind, but shortly after leaving the sheltered water in the launch, a heavy black cloud worked up to the north, and in half an hour we were running up the river in a blinding snow storm squall, with half a gale of wind. This sort of thing continued all day, and although we kept on the punting ground until dark it was impossible to launch the punts with any chance of success. It was not advisable to anchor up for the night in such an exposed place so I steamed off towards the lights of a harbour some four miles off, and getting in had a comfortable night of it, which would certainly not have been the case outside in the estuary as the strong squalls and snow continued all through the night making it look something like winter when I came on deck in the morning, the pier and quay being thickly covered with snow, and the deck of the launch, even over the boiler being hidden by a mixture some inches thick of snow and ice. It was about half past six and still blowing hard but as we had steam I was determined to start at once and try a sheltered bit of water I knew of some eight miles to leeward of where we had spent the night. As we left the harbour, and got outside we found a good sized swell running but luckily right behind us and after an hour's steam we got into a small creek running at right angles to the main river where the water was smooth enough for the punts. About a mile up the creek we let go the anchor opposite a long island which presented one of those sights which are common enough to the eye of a puntsman, snow clad and with its edges lined by a thick fringe of drift ice, it was almost covered with birds right abreast of us. Not far out of shot were several hundred curlew huddled up together with their necks tucked in, thinking more apparently, of how many degrees of frost there had been the night before than of any possibility of danger from us. Away on the left, a vast congregation of oystercatchers trying to derive some benefit from the feeble rays of the sun now high enough up to throw some light if little warmth on the wintery scene beneath. On the right, on the extreme point of the island which was bare of rushes and exposed to the swell that came in from the wide expanse of water outside were a nice bunch of wigeon, and some fifty or sixty brent geese with them. It was just high water and I knew we ought to attack these birds without loss of time, but just at that moment the savoury steam of bacon arose from the fo'castle and I was reminded of the fact that I had been on deck for two hours on a tolerable cold sort of a morning. When we did get out after them the tide had ebbed a good bit and they were more scattered and the wind was still strong enough to send in a nasty swell. The result was that after two hours of hard work we came back having made an indifferent shot of a miserable nine wigeon.

The wind was however now rapidly falling away so after lunch, on the last of the ebb, we ran off some twelve miles down towards the sea to some banks that were sure to have fowl on them in this sort of weather. Here, sure enough, we discovered some 300 wigeon, in a very favourable position –half of them on the sand on the edge of the channel - the rest in the water close by. Everything was favourable; a light beam wind which made no lop, just enough to darken the water and under the shore the young flood running up in the right direction.

We launched two punts to set to those wigeon. Some of the birds on the bank flew up as we were approaching and joined their comrades in the water. This was rather favourable for us as we had to fire at them, owing to them having worked down towards us a bit; thus rendering the others pitched on the bank too far off. We got within sixty yards easily enough; they were not thickly placed together but in a long line, which of course gave the second gun a good chance, as they grouped on hearing the first shot. On hearing my companions' gun let go, at once I gave the word to fire. On the smoke clearing we saw we had been well into them and had a busy half hour with the cripples, wigeon being struck from sixty to a hundred and twenty yards from the muzzles of the guns. We let them all drift into the edge and collected them together to clean and count them – forty nine of them. We also picked up a wing broken one later in the day, so we can claim an even fifty for that shot. We had another straggling shot at wigeon later and got ten or a dozen and I killed three ducks after dark. They made such a noise I imagined there were at least a dozen of them.

The next morning on coming up I found a change. The air was much warmer. The wigeon were unapproachable and all we got was a long shot at some black geese which produced some half a dozen. This was March 1st, the 2nd was a Sunday. The frost however started again, as hard as ever and on Monday we ran up to another big estuary, some twenty miles north of where we were. Daylight was finished by the time we got to an anchorage that night. As there was a good moon however we went out with the last of the ebb to try the brent on some huge banks that lay beside us. The ebb took us rapidly down for some four miles. Then we turned in towards the edge of the banks to look for the geese in the direction of the place where we had anchored the steamer. At first however the ground was so flat we had not water to get within shot of the edge and though we heard plenty of geese we could get no chance of a shot. The ice too was forming with great rapidity on the shallow water.

About half way up, the bank became steeper and with the night glasses I made out some two to three score of brent. The moon was however, by this time, rather high up and they jumped when we were still over 100 yards off. They crossed our bows however at some sixty yards, well up in the air, so I dipped my gun and gave them a passing salute, which brought down nine of them with a mighty splash among the ice and shallow water ahead of the punts. Getting our

Tom Pike's steam launch *Bulldog* moored at Brouwershaven

hands wet in picking up these birds we began to discover how cold it was; the oars and decks of the punts were masses of ice and judging from the amount floating in the river next morning I should say the temperature was pretty well down to zero – at all events it was the coldest night I have been out in since 1881. No-one on board got any sleep after three o'clock. As soon as the ebb stream went again, till daylight, the ice went down, crashing against our bows with one almost continuous roar.

On coming on deck, about seven next morning, a fine scene in semi arctic style was visible; huge pans of ice in all directions – numbers of wildfowl on them floating down towards the sea- while great banks were turned white as snow, their smooth surfaces only broken here and there by the fantastic outlines of piled up ice, where on the edges of the slopes, the great fields of ice had been broken and heaped together by the fall of the ebb tide. The air however felt curiously warm and I said to my assistant, "I am afraid there is going to be another change". On trying the first lot of birds, by their behaviour, we were confirmed in our opinion - they would not have it at any price – kept flying up in twenties and fifties when we were a quarter of a mile away. On a small pan of ice close to us were ten wigeon, huddled up as close as they could get and paying no attention to our punts whatever. I had seen them and despised (sic) them some time before this, but now, with a turn of the wrist, the bow of the punt was put toward them and remarking to my companion, "May as well have something", I let go the big gun. Two of them managed to struggle off but the rest of them were soon in our hands. That was the only shot we got and after two hours incessantly trying birds to no purpose, we returned to the launch and dropped down to the mouth of the river.

Here too the birds were in the same wary condition, all we got was a straggling shot at some mallard. On the very outside edge of this bank, on the open sea, amid some piled up blocks of ice, we saw with the telescope some birds which we thought were grey geese and on getting up to them found they were curlew. Annoyed at the trouble they had given us we fired the big gun into them and killed twenty seven of them, scarcely a dozen of them escaped.

Snow and hard weather, Meneersche Creek, Holland

The wind had now come decidedly from the S.W. and the tide was full. It was a fine sight to watch, as the tide covered the banks, the huge sheets of ice that floated off and went seaward. The wind now rapidly increased and we were kept awake the best part of this night by the roar of a heavy South West gale; a pleasing variety from the night before, when a very similar noise was made in a dead calm by the ice pans brushing against the chain cable and bows of the vessel. The next morning the wind flew into the North West and we had to clear out in a hurry, as this shift in the wind would put in a nasty sea in a short time. Accompanied by our old friends the snow squalls, we ran up the river some twelve miles to the junction of the estuaries, where the channel which brought us home divided off. However, as it was still early I determined to follow the other river up some dozen miles, to an immense bank which joined the main shore. Under the edge of this one we could always shoot, as the wind was blowing right off it. It was also higher than any of the middle banks and after the latter were covered, the birds always came in to the higher one, as being the last ground uncovered by the tide.

For the next three hours nothing turned up but as I came on deck after lunch, about a hundred black geese came flying over from leeward and pitched on the edge of the marsh right abreast us. Something unusual about their appearance as they pitched made me take the glass to look at them and I at once saw that they were bernicle (sic). They ran up the sand on which they had pitched and, taking a few pecks at the grass on the marsh, all lay down apparently for a rest. We launched the punts and were after them in next to no time. It was so rough however, that we dared not run out our guns till halfway to the birds, then with firm sand under us we and our short setting poles, we advanced rapidly to the attack in spite of the head wind. On getting within 250 yards a slight contretemps arose. Another lot of about 100 geese flew over our heads and, after some uncertain sweeps round, pitched down, some twenty yards nearer than the first lot.

They of course had seen us and remained standing up, regarding us with a considerable amount of interest. We ought, of course, to have waited some minutes, but this was impossible. In ten minutes the whole marsh would be covered and with a strong wind now blowing, the thing was not to be thought of. All this passed through my mind in a second and I whispered my companion to get on as quick as possible. On getting within 120 yards they assumed a most threatening appearance, with thin long necks stretched out their full extent, like so many double magnums of champagne. My man said, "They are going Sir." "Push on till they lift," I replied. The unexpected often happens and to our intense surprise these birds let us run in to within sixty yards of them before their wings opened. At this distance our two and three quarter pounds of shot hustled through them with fatal effect, and, as the smoke of the half pound of powder we had burned, clearing, we saw the marsh well covered with dead and crippled geese. Several of them soon began to recover themselves and began flying up and dropping in the water to leeward. After them I sent the man and paddled up to the marsh to attend to the main business. I found it an awkward job the ground being covered thickly with ice and snow while the tide was rising rapidly; and what was worse a great number of narrow but very deep drains intersected it: the result of this was I lost several birds, which were of course running in all directions and owing to the above named obstacles able to go faster than I could. In the end I had 28 fine birds laid out on the bank to which the tide had now risen. The other punt returned with eight droppers and reported two more dead ones that had fallen too far out for him to venture, so we had 36 splendid bernicles (sic) laid out in a row and a mighty array they looked.

It hardly seemed credible that two guns could cover ground sufficiently spacious for their great bodies to stand on. We had to hurry off as the rising tide made it rougher and rougher to go off to the launch again as it was heavily laden with geese. We shipped plenty of water before getting safely on board. We saw two more crippled geese washed out by the tide but they were picked up by two professionals in a punt that had come out of a little creek on the main shore, a little too late for them as it turned out. The two birds that had dropped dead outside us were picked up by a man passing in a smack who stayed his vessel for that purpose. So we had 40 of these fine geese picked up on the spot from this one shot of ours. We had now to get home the best part of forty odd miles, with the best part of a gale blowing and only three hours of daylight. We managed this alright but the last two hours after dark, with a falling tide and occasional snow storm. It was a somewhat anxious period as a mistake meant another night out reclining on a sandbank at a very uncomfortable angle. As I crossed over that night from the yacht's mooring in the channel to the hotel I felt that a good night's rest in a place where the ice pans ceased from troubling and sou' westers are at rest was a very agreeable prospect. Our bag for the six days amounted to wigeon 77, bernicle geese 36, curlew 27, brent 21, ducks 9 total 170.

The above gives a tolerably fair impression of the sort of time we had of it after wildfowl in big estuaries in winter. There is a good deal of hard work some anxiety and loss of sleep but we usually managed to get some birds. Also it is a form of sport which one does not get tired why this is I do not know but the fact remains. Possibly it may be found in the circumstances that it affords a considerable amount of occupation to one's brains as well as one's hands and there is no considerable amount of difficulty attached to it."

Footnote: T M Pike of Fascadale, Ardrishaig died 5 February 1908 aged 56

RPG's Diary continued

1889/90. RPG returns to Holy Island

At the start of the wildfowling season in 1889 RPG did not join George Gould for their usual foray to Holland as Gould had gone to Morocco with Mr H. D. Scath. He wrote to RPG in November recording the bag for 24 days shooting during his visit in late November and early December.

In January 1890 Steven Shuttler was again employed by RPG to act as his puntsman at Holy Island. Shuttler was not restricted to going afloat only when RPG was at Fenham; in fact RPG seems to have positively encouraged him to go out every day and on occasion at night under the moon. This was not uncommon at Holy Island and by the time RPG arrived on 21 January Shuttler had accounted for 5 brent, 21 wild duck (mallard), 1 goldeneye, 1 wigeon, 39 knots (a single shot with the double gun by Frank Payne-Gallwey, RPG's cousin) and 2 godwits.

On arrival that day RPG added 2 brent geese but try as he might the next three days were a disaster with flat calm weather and all the fowl safe out at sea around the Farne Islands. So he went home!

Summarising the season he writes, "a simply disastrous season for fowl at Fenham. Three white frosts and no snow or real east wind all winter. All we killed at Fenham was 49 brent, 21 wild duck, 1 goldeneye and 1 wigeon."

Captain Gould's bag shooting in Morocco

RPG returned in mid-February but he records that, "Fenham is perfectly hopeless". On 22 February 1890 he instructed Shuttler to put his punts in store and return the guns to Thirkleby.

1890/91 WILD FOWLING SEASON. FENHAM LE MILL, HOLY ISLAND

It was not until after Christmas 1890 that RPG returned to Fenham. He arrived on 31 December bringing his double Holland and Holland to Beal station as passenger luggage. Shuttler was there to assist him transport the gun by carriage to his fowling headquarters at Fenham Mill. The punt and gun were then launched into the Mill Burn and they went afloat together that afternoon and got a good shot of 7 brent geese. An equally successful day followed: they were afloat from 7 am and returned at 4 pm, a long day but their reward was 15 brent geese, 7 scaup and 1 Slavonian grebe. The next day was mild and warm and scaup were the focus of RPG's attention. He remarked that although they got well within range and knocked off feathers, their skins seemed made of tin or some other shot proof material. However, they managed to bag 7.

On 12 January, following a short break back at Thirkleby Hall, RPG returned accompanied by Frank Payne-Gallwey, just in time to watch Shuttler make a great shot of 25 brent geese. This shot was later to be depicted in an oil painting that RPG commissioned by the artist Anthony de Bree. Despite, "garden party" weather the week progressed well and several good shots at brent were made. Working the tides they would launch at 8 am and pass the day afloat, returning to Fenham as the tide ebbed around 4 in the afternoon. The record for 14 January states, "a delightful day, just right, gale from the north, driving sleet and snow, heavy squalls and bitter cold. Nearly made really good heavy shot at wigeon, 500 about. Trying for shots all day. 8 brent, 9 wigeon, 4 scaup." The weather improved for them on 16 January and RPG records, "A fine wild day. Very cold, gusty east wind with snow. A good many geese about but with several punts and sailing boats out, and their black coated occupants popping off at all ranges continually all day. I could not get a fair chance though I bagged three times as many birds as all the other, 'frighteners' put together. What delighted me immensely, I cut some geese down right under their noses!" Total bag for the day was 14 brent, 2 wigeon and 1 longtail duck.

Horse and carriage on the Pilgrim's Way, the route across the sands to Holy Island

This is the first entry in the diary indicating the competitive element of fowling at Holy Island. Criticism would not have been one sided. After all, the Island's fisherman/fowlers were trying to make a living taking 'gentlemen' out punting and selling fowl that came to hand during the winter months. RPG could not have been the most popular person on the Island and we shall see that Abel Chapman had words of advice for RPG.

Indifferent weather again led RPG to return to Thirkleby leaving Shuttler to continue his daily forays in pursuit of brent geese. The geese would have been very wild by now and the bags achieved were small.

The 26 January saw RPG back at Fenham but the weather was again against him. This time it was, "nasty, muggy, fuggy, drizzly and calm." Fowling on the 28 January he records a sad occasion. He had been out with Shuttler since 6.30am that morning and they had made a good shot of 7 brent geese, when returning home, after the shot, a messenger on horseback came galloping over the sand banks, bringing the sad news of the death of RPG's brother Lionel. Evidently he had contacted malaria whilst serving as Colonial Civil Engineer and Overseer of Public Works in Demerara, British Guiana.

With the news of the unexpected loss of his brother, RPG returned home to arrange family affairs. However, he went back to Fenham on the 9 February recording that the weather was against him making a successful shot for his friend, Mr G.D. Whatman who had come to stay. He returned to Thirkleby on 14 February.

In summarising the season he writes; "So ends my campaign at Fenham for this year, a season that commenced favourably but ended miserably. I have never seen at most more than 400 to 500 geese on the flats where a year or two ago there were thousands (7,000 to 10,000). I imagine the severe weather abroad sent these birds due south without their coming across as usual to Fenham or else the birds crossed to the east coast of Scotland and, as there was no frost in the north this winter, perhaps they remained there. In mild seasons the geese come to Fenham as a rule in thousands, and when they have safely arrived about the middle of January then we want hard weather so as to tame them, for once with us they remain. Frost in February and the latter half of January, not in December as this year."

One interesting observation came this season from the Holy Island fishermen who had observed many thousands of geese at sea feeding off shore on the drifting weed (Zostera). The weed would have been torn out of the Zostera beds by gales and floated out to sea allowing the birds a plentiful supply of food without the risk of being disturbed by the threats of punts on the Holy Island Flats.

1891 February. RPG visits Beaulieu Lodge, Hampshire

Before the season finally closed RPG was invited by Mr John S. Montagu to stay at Beaulieu Lodge (Palace House) Hampshire, the plan being to punt the Beaulieu Creek. Arriving on 24 February 1891 he describes his findings, "A charming and perfect sporting estate of 10,000 acres, beautifully wild and to all appearances it might be in Scotland though under 100 miles from London. 3,000 acres of lovely woods for game, a tidal creek 6 miles long, strictly preserved for duck shooting, a large lake (Sowley) of 100 acres also some 1000 acres of marsh and snipe land by the sea. The estuary was good for sea trout, grilse, oyster beds and sea fish; all at the door of a wonderful old Manor House."

"They kill in a season, about 3,000 pheasants, 1,500 partridges, 500 ducks punting in the creek. (this year 650) 100 woodcock, as many or more snipe, about 100 grilse (netted and caught with rod) and some 3,000 sea fish with a trawl. What more could a sportsman wish for? Many hundred pigeons are shot here in a winter and Mr J. S. Montagu has twice killed a 100 and more in one day to his own gun."

Beaulieu Lodge, John Montagu's home

Steven Shuttler

The next day they drove down to the mouth of the Beaulieu Creek, a distance of about 5 miles where a small yacht was moored. They then sailed up river towing a fowling punt astern in the hope of finding a shot. RPG was disappointed that no worthwhile shot was seen. That same afternoon they visited Sowley Lake where they spotted five wild swans. Evidently, another fowling punt was on hand and, on going afloat, they were able to stalk within 70 yards of the swans which then bunched! RPG was on the gun and describes what happened, "I took steady aim and the result was a miss fire! I must have dropped three swans at least and possibly the whole five."

The quality of care of the fowling equipment was again called into question when the following day they experienced a bad hang fire when stalking a company of wigeon.

Clearly RPG enjoyed his visit to Beaulieu. Lord Montagu had shown him around the house which he much admired. Although they had not seen many duck, RPG could see the potential of the small estuary. He was not surprised that excellent shots of 46 wigeon and 63 teal had been recorded in the 'Estate Gamebook' by John Montagu.

On leaving Beaulieu on 28 February RPG travelled to Lymington, the home of Steven Shuttler. He regarded Shuttler as the best puntsman who had ever accompanied him. He praised his sober, steady and honest nature and writing in his main game book he states, "Shuttler is always anxious to please and clever and careful at his work and in his care of my guns and boats! Never out of temper and always willing and cheerful through the longest day or the darkest night." Shuttler was, of course, still at Fenham and did not return home until the first week of March. Leaving Lymington RPG travelled to Keyhaven, a place he had always wanted to visit as it was the fowling headquarters of the celebrated Col. Peter Hawker. On arrival he describes it thus, "I found this place just as depicted in the frontispiece to 'Instructions to Young Sportsmen'… a cluster of small houses, including Col. Hawker's on the verge of the sea, a lovely desolate spot, just the place for punting from, were the fowl still present as in bygone days. Now there are next to none. I casually met Old Shuttler, who was formerly in the employment of Col. Hawker and with whom I had a long and interesting yarn about duck shooting at Keyhaven long ago and of Col. Hawker's success in those days."

1891. Testing W.W.Greener's repairs to the double gun

The double-barrelled Holland and Holland had been completed in March 1885 and had since seen service in all weather conditions every year either in Ireland or Fenham. RPG had experienced a problem with the top rib on the gun in 1888 and he sent it down to Greener's in Birmingham. They had taken the old rib off and re-jointed the barrels. RPG suspected that, in undertaking this work, insufficient care had been taken by Greener's in resetting the barrels parallel so that each shot to a centre with the two circles overlapping one half at 70 yards.

On 30 April 1891 he set up the double gun in Thirkleby Park to establish to his total satisfaction exactly where the gun was shooting. Over the next two days he fired a series of 20 shots at a target 14 ft long by 2 ft. high. He soon established that the right barrel centred its pattern 5 ft. to the right of the point of aim and the left barrel 2 ft. to the right of the point of aim. He also found that the gun shot very high. He set about filing the sight at the breech until he found that the elevation was correct and the following day undertook further alteration to re-establish the correct overlapping centres. The results were summarised in tabular form opposite.

On the afternoon of 2 May he summarised his work, " the above capital and regular shooting was achieved this afternoon and is the result of my having carefully altered the sighting of the gun on the ground, shot by shot till I was satisfied. The result is very different from the other day!"

1891. RPG with Captain George Gould aboard the '*Watergeus*'

In October 1891 George Gould once again invited RPG to join him on board '*Watergeus*.' He arrived on 5 October travelling by steamer from Queensborough to Flushing, and thence "arrived Leeuwarden at 4.30; and so on by carriage to Holward (17miles) and on board the yacht at 8 o'clock."

Day after day they toiled in pursuit of fowl, often rising at 5 am and only returning at 3 or 4 in the afternoon. They saw thousands of wigeon but the weather was fine, and winds were light which made it impossible to approach anywhere near the large flocks of birds. In despair he started for home on 14 October and even this did not go well: a hurricane blew up which he reported as, "the worst gale on the English coast for 10 years." He ended up returning via Brussels and Calais. A short diary entry sums up his feelings, "I travelled quite 1000 miles and spent £30 in obtaining three wretched ducks and yet sundry idiots condemn the sport of punting as easy and idle slaughter."

The results of the pattern testing of the double gun after it returned from Greeners

Gould later returned to Ireland and visited the Shannon estuary.

Gould records his total bag for the season, including his trip to Holland and his days afloat in Ireland 613 fowl and 58 plover and curlew.

1892. Back to Holy Island

The season had not started well in Holland but after Christmas there was the prospect of better wildfowling at Holy Island. RPG and Shuttler arrived together on 28 December, carrying with them the double Holland that promised to shoot to the now corrected point of aim. They were ready to go afloat the following day and launched at 10 am. They were out all day and saw very few brent geese. On the way home RPG, anxious to try the gun, sighted a shelduck which he killed at 80 yds. No doubt he did not fancy eating the shelduck for his tea so he ended the day by adding two plover to the bag with his 12 bore. The following day he concluded that there was no chance of sport at Fenham and went home.

By early January 1892 the weather had improved and he was all set to return to Fenham but then received news that Shuttler was laid up with influenza and rheumatic gout. It was not until early February that Shuttler was properly recovered although he did struggle out and shoot 7 brent geese on the 29 January. RPG arrived on Monday 1 February. There follows a wonderful entry in his diary;

"Hurrah! At 'em at last. Left Thirkleby at 7.30 this morning, afloat at Fenham at 2 o'clock same day. Went to some 300 geese that pitched close to my house. We set to them at once, brought in eleven. All the house turned out to see the sport except the infernal cat who ate the fat pheasant roasting for my dinner." A note added later mentions that 9 more dead geese were picked by the Holy Island fishermen.

RPG then alludes to six days of really enjoyable sport which involved leaving the fowling headquarters at Fenham around 7 am, often returning for a bite at midday and then punting until seven in the evening. Although there were many more brent geese on the slakes (local name for mud flats) than they had seen for the last two seasons they remained very wild. Weather conditions were changeable, one day favourable northerly wind and then as he puts it, "Garden Party weather", hot bright sun and west wind. A good shot was made on 5 February of 6 brent geese but after that RPG returned home as the weather was against him. He did return on 15 February with Frank Payne-Gallwey but by now the season was nearly over and the best shot they made was 13 mallard on 18 February.

Summarising the season he writes; "we had three weeks of very severe weather, about Christmas time during which, and for some time after, my puntsman was ill and confined to the house. Since then we had one good week of east winds with snow and hard frost. But, I did not do well somehow that week, though had I been afloat myself each day, I should have done better. Frank was staying with me and missed a fine shot at wigeon! Very few wild duck and wigeon this season at Fenham compared to former years; but a fair show of brent geese, perhaps a 1000 all told. Myriads of wigeon in Holland but quite inaccessible. Oh for a good old fashioned January again!"

Just before the end of the season RPG notes the arrival at Fenham of Mr de Bree, who had travelled from London to paint a picture of him and Shuttler out on the slakes with his punt and double Holland and Holland. Two days were spent, "paddling about" as he put it, to try and get a good aspect to paint the picture. In April RPG reports that the oil painting is finished, "Mr de Bree completed the 4ft x 2ft oil painting under great difficulty, heavy snow storms, gales of wind and bitter cold. He stuck to it like a hero, though he was often stood for several hours at a stretch over his knees in ooze, painting a half mile from the shore. His picture is admirable, the geese, the punt and the gun, myself and especially Steven Shuttler and the scenery, being a perfect likeness. He is painting a duplicate of the picture for my friend Capt. George Gould."

Today one of the Anthony de Bree's oil paintings can be seen at BASC Headquarters, Marford Mill, Rossett, near Chester.

1892. RPG's correspondence with Abel Chapman

In 1892 RPG was anxious to know how his own fowling successes and observations about brent geese, at Holy Island, compared with those of Abel Chapman. The response he received was not only informative but, in the politest possible way, gives a vivid insight into Abel Chapman's thoughts about RPG's behaviour at Holy Island.

Abel Chapman writes;

> "Your own scores at Fenham ought, I think, to make one envious - that is if any of that quality exists in one's composition. There is no doubt that through your being able to, operate from the Fenham shore you have an envious advantage, dominating the whole line of the slakes and three miles nearer the ground than the rest of us. Also, as you say during westerly gales you have the whole place to yourself since no punt can then cross the deeps- not even in tow. I cannot keep thinking though- if you won't mind me saying so –that there would be a very much better chance of sport both for you personally and for the rest of us, if the birds were only shot from Fenham when you are there yourself. This would give them intervals of rest and time to , "tame" such as they used to have in the days of the ' fisherman–gunners'- but which they never get now . I don't of course wish to infer any single thing as regards your puntsman, whom I have never seen and who I believe is a good sportsman- but it is natural that living at Fenham and having (I suppose) nothing else to do, he should keep pretty constantly on the lookout for a shot whenever an opportunity occurs. I may be wrong but I attribute the present extreme wildness of the geese to this, more perhaps than to any other cause and trust that you will forgive my mentioning it."

The letter closes with notes on pintail records, dates seen and asking if RPG had shot any young birds.

RPG was quick to reply;

> "My man is a most accomplished punter, single or double, and since he has been here I should say he alone has killed three times as many fowl as all the local gunners together."

Abel Chapman comments;

"I took no exception to my correspondent's own shooting, nor to his vicarious boasting; but on remonstrating in mild terms against his employing a paid servant, who practically monopolised the locality, in the face of his promise and the quoted assurances."

RPG's reply is then quoted;

"Do you wish me to tell my man to idle about and do nothing when I am away? Surely he and others have equal chances."

The latter remark we know was wholly incorrect as RPG knew that he had a distinct advantage punting from the west shore at Fenham!

Abel Chapman concludes by saying;

"Alongside 'mala fides' such as this, the petty jealousies, spite, and unfairness of local fowlers sink into insignificance; but comment is superfluous, so I will content myself with repeating the advice to tell nothing- not even to your best friend."

From the correspondence the reader is left in no doubt what Abel Chapman felt about RPG's exploits at Holy Island. As if to underline his feeling he wrote a short piece for 'The Field' magazine in 1892 under the heading, 'Wildfowl and the past winter.'

"The need now is for Arctic weather to make the brent geese accessible with a punt gun. This due to the use for the past few years of a monster gun firing 3lbs of SSG shot, firing several shots

Anthony de Bree's painting of a shot of 25 brent geese with the double gun

a day irrespective of distance in the hope of wing tipping a couple at each discharge. No sense of fair play. Probably the old fashioned fowler with his 60 or 80lb muzzle-loader is expected to die gracefully, to recognise that he is out of date, outpaced, left stranded on a mud-bank by the ebb of time, but one hardly cares to be snuffed out in silence, when the extinguisher is seen to be so faulty; or like the dying swan to sing paeans in horror of our threatened destroyers. Some of whom may perhaps sigh."

> *"Swans sing before they die, me thinks t'were no bad thing*
> *Would certain persons die before they sing."*
>
> (S.T. Coleridge's epigram)

This vaguely shrouded insult was too much for RPG. It was now all too obvious who Chapman was referring to and he demanded an apology. This was never likely to be forthcoming from Chapman but in June 1893 a short note appeared in 'The Field' which we reproduce here headed, 'Wildfowling on the North East Coast.' "In an article which appeared in our issue 20 May on the above mentioned subject there was a paragraph in which an attack was made on some person concerning whose identity no hint was given. Since the publication of the letters which leave for doubting that the accusations were directed against a well-known sportsman, who from our own knowledge of him, we should say could not possibly be guilty of the conduct imputed to him in this article. We much regret that the paragraph in question was inadvertently printed."

As a reader of RPG's diary entries, detailing his activities at Holy Island, over a hundred years later, you must now form your own opinion about RPG's behaviour. What is absolutely certain is that animosity continued, and although RPG went wildfowling at Holy Island until 1896, he would not have been welcomed by Chapman or any of the local gunners.

1892. Unresolved problems with the double Holland and Holland punt gun

Towards the end of the season 1892 the brazed top rib on the double gun had again begun to lift. RPG put this down to the two 9 ft. barrels flexing to varying extent when either barrel was fired singly or when both barrels were fired together. This was a matter of conjecture but in any event the gun was sent to London where Holland and Holland were told to remedy the problem once and for all, after Greener's abortive attempt! The gun went to Holland's on 14 April and remained there until 23 May. They undertook the setting down and re-brazing of the rib and in accordance with RPG's instructions, removed the choke from both barrels and also nickel plated both locks. To avoid the brazing fracturing again a 5 inch piece of iron was inserted at the muzzle before resetting down the rib.

Once the gun was returned to Thirkleby Park RPG set about new trials. The gun did not balance to RPG's satisfaction so he bored a small hole on the underside rib between the barrels and poured in three pounds of beeswax at the muzzle, that done, shooting trials commenced in the Park on 10 June 1892. The results are summarised in the table below;

The results were regarded as excellent; both right and left barrels shot independently true to centre of the target with the centre sight, and both barrels together made a wider even spread-pattern.

1893. RPG and George Gould return to Southern Ireland

The 1893 fowling season started for RPG and George Gould with a trip to Ireland. They met up together on 12 October at Foynes, Co. Limerick. It had been 6 years and 8 months since they were last there.

RPG's caption was 'Another sportsman on the scene', or 'Take one and welcome, you splendid fellow'

RPG was the first to go afloat; prospects appeared to be excellent as they had observed good numbers of wigeon and teal. RPG writes," we saw today quite 3 to 400 teal , 200 wild duck and at least 600 to 700 wigeon, all save a few, in a bay round Aughinish Point."

"I fired two shots, the first for 13 teal, 1 wigeon, and second for 18 wigeon. Regarding the shot at teal, had there not been some half a dozen wild ducks between me and the teal I should have killed 50 easily, as they were very tame and splendidly placed , but the ducks frightened the teal up and I had to take a long flying shot at the teal."

A further note in his diary tells of a peregrine falcon 'watching on' after the shot at the teal and the incident was later to form the basis of an illustration by Charles Whymper in the third series of 'Letters to Young Shooters,' published in 1896', seen above. A spell of rough weather resulted in some unspecified damage to the punt. By 17 October it was decided to move to calmer waters and join the yacht *'Scoter'* anchored in the Clare River, 2 miles below the estuary of the River Fergus. RPG accompanied the two Grimes (Gould's puntsmen) and had a rough voyage rowing and sailing the following boat a distance of 17 miles.

'Scoter' was formerly the property of Mr Vincent who used her as a fowling headquarters and punted from her for 15 or more seasons on and around the Fergus estuary. He was a famous wildfowler in the area and enjoyed great sport with his well-known puntsman, 'Sambo' (Peter Considine). He is recorded as having made many notable shots and one magnificent flying shot

at teal on the Shannon Estuary, picking up 106. We believe that Mr A. Vincent owned and used 'Irish Tom', the largest punt gun ever made and on his death the gun was sold to Mr Graves of Limerick who was also a professional wildfowler. The gun later passed into the ownership of James Robertson Justice (of which more in Chapter 18).

Returning now to October 1893 on board 'Scoter', they settled into a daily routine of going afloat at 7.30 each morning, weather permitting and then remaining out until 4 or 5 in the afternoon. Bright, calm days frustrated them but Gould got a good shot of 14 wigeon on 18 October and another of 21, on 21 October, below Coneg Island. RPG had a small shot of 8 mallard off Boland's Rock on the 18th. They experienced thick fog on 24 October which was hopeless for fowling, but that day they bought a fine supply of salmon at 6 pence per pound! On 26 October Gould went off to Dublin on business, returning on 31 October. Meanwhile RPG went to Limerick and on to Dromoland Castle where he enjoyed three days of pheasant and rabbit shooting. While RPG was away, as luck would have it, sport aboard 'Scoter' improved, Gould managing two good shots of green plover, one of 67 and a second of 24 then a shot of 13 wigeon. Finally, just before RPG returned to Yorkshire, Gould managed further shots of 27 wigeon, 37 plover and 2 bean geese.

Gould continued shooting on the Shannon until 8 January bringing their joint totals to 605 ducks and geese, 201 plover and 135 curlew. Gould then went to France to join Walter Pope at the end of January and enjoyed punting for the rest of the season, adding a further 500 ducks and geese with shots of 85 and 53 wigeon .

Over the years nothing appears to have changed when it comes to journalistic nonsense. Here is a paragraph from the contemporary Irish newspaper 'Longford Leader'. It is headed, "Duck Shooting at Clonfinlough" and runs as follows, " During the past week these lakes have been visited by several lovers of the rifle who obtained excellent sport, and brought down some fine birds including Mr Patrick Kerr, of Stokestown and Paddy Covahv." We must expect accidents of this kind if people go duck shooting with rifles!

1893. An account by Walter H. Pope and George Gould punting from Chateau De Truscat in the Gulf of Morbihan

"Wary they gaze - our boat in silence glides,

The slow moving paddles steal along the sides."

Alexander Wilson. "Father of American Ornithology." 1766-1813.

Walter Pope was well known and respected as a wildfowler. He contributed to the section on wildfowling in the book 'Wild-fowl' published in 1905 in the Fur, Feather and Fin Series and often wrote about wildfowling in France. He describes ideal punting conditions in the Gulf of Morbihan on the southern coast of Brittany.

In the winter of 1890 he recorded great success wildfowling from Chateau De Truscat where, using a small punt gun firing 16 oz of shot, he killed 1,425 brent geese, wigeon and mallard. In 1892-93 with a 2 inch Holland and Holland firing 32 oz of shot, he bagged 630 brent geese, 1307 wigeon, 40 mallard, 1 teal, 1 pochard and 82 various birds most of which were coots, a total of 2,061 head from eighty-five shots.

George Gould was a close friend and visited Chateau De Truscat as Pope's guest. This is a description written by Walter Pope of what it was like fowling during the winter of 1893 - 94.

"It will be in the recollection of every lover of wildfowl shooting that the type of weather prevailing in the latter part of December and the first fortnight of January 1893 was exceptionally favourable for the enjoyment of this grand branch of sport, and sportsmen all around the coast, both ashore and afloat, hailed with glee the ice and snow, which bound up the greater part of northern Europe in its iron bonds for so long a spell."

Walter Pope was residing at the Chateau De Truscat, his regular winter wildfowling headquarters overlooking the Bay of Sarzeau. His 2 inch Holland and Holland breech-loader, 'London' gun was formerly the property of George Gould. This gun was breeched onto his double punt and moored close to the Chateau. Gould joined Pope at the end of January 1893 and later exchanged letters with RPG who was afloat at Holy Island in equally demanding weather conditions.

Pope describes this area of the Gulf of Morbihan close to the Chateau where he stayed; "The bays in the neighbourhood of the house are of considerable expanse, and here and there they are studded with islands of larger or smaller magnitude which cause the tide in some of the narrow guts between them to run very hard at times. In many of these bays there are no mud flats whatever, water being of great depth all over, but in others, fine banks of ooze run out from the shore for a mile or more, which are covered in wigeon grass, and the outside edges of same with the coarse broad leaved weed known as Zostera Maritima. Round many of the islands and clusters of rocks, where the flats exist, the vegetation is more or less luxuriant. Naturally with these attractions this spot is specially patronised by wigeon and brent, though unfortunately they are not the sole occupants as thousands of coots are to be met with which have spoilt many good chance for us when in search of more valuable fowl. There are a considerable number of big channels also but the creeks intersecting the flats at low water run dead in most cases very quickly. The high ground of the mainland or the loom of the islands often gives a certain amount of background from which to make an approach, to a gunner who knows his business.

Numerous small villages with a population principally of fishermen, are posted upon the hills around the bays so that the difficulties of getting to the birds are greatly augmented by the presence of fishing boats and canoes which often appear at the wrong moment and dissipate all chance of a shot. Native gunners are also to be seen at all times of the tide but as I am on particularly friendly terms with all of them, by reason of my long residence amongst them they are generally content to act the part of 'retrievers' thus enabling us to catch the birds which on this soft mud, must otherwise on many occasions escape from us."

Many of the shots made by Pope were made under the cover of darkness and considerable skill was needed to achieve success when punting at night. Pope's description of one particular night gives the reader a vivid insight into the conditions endured by the puntsmen and their determination to achieve a good shot.

"Until now the weather had been somewhat changeable, but certain indications of what was coming appeared a few days before the end of the year (1892). The wind went to the east together with more settled conditions all round. Under the influence of bitterly cold nights the bays now rapidly froze up and ice flows were to be seen drifting about in all directions. The tides now were very steady, being neap, so that the surface of the ooze whilst uncovered became frozen as hard as boards and as the advancing tide lifted the ice crust that formed the thin surface coating. This ice was then driven shoreward and united itself with the solid sheet which fringed the snow white border of the main land.

Now commenced to arrive all those foreigners who seldom pay us a visit except under extremes of weather. Mallard and pintail might be seen in smaller or larger bunches, flying and pitching here and there with a few teal and pochard on and amongst the 'bergs of ice having been driven out to the coast by the frozen up state of things inland.

About the fourth day after this weather had set in the cold became most intense and everything in or out of doors in liquid form was turned into ice. The spring tides had begun to make up for the full moon, and set at liberty a considerable quantity of huge flows from the shore so that shooting was carried on under great difficulty. It was necessary to pay great heed to these frozen masses which were grinding and crashing against each other at the mercy of the tide. The scene all round was indeed arctic and as each nights frost increased in intensity it seemed quite probable at one time that we should be blocked in at our mooring."

The wintery surroundings prompted Pope to change the punt colour from a dark grey to a very light French grey which was more in keeping with the prevailing surroundings. There followed an abortive early morning foray when enormous masses of drift ice prevented them from going afloat until the receding tide gave them an opening through the ice.

Pope continues the story; "In the evening of 1 January 1893, profiting by the morning's experience I took the precaution to cut my way out into open water before the ebb tide began to run

Chateau De Truscat, with the punting grounds of the Gulf of Morbihan beyond

hard and in this manner we got away of all obstacles. The moon was one day off full, rather too full for night shooting but not high up as yet. A slight breeze from the east caused a nice ripple on the water astern of us, so that although fowl were plainly visibly distinguishable under the moonbeams we were able to conduct our operations with the assistance of the loom of the shore, entirely in the shade. Hearing but a few birds our end of the bay, we rowed to windward hugging the ice girdle as closely as possible. We were not long in falling in with a big lot of wigeon which had evidently drifted up on the last tide, and whose presence was made known to us by incessant calls, coming from the direction where the weed would first be exposed.

The tide was still high so we moored ourselves to an oar stuck into the mud in order to locate the position of the pack. A huge gaggle of brent were still further to windward yelling like demons and apparently not far from the small island called Shark. Their calls tempted us to go and look at them. Laying down, we passed wide of the wigeon and got within easy shot of the geese but as they were so spread out we declined to pull on them fearing to lose a better chance at the wigeon later on. Still in the recumbent position we sculled across under the moon with the object of going ashore on the island to warm our hands and feet but this manoeuvre had to be executed most cautiously in order to avoid driving up packs of fowl to leeward which might possibly both wind or see us.

We are within a gunshot of the island when a roar startles us and immediately the air is filled with the shrill whistling in every direction and a goodly amount of quacking denoting to us that another mass of wigeon and ducks not previously heard had suddenly seen us under the moon and had risen from the shore of the island where they had probably been reposing since nightfall.

As they pitch again within two or three hundred yards, and the cause of their alarm was now invisible to them, we move close inshore and wait to see where they will collect to feed. The rendezvous selected by the company nearest us is a high patch of mud running out not far from our hiding place. We can with the aid of the glasses see them looking as black as coots under the bright clear moon all swimming up to this point where the first peck of the weed can be obtained. Beyond them lies the mainland shore fringed with solid sheets of ice which glisten and sparkle in the moonlight. Oars, setting poles and all movables that have been in contact with the water are wrapped in a coating of ice and the crisp air does not pass over moustaches or hair without leaving traces of ice behind.

As the scene around us is taken in another quarter of an hour passes and the increasing chorus tells us that the ranks are closing up. Some wigeon are attending to their toilet whilst others may be seen standing on their heads in an attempt to get in touch with the weed as the tide recedes. We have not much longer to wait as we must move out to our shot unless we wish to risk being left high and dry on the mud.

The glasses show to us that we cannot get to the end of the line as there are a lot of stragglers on the outside of the main company which will surely fly up in an approach from our present position. In the still white water there will be no difficulty in seeing them so I determine to go to them with the moon on our beam in order to get at the thickest part of the pack. A few strokes of the setting pole astern takes us out of range and then turning the punt's head gently and in such a way to avoid the moonlight flashing on the punt, we are soon up opposite the middle of the company now busily engaged in feeding. A final look through the glasses showed a long patch of birds but not close together, there are some coots in with them so it is necessary to be careful where we place our shot. We are within forty five yards, quite close enough to kill birds far into the pack and so with a tap of the side of the punt, to lift their heads, I pull on them. A belch of flame shoots out of the muzzle of the big gun, a noise like that of a cannon echoes around the shore and then the air is full of birds complaining bitterly that their sentinels had not been more vigilant. Our charge of shot had found its mark and we observed a mass of wigeon, nearly all dead outlined by the white water. Our following boat quickly rows round the head of the creek beyond in order to secure any birds that may make off shoreward whilst we pick up the dead birds shooting with a shoulder gun any likely to prove troublesome. The water is now getting very short under us and the punt runs dry. We have then to submit to the unpleasant trudge through mud and water with mud-boards on to pick one final bird at the head of the creek. On counting over we find we have bagged fifty one wigeon and only one coot. We feel ourselves amply rewarded for the long weary cold wait. There being no further chance of a shot we came home just before low water and turn in at 1.30 in the morning."

Thereafter Gould wrote to RPG on the 8 February from Chateau de Truscat.

My dear Gallwey,

After writing to you last Monday we started in a thick fog to try for geese, but with very little hope of getting any, we soon heard widgeon and polled about till we found them and let them have it at about 60-70 yards,- we got 85. I daresay a few got away in the fog but not many as we had three of our followers and they don't let many off. Yesterday we got at a small lot of about 200 via a creek close here and got 53 of them; they were in the water and I did not expect to get more than 30 when I fired. I think I told you that Pope had bought a big gun that formerly belonged to me; it is the best gun, by a long way, at making a big hole in a pack of widgeon that I have ever seen and I am rather sorry I parted with it. The tides are now about right for geese and we are going to devote ourselves at them for the remainder of the week.

There are very few widgeon left and the natives say they will all have left by the middle of the month, but we expect to get a good lot of geese still.

Pope's punt is only 20 ft 9 in. long and very low, but carries us well tho' as he is a couple of inches taller than I am, it is rather a tight fit - she is a very nice punt and I expect its great success is due to her being so low and fast; he always punts and is a first rate hand at it. The mud here is simply awful; a 7 lb pressure on top of an oar will put it almost out of sight - I had my first trial of mud boards on Monday and got on as if I had been wearing them all my life.

How are you doing at Holy Island? Of course I don't want anyone to know of this place so please don't say anything about it.

Yours sincerely,

G.J. Gould

1893. The hazards of travel in search of sport

In December 1893 we find George Gould once again staying at Chateau de Truscat. He had already been in residence for a month but wigeon and geese numbers were unusually low and he had only fired six shots during the whole time he had been there. Walter Pope joined Gould on 20 December and punting remained poor until a change in the weather in January 1894. Pope tells the story of how they chartered a rather unseaworthy sailing craft to try and get on terms with fowl they had observed around Mean near the port of St Nazaire. In severe weather conditions the river became blocked by drifting pack ice and icebergs. Through perseverance they eventually managed to get a nice mixed shot of wigeon and teal but then conditions became hazardous.

Pope explains; "following the shot the water became so rough with the strong tide running against us together with half a gale of wind, we were in immediate danger of being swamped at any minute. The leaky sailing craft which we had hired as a following boat proved a veritable death trap for us, and it was only by constant bailing we kept ourselves from sinking." However, all ended well and they made it ashore with their bag of twenty four wigeon and teal vowing that they would be more careful in the future when hiring a seaworthy boat and a trustworthy skipper."

George Gould was in trouble again two years later. This time he was not punting but sailing to South Harris to shoot woodcock. In a letter of 8 October he writes to RPG;

My dear Gallwey,

I have had an experience which you will appreciate. Coming in to Rode (South Harris) yesterday the steamer ran on a rock and remained. The first voice I heard, after stopping, was the engineer who said, "water's coming in, draw the fire." That set my mind at rest as I knew the only danger was the boiler might explode. It was quite smooth at the time and we were all ashore in about half an hour. The steamer is a total loss and only a small piece of her stem is above the water now; that could disappear as it was blowing hard right in to the bay. I am now in the shooting lodge here, the Factor very kindly having taken me in, and put up and fed the crew -22 men.

This is the most destitute place and consists of a lodge, a gardener's house and an old church. If the Factor had not been aboard I don't know what we should have done. I hear the steamer will be here tonight to take us off, but unless the wind moderates considerably she will not be able to do so.

This is my first shipwreck tho' I had three very narrow escapes in Holland. I have been speaking to the Keeper here; he says this is the worst year he has ever known for woodcock and is worse than last year. Three is the most he has seen in a day.

Yours sincerely,

G. J. Gould.

We could find no record of whether it was Gould's intention to shoot woodcock and snipe on South Harris or perhaps he was heading for another of the Outer Hebridean islands. What is clear is that his enthusiasm for shooting truly wild birds had taken him to the Outer Hebrides, a remarkably long way when you consider that he must have relied on a small steam passenger boat which would have been largely used for commercial purposes and then horse drawn transport to carry guns, cartridges and luggage from Ireland.

RPG's diary continued

1893. The new year at Fenham le Mill

In January 1893 RPG and Shuttler were back at Fenham. Everything had been prepared for RPG's arrival on 2 January when they had their first day afloat. They launched at 6 am into a gale of north-east wind and blizzard of heavy snow, but they were back at the house by 12.30 pm with boots full of water and freezing cold! Undeterred they were off again at 2 pm and sailed north in search of the geese which numbered about 300. Despite toiling all day their only reward was 6 wigeon, 1 goldeneye and 1 shelduck.

Sport did not really improve; the weather was desperately cold, the frost lasting all day with ice building up on the sand banks along the channels. They missed a good chance at wild

Bewick swans which, had they been luckier, might have been a record shot. By the afternoon of 7 January matters were deteriorating and RPG writes, "Home to Thirkleby with much regret, but am short of provision, my clothes all saturated with water and mud and my long boots leaking like a sieve!"

He was back on 9 January to find Shuttler had lost no time in having another shot at the Bewicks, having downed 5, picked 3 with the other 2 being picked up by a passing sailing boat. A second flying shot that day accounted for 12 brents. RPG weighed each of the swans; 13, 12 ½, and 10lbs.

The north wind continued for the next two days but only two small shots at geese were made.

Two pairs of fine new 'Fagg Brothers of London' leather boots arrived for RPG on 10 January but poor Shuttler's did not arrive until 14 February. India rubber boots, although available were regarded by RPG as most unhealthy, "a tramp on the ooze will induce your feet and legs to perspire profusely, and as these boots are ready-made, they never fit, and will chafe the heels if you run or walk in them."

The weather turned mild again, but by the middle of January very large numbers of brents arrived which was put down to severe weather on the continent. By 18 January there were an estimated 1200 brents feeding on the flats. Prospects for a shot improved with heavy snow on the morning of 17 January and on 18 January they were out at dawn. RPG comments;" followed the geese for miles today and after many attempts I made a nice shot of 14. Total for the day was 1 scaup and 18 brent geese." They had little success thereafter and RPG left Shuttler to go afloat alone until he returned on 31 January. In fact Shuttler had a close shave on 29 January picking up after a shot at brent geese he experienced rough water and he struggled home with the punt half full of water.

RPG achieved a good shot of 6 brent geese on 1 February and then on 2 February he writes, "the only thing I fired powder at was a salmon that I killed with the shoulder gun as it swam down a shallow creek."

Notable comments in the diary include, "5 February. - Afloat at 6 am and went in to the North channel by dawn, saw nothing, so walked home 2 miles across the sand in long heavy boots (the new ones!) and left Shuttler to wait for the flood tide. Here ends the most dismally barren week of sport I ever had here, owing to this abominable spring like weather and calm winds. The worst of it is that there are geese all over the place."

Then an amusing note on 17 February, "afloat at 6 am and for 10 hours afterwards, summer weather. Had one or two narrow escapes of making a good flying shot at the geese as they wheeled over the 6 decoy birds I had set up on the bank, under which I was concealed in the punt! A new dodge this!"

And finally to add insult to injury, while RPG was away, Shuttler made a wonderful shot at wild duck (mallard) on 20 February, picking 17 with a further 13 picked up by a fishing boat. By the time Shuttler got his new Fagg boots it was a bit late in the season for him!

Punt and double Holland were returned to Thirkleby on 1st March and then Shuttler went home. There was repair work to be done to the punt and the gun needed to be thoroughly cleaned and put in store.

1893. A Royal Salute and a shot at starlings with the double gun

On 6 July RPG writes, "After three months of 'tinkering' at my double duck punt I launched her in the lake at Thirkleby last evening, she now appears as good, or better than new. She is now eight years old and is the one that with my 'Double Duck Gun', was exhibited at the sporting Exhibition, London 1885. Today at 12 noon I fired a, 'Royal Salute' when afloat on the lake in honour of the wedding of Prince George and Princess Mary (8 oz. of powder at each discharge)."

On 29 October 1893 just when thoughts were once again turning to the new wildfowling season RPG again rolled out the double Holland. A horse and cart and three men laboured with RPG all day to make everything ready for an attack on the starling roost in Quarry woods. The first evening the starlings arrived on schedule but the gun could not be elevated high enough. The result of a double discharge resulted in 40 starlings picked.

The gun was left in the wood overnight and the following evening prepared for a further assault. RPG writes, "There were not a quarter of the number of last night; but I took a shot at them flying high past me over the tree tops at dusk. The result was an improvement on the previous evening, 103 picked." The charge used was 6 oz of powder and 32 oz. of number 1 shot. RPG thought that if the gun had been loaded with number 5 shot, he would have doubled the bag!

1894. Holy Island with Steven Shuttler

There was no early wildfowling trip to the Continent this season and it was not until after Christmas that Shuttler was sent to Fenham to prepare for RPG's arrival on the 9 January 1894. A spell of very severe weather had left the Fenham flats looking like the Arctic, 20 degrees of frost resulted in the whole shore line being scattered with ice. Shuttler reported that the geese had not arrived in any number but he had made two small shots of 6 and 5 brent geese to date.

10 January saw them afloat at 7 in the morning and back to the house at 4 pm. As it turned out it was the best day RPG was to have all season. A bitter cold south east wind blew followed by a deluge of rain. Small lots of brents were arriving and they were able to make a nice shot of 8 at the tide edge opposite a low water sandbank named Seal Point. The severe weather had caused a movement of birds, with good numbers of wigeon and mallard, all in the air to add to the excitement. Shorebirds, including knots, godwits and dunlin passed overhead in large numbers and RPG shot with his shoulder gun the only little auk he had ever come across.

However, the cold weather did not last and RPG left for Thirkleby on 12 January. Frank Payne-Gallwey made a short visit between 22 January and 26 January securing two shots with Shuttler, one of 10 wigeon on 24th and then 3 shelduck on 25th.

RPG returned for a final foray before the season ended, staying at Fenham from 20 February until 24 February; he did get one shot of 8 brent geese but for reasons that will become clear we will not dwell on the rest of the season. Here is RPG's summary as written in his diary:

"Here ends the most disgusting and miserable wildfowl shooting season I ever experienced. At Fenham there were never at most more than 400 brent geese instead of the 4000 common to the place in former years. There were about 500 wigeon and duck about in January but these left in early February and the weather utterly prevented any chance of a shot at them. The everlasting westerly winds quite prevented the geese this season migrating to Fenham as usual, and there was no continuous hard weather abroad to send them over the North Sea. In the first week of January we had a severe week of frost, but then this was too early for the geese and there were none then at Fenham, and the frost did not last long enough to send them over to the Scottish and English Coasts. A vile foul season for wildfowling."

1894. Pigeon shooting with the double Holland and Holland punt gun

As part of the history of the double Holland, we are including this extract from the diary on 13 December 1894, although it has nothing to do with wildfowling.

" I this morning at dawn arranged my big double gun (on its new four wheeled recoil carriage) so as to command a long strip of chaff and corn on which a number of woodpigeons have been daily enticed to feed for some time. I placed the gun, (as I thought) to strew the charge of 2 ½ lbs. of shot all along the strip of corn. I then fastened a 150 yards cord to the trigger of the gun and held the end as I hid in the hedge. The pigeons came as usual to settle on and feed on the corn; I pulled the string and fired the gun, but unfortunately the muzzle was raised an inch too high, and the charge only just touched the farthest birds, else I should have killed 40. The result was six. The Revd. Mr Higgins, (our new vicar) and his friend Captain Brooksbank, 14th Hussars came to see the shot and were much interested."

1895. Holy Island with a new puntsman

In 1895 the New Year started with the bad news that Steven Shuttler was unable to come to Fenham as he was suffering from rheumatism. In his place RPG invited John Bran to act as his puntsman for the coming season. Bran came with good references; he lived at Lymington, his father was a professional puntsman and he had in previous seasons assisted Arthur Kavanagh punting on the Solent. Kavanagh had also employed Bran to travel abroad with him from time to time.

On 2 January 1895 RPG spent the day, 'cruising' the area to show Bran the extent of the punting grounds. The following day they went afloat in calm westerly wind conditions but by the afternoon the wind went north-north east bringing a gale with driving snow showers. In the afternoon they set to a fine pack of wigeon but due to the weather conditions could not get closer than 150 yards. RPG hallooed and put them up and then took a long flying shot which resulted in at least 25 dropping out into rough seas, there followed a long cripple chase and only 10 birds were picked. On the basis of this behaviour it is little wonder that Abel Chapman was so critical of RPG.

They then had to get the punt back to Fenham Mill which proved to be a stiff challenge. It was a close run thing; RPG writes; "we came home by moonlight and found the Mill Burn with some difficulty, boots full of water, and punt with several inches of water in her and John Bran and myself soaked!" It proved that the Holy Island slakes can be a very dangerous place if the prospects of a shot entice a puntgunner to cross deep, unsettled, rough water when wind and tide are running against each other.

Julian Novorol
2012

Sir Ralph Payne-Gallwey and Steven Shuttler with the double 1½" breech loader by Messers Holland and Holland, Holy Island 1889

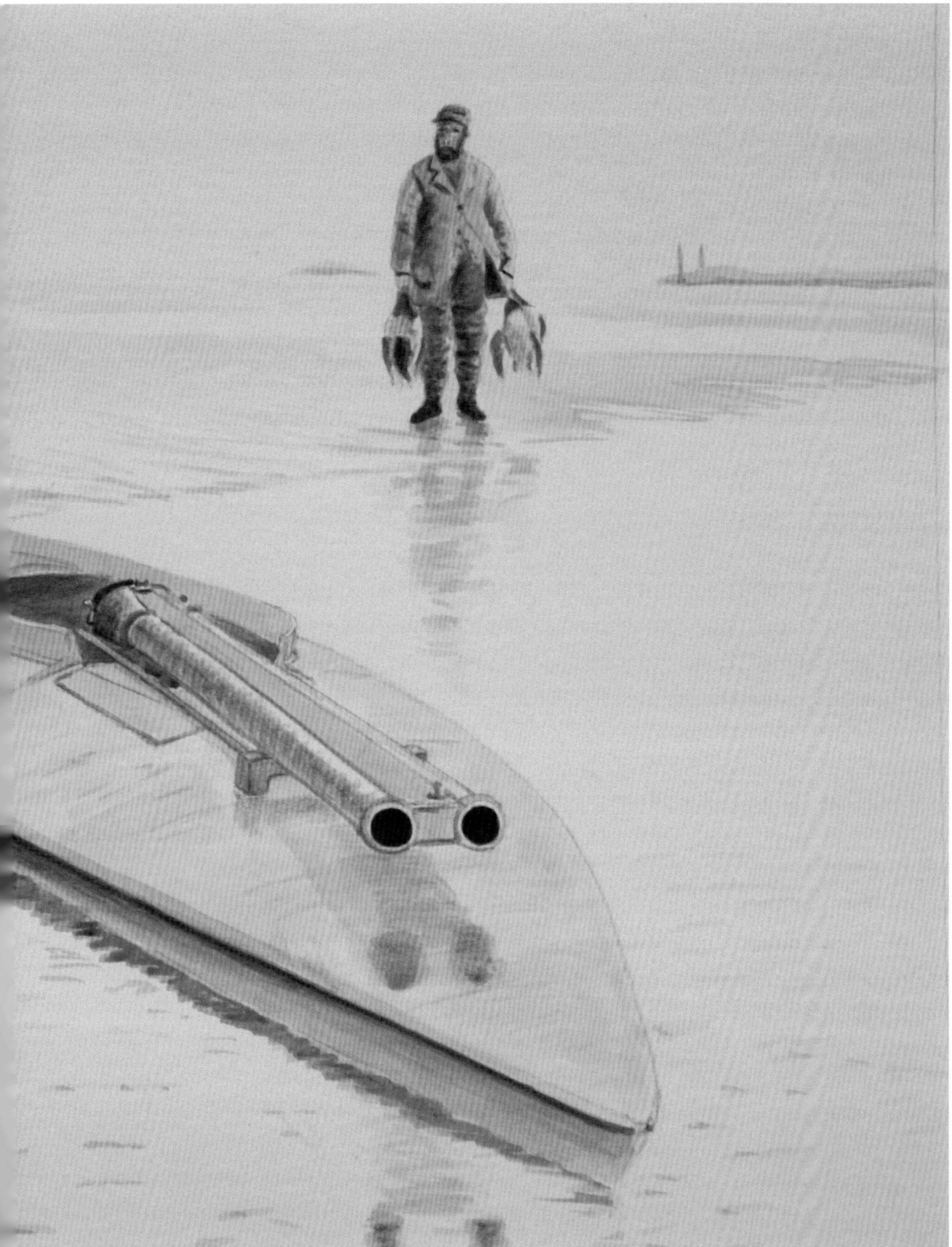

The next day was equally rough. Another long shot resulted in 9 wigeon picked but the Holy Island fishermen had spotted the droppers and lost birds. It was reported later that they had picked a number of wigeon around the Harbour entrance. After another small shot, again at long range, one begins to sense that RPG was already beginning to have doubts about Bran!

On 5 January RPG had to return to Thirkleby and was unable to return to Fenham until 28 January. They got afloat that day but did not get a shot, however, there is an interesting note in the diary, "Selby Allison*, Holy Islander and Abel Chapman's puntsman called; he had in his punt 26 wigeon and mallards and 6 brent geese and reports more wigeon and ducks here now than ever seen before." The diary also records that Bran had done nothing while RPG was away.

On 30 January there was a hard frost and many ducks and geese about. RPG was due to depart for Archerfield, North Berwick where he had been invited to shoot pheasants. He went afloat at break of day but did not get a shot. When he got back to the house he had lunch with Adam Martin, a punt gunner from Holy Island, who had come over from the Island to seek advice about a swivel-gun that had burst and nearly blown his head off! RPG comments, "it was a real old rusty dangerous gas pipe that was not worth a pound."

RPG did not return to Fenham until 14 February due to his health taking a turn for the worse whilst pheasant shooting. It took some time for him to recover his strength and all this time there were thousands of brent geese at Fenham due to very severe weather on the Continent. He went afloat on 15 February at daybreak and fired one shot killing 7 brent geese and 3 wigeon. He noted two other brents were lost in the tide, only later to be picked up by fishermen. On 16 February he again launched at daybreak and had a small shot of 3 brent geese with an additional 2 birds stolen by the occupants of a sailing boat!

Towards the end of February there were an estimated 5000 brent geese feeding on the slakes. The end of the season came and went all too quickly and RPG summed it up in despair;

"A glorious winter after Christmas. Two months of deep snow and hardest frost with east and north east gales week after week. Thousands of geese at Fenham and many hundreds of wigeon, and scores of mallards in all directions. Yet I did nothing, absolutely nothing. One week we had a party at Thirkleby and I could not leave home. Another week I was ill with influenza. But, the worst of all my new puntsman John Bran was no use whatever, though he came to me with a flaming character. He was nearer 60 than 50 years of age; was as weak as a child, easily caught cold and did not know his business. He only killed about 12 birds in 7 weeks though they were in abundance all round him. Steven Shuttler would have bagged 130 or more this glorious winter. John Bran, through his ignorance of how to take me up to fowl lost me some of the finest shots I ever saw."

RPG did not suffer from colds and had little time for John Bran who continued to complain about his cold. He offered this advice to anyone who feels a cold coming on, "Stick a postage stamp to the bedroom wall opposite the bed. Once in bed, drink whisky until one can see three stamps. All symptoms of a cold will be gone by the morning."

RPG's disappointment was not helped when he heard from Sir Charles Ross who lived at Balnagown Castle near Tain and punted the northern firths. Ross had enjoyed an exceptional punting

*Footnote. Old Selby Allison died on 21 June 1945.

season shooting 300 brent in 3 days (52 with one shot) using a gun loaded only with a pound of shot. That was depressing enough and then he had a letter from Mr Leonard Brooke who punted the Dee Estuary who reported shooting 500 wild duck and 150 various during the past winter. RPG writes, "Everyone seems to have enjoyed splendid sport except myself."

1895. RPG visits Broomfleet Island on the Humber Estuary

On 11 October 1895 RPG secured a lease on Broomfleet Island near the north shore of the Humber, 4 miles west of Brough and close to the remote village of Broomfleet. The total area was about 1000 acres of marsh and mere, ideal for wildfowl and wader shooting. RPG describes it, "A perfect Paradise for a wildfowl shooter or a lover of birds of all kinds and I secured the lease for £25 from the Humber Conservancy Board!"

After an initial visit to establish the lie of the land in November, RPG invited Gould to join him on 2 January. Gould had arranged to send his punt and 2 inch Holland and Holland all the way from Holland. They were ready to go afloat on 4 January. Both men met with success; Gould picked up two shots (6 and 9 mallard) on the Humber River and RPG a single shot (4 Mallard). They also walked the marsh and between them shot 65 snipe, 4 pinkfeet, 2 water rails and 2 golden plover.

RPG summarised his thoughts, "the tides are very rapid and even dangerous if care is not taken. The stretch of water we shoot over with the punt and gun is from Humber Lock down to Brough, (about 6 miles in length by a mile in width). There is no feeding ground for the birds on the Humber, but many large sand flats show at low water. The ducks that come here are chiefly migratory birds in autumn or mallards driven from inland waters by frost."

Patrington Haven to the east was where Stanley Duncan (founder of WAGBI in 1908) punted and it might have been on this visit that RPG first met Duncan. In any event a later meeting was to change the history of wildfowling as Duncan asked RPG if he would become the first President of WAGBI when it was formed.

RPG noted that he employed Mr Henry Fordham from Broomfleet as a 'watcher' for the Island and as puntsman when they were there. Both men would certainly have met Duncan. Apparently Fordham had worked a single handed punt at Broomfleet launching at the mouth of the Market Weighton Canal and knew the punting grounds very well. Broomfleet Island was drained, so RPG gave up the shooting lease in April 1897.

1896. RPG visits Fenham le Mill with Sam Croutear, puntsman

On 11 January 1896 RPG employed Sam Croutear to punt single handed at Fenham until such time as he could join him. However, this was not until 28 January as RPG was game shooting at Taverham Hall in Norfolk. Croutear, who was also a Lymington man, is described as tall, young, strong and a good boatman, who was a professional puntsman during the winter months.

The big muzzle-loading 2 inch Bentley and Playfair, which was far too heavy for a single punt, was replaced with a 1¼ inch breech-loader borrowed from Gould, making the single punt a lot more seaworthy. The double gun was used only when RPG was punting.

Although RPG went afloat in excess of twenty days, the results, in terms of ducks and geese, were very disappointing. The seven weeks of sport at Fenham was a disastrous season in which RPG only got one shot. Although Croutear was held in very high regard by RPG, the whole season was mild and very few brent geese and wigeon visited the Holy Island slakes. Perhaps this was the reason why it was the last visit that RPG made to go afloat at Holy Island. The very last shot recorded there was taken with the double Holland on 26 February 1896, and the result was 8 wigeon.

1896. The opening of Holland and Holland's new shooting school and RPG completes his new book 'Letters to young shooters'

During the ensuing months a number of notable events occured that, though not directly associated with wildfowling, seem appropriate to record.

11 June 1896 saw RPG opening Messrs. Holland and Holland's new shooting School at Kensal Rise. On 3 July he hired the ground for the day, inviting Lord Walsingham, Lord Ashburton, Sir R. Gresley and Mr G. Tennant amongst others. They enjoyed a pleasant afternoon shooting several hundred shots at all manner of curious and cleverly contrived targets, including live and clay pigeons.

On 1 October 1896, RPG records the completion of the last pages of his book, 'The third series of Letters to Young Shooters, Wildfowl and Wildfowl Shooting.' "It has taken me three years of constant hard work, frequently 8 hours a day, for weeks at a time. It has also cost me in expenses and in extra illustrations I inserted at my own cost £350. I was determined to produce the best book of the kind ever written and I am confident I have succeeded in doing so." The new book was published on 18 November 1896. The effort put into the book would suggest that RPG was, in the second part of the nineteenth century trying to emulate Colonel Peter Hawker's role in the first half of the century when he wrote;' Instructions to Young Sportsmen'.

Invitation to Holland and Holland's shooting ground, 1896

1896. RPG visits Glynllifon, North Wales

Later in October 1896 RPG visited Glynllifon, near Caernarvon, an estate owned by his friend The Honourable Frederick Wynn, where he had been invited game shooting. Frederick Wynn had inherited the estate from Spencer Wynn in 1889, whereupon he set about enjoying his new found wealth. One such indulgence was his love of yachts. In 1891 he commissioned D.J. Dunlop to build a 329 ton steam yacht designed by G.W. Watson, a leading yacht designer of the day. The yacht, named *'Mira'*, was completed in 1892 and reputed to have cost in excess of £11,000 to build with additional running costs of £1,000 per annum. She had a crew of 18, five officers, three stewards, a cook and nine seamen/stokers. The aristocracy have always been fiercely competitive and building this wonderful yacht enabled Frederick to look his local rivals firmly in the eye.

RPG was in his element surrounded by guns and boats and he and Frederick quickly became close friends. He noted in his diary on 30 October that he went to the nearby coast with a view to assessing punting opportunities at a future date. The result was obviously favourable as on 18 January 1897 he returned to North Wales where he had arranged to stay at Belan Fort situated overlooking the western entrance to the Menai Straits.

The fort was built by Thomas Wynn to defend the entrance to the Straits at the time of the Napoleonic Wars (late18th early 19th century). It was now owned by Frederick Wynn and he lent the entire fort to RPG to use as his new fowling HQ. RPG's description follows;

"Belan Fort is beautifully situated, almost surrounded by sea, the Snowdon range of mountains about 10 miles off, and Caernarvon and its castle in view three miles away. Belan is a first rate house with many rooms that are beautifully furnished. The fort is in complete order, drawbridge, moat, battlements, and armoury with 50-60 cannons on the defences. Large store houses, dock for yachts and workshops. Models of cannon, ships, and quaint old pictures and many books inside the house. I have every convenience here for fowling, boats, and steam launch. My staff consist of Alec McKay (valet), a sailor puntsman Sam Croutear from Lymington, a cook, a housemaid, and a man in charge of the fort who also sets fishing nets. I have here two punt guns, a double handed fowling punt and all that is necessary for sport. The water and mud flats look good for punting."

By the nineteenth century the fort had been adapted for leisure activities rather than used in its former role as a military installation. The whole complex was now managed by Richard Roberts who was said to be a fine man who lived all year round in one of the dock cottages. His son Evan was later (1913) to act as RPG's puntsman.

RPG clearly liked his new wildfowling headquarters. He had observed that in the Voryd Bay, an inlet over looked by Belan Fort, there were good numbers of wigeon, a few brent geese, plover, curlew and oyster catchers all of which could provide sport. Added to this, Frederick Wynn owned Bodfuan Hall an excellent estate where he was to enjoy fine woodcock shooting in late January and good snipe shooting on the famous bog at Bodfuan on the Llyn peninsular. Here there was another large house built originally in 1736, but rebuilt in the nineteenth century.

Richard Roberts

From January onwards, he went afloat 21 days from Belan. The early days were exploratory, a small shot of 4 wigeon on the 18 January but the very next day he rejoices in making a fine shot of plover (39 green and 6 golden). Frustrated by a spell of strong easterly winds and hard frost he went woodcock shooting at Bodfuan Hall and records a bag of 28. Whilst he was away Croutear went afloat and had two shots, one of 7 wigeon and another of 9 wild duck (mallard). A note in the diary indicates that Croutear was struggling with the large double handed punt and gun on his own and on one occasion missed a chance of getting up to a large sitting of wigeon, "Unaided he could not manage the punt and gun."

On 29 January fortune at last shone for RPG; "I made a good shot of 25 wigeon this afternoon. Unfortunately, I only had the small full-choked Holland punt gun loaded with 1lb of shot on board (Gould's gun). If I'd had had my 2 inch muzzle-loader I should have bagged at least 50. There were 300-400 wigeon along the edge of a shallow bank, as thick as bees, and I ran up within 60 yards of them. A fine lot of birds about today. It was cruel ill-luck my having so small a gun in the punt when I had such a splendid pack of birds to fire at, so beautifully placed for a shot, so tame, and so close together."

RPG invited George Gould to join him at Belan and he arrived from Dublin on 2 February. The weather was hopeless for fowling so they amused themselves by walking the marshes and dunes along to Dinas Dinlle picking up snipe, partridge and teal. On 6 February the pair went by boat to Caernarvon and then by train to Pant Glas station (10 miles) where they shot the Pant Glas marshes. RPG wrote; "It was a fine days sport that we enjoyed together picking up 23 snipe, 6 mallard, 1 golden plover, 2 teal and a goldeneye." The following day they crossed the Straits by boat arriving on Anglesey at Aber Menai Point and then walked to LLanddwyn Island Lighthouse, four miles to the north-west.

Gould returned to Ireland on 8 February having not fired a shot with the punt due mainly to the unseasonably warm weather that resulted in the birds sitting out at sea all day. But Gould does report that he had not been idle between 4 November and the end of January as he gives details of his recent trip to the island of Tiree off the west coast of Scotland. He gives no account of the daily sport but he does record his bag: 6 teal, 72 golden plover, 13 hares, 9 woodcock, 890 snipe, 10 ducks and 4 various. The total number of cartridges he fired was 1864 giving a 53% cartridge to kill ratio. He also records that he was shooting for 39 days and out on an average day walking for between 5 and 5½ hours each day. The best day's shooting, to his own gun, was 41 snipe.

Belan Fort drawbridge

Belan Fort interior

The figures suggest that he was more than able to hold his own when shooting in the company of RPG and it confirms Gould's love of shooting wild birds as opposed to pheasant shooting.

RPG's stay at Belan was coming to an end, but on 9 February, following a south westerly gale, the weather for fowling improved. He went afloat at 8.30 am and almost got up to a lovely sitting of wigeon only to go aground at long range. When the birds saw the punt he took a long flying shot resulting in 7 wigeon. That night he and Croutear went afloat at midnight. It was a moonlit night, and they took a shot at wigeon picking up 6.

Boat shed No3

Belan Fort dock

RPG left Belan Fort on 11 February travelling by boat to Caernarvon towing punt and guns and carrying the household luggage.

He summarised his first visit to North Wales, "My visit to Belan has been most pleasant except in the matter of sport. The weather has however been much against me. That some really heavy shots at wigeon (50 – 60) are to be made at Belan I have not the slightest doubt, and I hope to succeed in doing so another year."

A short medical note was added by RPG to his diary which may assist those wildfowlers of a certain age who suffer from rheumatism; "boil one ounce of celery seed in a pint of water till reduced to a half pint; bottle and take one teaspoonful in a little water twice a day." Perhaps this recipe was sent to Steven Shuttler whom you will remember was suffering from rheumatism! Many wildfowlers will, in preference, regard a large glass of whisky as a better cure.

1897. RPG acquires Colonel Hawker's scale model of his punt and gun

On 13 April 1897 RPG spent two days at the late Colonel C. Birch Reynardson's home, Holywell Hall, near Stamford, Lincolnshire. Reynardson had bought Colonel Hawker's famous double punt gun from the executors of the Hawker Estate when it was advertised in January 1855. The

Colonel Hawker's model duck punt and carriage in the gun room at Thirkleby Park

Hawker gun later came up for sale at an auction in 1889 at which time RPG purchased it. The significance of this visit was that the Reynardson family either presented or sold to RPG a scale model of Hawker's double gunning punt and punt carriage. This had belonged to Reynardson who had presumably purchased the model at the time of the sale of Hawker's effects. An engraving of the model was used as an illustration in Hawker's book, 'Instructions to Young Sportsmen' Page 456, 9th Edition and page 410, 10th Edition. The model can clearly be seen in the famous picture of RPG in the gunroom at Thirkleby Hall painted by Anthony de Bree in 1914. This picture currently graces Holland and Holland's Bruton Street Gun Room. Today the whereabouts of the model is unknown.

1897. A NEW DUCK PUNT COMMISSIONED

The last double handed gunning punt that RPG commissioned was in 1885, at which time the new punt and double Holland and Holland punt gun were exhibited at the Inventions Exhibition. At the end of each season, repairs, as necessary, had been made to the punt which was now 12 years old. Following the return of the punt to Thirkleby in 1897 RPG decided it was time to instruct John Pickett of West Quay, Southampton, boat builder, to build a new gunning punt. The 23ft. 4inch punt with a 3ft 9 inch beam was completed on 9 July, built to the exact measurements as described on Page 493 of the 3rd Series of, "Letters to Young Shooters." The total cost of the undertaking was £25.

The workshop at Thirkleby was also busy making a new gun carriage to take the punt and gun either by road or rail.

Converting the Bentley and Playfair punt gun into a breech-loader

It was noted that RPG did not have either of his heavy punt guns at Belan Fort in 1897, the reason for this now becomes clear for he had instructed Holland and Holland to convert his 1⅞ inch muzzle-loader into a breech-loader. He notes that the gun had originally been made by Bentley and Playfair in 1880 and he regarded this gun as the finest he had ever used.

The converted gun was delivered to Thirkleby on 20 July and shooting trials then commenced in August. There is no mention of the cost of the conversion. RPG reports on the trials as follows, "I had a grand trial today of punt guns at a twenty foot square target which is probably the largest target a sporting gun has ever been properly tried at. I used the gun just received from Holland and Holland of London. This gun was my favourite old muzzle-loader. Bore 1⅞ inch, weight 180 lbs. The gun has this year been converted into a breech-loader. I fired several shots. The three best patterns were 1185. 1170. 1217. The charge used was 6½ ounces of coarse powder and 34 oz of shot (BB, 60 pellets to the ounce). The gun made a splendid regular pattern."

1897. Early season visit to Belan Fort

In October 1897 RPG was invited back to North Wales for three days pheasant shooting as a guest of Frederick Wynn. He stayed first at Glynllifon, his host's house, but on 29 October once again took up residence at Belan Fort. Here, awaiting him was his new gunning punt mounted on the new carriage and his faithful 1⅞ inch Bentley and Playfair newly converted to a breech-loader.

All was wonderfully prepared but the weather was fine, calm and warm and of course there were no birds! His diary records; "Ate! Slept! Smoked! Drunk and wrote letters. But, I have got all ready for a later visit in the winter."

RPG's new punt and carriage now in the Liverpool Maritime Museum

Belan Fort and dockyard

However, on 1 November there was an opportunity to try the newly converted gun, the first shot accounting for 1 shelduck and 4 godwits. In the afternoon he spied some good sittings of plover, "I fired three shots and killed, 1st shot, 22 golden plover and 1 knot, 2nd shot, 23 green plover, 3rd shot, 13 green plover".

The newly converted gun was not totally satisfactory as a number of misfires are recorded one of which was at another fine lot of plover.

He concludes, "A fine days sport, weather calm and bright and hot as midsummer. I also got a fine plaice and my valet caught 6 pollock."

The next day was spent exploring the coastline in the following boat, towing the gunning punt, "we went outside the Voryd Bay and round by sea to beyond Dinas Dinlle towards the mountains called the Rivals, a splendid trip but no shot to be had."

In his diary RPG recounts a story about the residents of Bardsey Island, which was owned by the Wynn family and a few miles along the coast from Dinas Dinlle. There were very few residents on the Island but they were plagued by a visit from His Majesty's Tax inspector. A fisherman was compelled to row the taxman over to the Island for which he charged the taxman one pound. The taxman then visited all the poor residents and netted five pounds in taxes. But, the original boatman had already returned to the mainland so the taxman had to negotiate, with the Islanders, for a boat to get back. No one could be found who would make the return trip for less than six pounds. The Islanders made a clear profit of one pound!

On 10 November news came from North Holland. His old friend and fellow shooter George Gould was once again fowling at Zoutkamp and had enjoyed a remarkable spell of good sport. He reported he had many good shots resulting in a total of 638 ducks in eleven shots!

At first it may seem strange that RPG was not with Gould in North Holland for doubtless he would have been invited to join him aboard *Watergeus*, however, on studying RPG's Game Book it seems fair to speculate that game shooting, with the Victorian Country House Set, was now playing a very prominent role in his life. He records sixty days game shooting between 30 August and his return to Belan Fort on the 18 January 1898. He was shooting either at Thirkleby or as a guest on some of the finest shoots in the country and in the company of the shooting aristocracy of the day. But, we cannot help wondering if, after he received Gould's letter, he would have swapped a few of the 1000 bird pheasant days to have been with Gould aboard *Watergeus*.

1897. RPG visits Adare Manor, Southern Ireland

In December RPG records a brief wildfowling trip following four days game shooting at Adare Manor, Co. Limerick, Ireland the seat of Lord Dunraven. The house was beautifully situated on the banks of the river Dee two miles upstream from the Shannon Estuary. He had arranged to meet Lord Dunraven's puntsman Shanahan at Askeaton (14 miles from Adare). Shanahan had his punting outfit ready together with a following boat skippered by his son. They spent the day afloat around Foynes seeing thousands of wigeon and to RPG's delight they managed to get two good shots. One of 20 and a second of 14 wigeon achieved by young Wyndham (Dunraven's son) who was serving with the 17th Lancers, and on leave. He summed up the day, " Returned to Askeaton and drove back to Adare by 5 o'clock. A successful expedition."

RPG writes that the day before this outing he had been knocked off his feet by a downwind pheasant he had shot at Adare Manor. As he swung, and fired the second barrel, the bird he hit with the first barrel knocked him on his back. He thought one gun barrel had burst and the on-lookers thought he had been shot! In any event he suffered a painful black eye and an inflamed cheek. He had already been hit on the head, that same day by one of Lord Dunraven's falling birds so he was not expecting a second incident.

1898. RPG explores Anglesey

After Christmas on the evening of 19 January 1898 RPG travelled from Thirkleby to Belan Fort. Sam Croutear was there to meet him and they were all set to go afloat at dawn the following morning. The entrance to the Menai Straits are notoriously dangerous and the weather was rough, but RPG was determined to cross to the Anglesey shore in search of a shot in a sheltered bay known as Traeth Melynog. He recounts crossing the entrance in the following boat towing the punt with Croutear and two other men accompanying him and once safely across he went in search of fowl.

Their efforts went unrewarded and this misfortune continued each day until the 26 January. RPG decided to try pastures new. He instructed Croutear to ship the punt and gun on the new carriage to the Isle of Anglesey shore, then transport everything across the Newborough Sand Dunes and onwards across the island to the Malltraeth Estuary. Not an easy task when you consider that the carriage was horse drawn and the whole outfit had to be transported across the Straits on a large boat and then 6 miles by road to the village of Malltraeth.

RPG was joined by his cousin Frank and while Croutear laboured with the punt he and Frank walked the marshes shooting 5 snipe.

The prospects for sport now looked better. Frank and RPG rose early on 27 January crossing the Straits and arriving at Malltraeth in time to go afloat and make a shot of 10 wigeon and a shelduck. That evening they both returned to Belan Fort where they stayed over the weekend.

Frank departed leaving RPG and Croutear to try for a shot at Malltraeth on 31 January. There follows RPG's account of the day; "Came here from Glynllifon early this morning; went afloat at once. Came in fair shot of several hundred mallard, wigeon and pintail sitting as thick as they could stick on a sand bank. On pulling the trigger the gun misfired, most damnable luck. I never saw a finer shot or one more likely to result in at least 70 birds. I then hastily re-cocked the gun but I was of course too late. The birds rose. I fired a long despairing silly shot and bagged six.

My lodging is at Captain Owen's (an old sea Captain). Malltraeth Bay, is very safe, which Belan was not, there being sometimes an awful sea in the Straits. I have seen fully 2000 duck and wigeon in it on each of the three occasions I have been on it. No one else punts here, there are no shore shooters and hence no jealous interlopers to spoil my chance of sport. Daily post and railway 2 miles away. A very heavy shot is to be made here with care and patience. At Malltraeth I can launch, land and moor the punt within 20 yards of the door of the house I

Crossing the Menai Straits with punt and gun

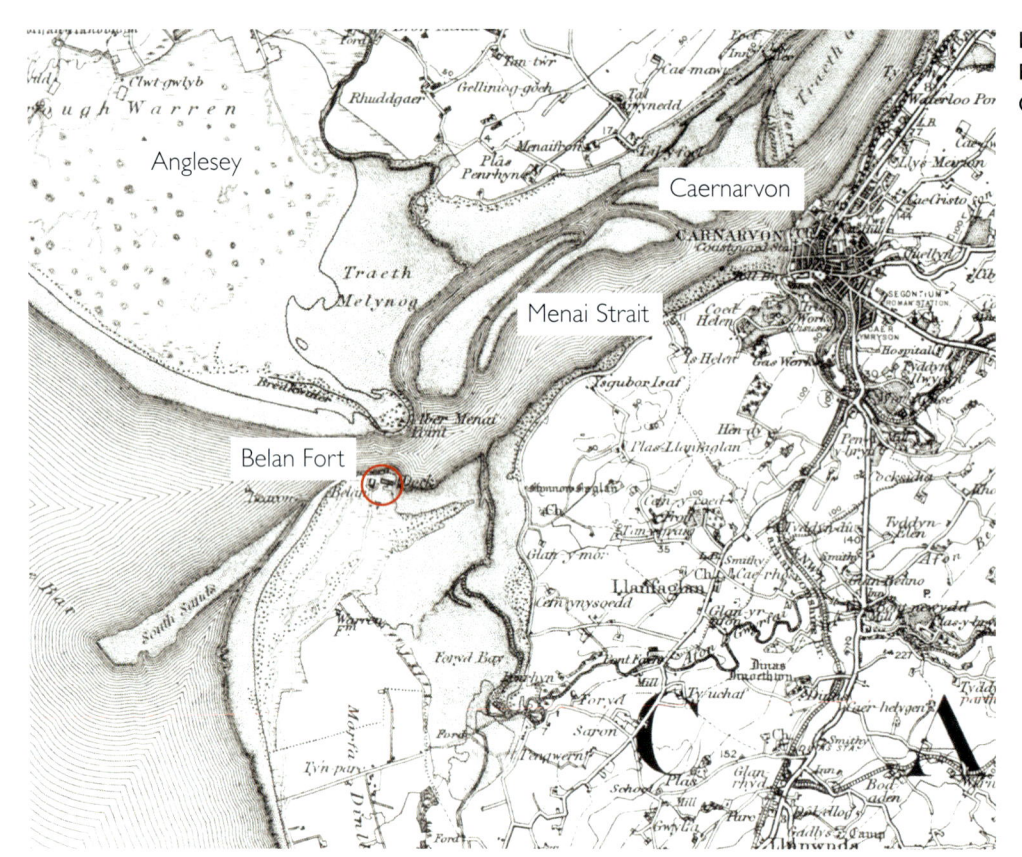

Location of Belan Fort and Caernarvon

am staying in, at all times of the tide. Belan Fort is hopeless, I never scarce saw a duck all the time I was there."

Fortunes were mixed for the next five days. On 1 February they got a good shot of 12 in a gale of westerly wind. 10 mallard, 1 shoveler and 1 wigeon. On the 2nd the wind went north and despite being afloat all day they did not get a shot. On the 3rd they made, "a beautiful shot at a small lot of birds sitting on the sand near the bar at the entrance to the bay; 23 wigeon, 4 shoveler and 1 mallard. Total 28." After that success the next two days proved to be fruitless as all the birds had left the Bay!

A day chasing wild snipe at Bodfuan proved to be equally frustrating, "The birds kept rising in front of me at 80 yards. The bog was flooded and it was blowing a gale of wind, and there was no moon the previous night. Bag - 7 snipe and 1 mallard."

Finally, on 8 February they made an unsuccessful attempt to get a shot at Malltraeth. They then decided to make tracks for Fort Belan which involved a trek of 6 miles across the sand dunes via Newborough, then crossing the Menai Straits by boat and reaching the Fort by 3pm. If this was not enough they went afloat that night, RPG reports that they heard plenty of wigeon and tried to fire on sound, only to have another misfire.

On 9 February RPG evacuated Belan Fort and reached, 21 Cadogan Place, London in the evening. RPG summarised his thoughts about Malltraeth; "This is a splendid place for punt gunning in certain weather conditions. The birds only come in large numbers with a west to south west strong wind. I several times saw 1500 duck and wigeon near the sand bar, and there is an extraordinary heavy shot to be made here. What is wanted is a gale from the sea and a very hard frost, also spring tides are the most favourable."

An amusing note is added; "I really believe that the people of Anglesey who live in this wild lonely Island thank God every day that they do not live in England, Scotland, Ireland or Wales."

There followed a short lament about the cost of the visit to Caernarvon estimated to have been £36, not including ammunition, £3 for carriage of punt to Caernarvon and other small items.

1898. George Gould visits Holland

The 19 October 1898 brought word of Captain Gould's sport on board '*Watergeus*' at Zoutkamp Holland. On 11 October RPG's old friend reported that he had made a shot of 149 wigeon and the following day, a flying shot of 89 wigeon. A record that RPG thought would never be beaten. RPG might have lamented not being with him but as his Game Book shows, grouse and partridge shooting had been the focus of RPG's attention. A short footnote is then added, "since first hearing from Gould I have received another letter telling of two more splendid shots of 133 teal and 122 wigeon."

A week later Gould wrote again to RPG on headed note paper from The Union Club, Trafalgar Square, his London base. In fact the letter was sent from Dalkey, a suburb of Dublin so he was back in Ireland. Gould tells RPG of two new Decoys that have been constructed four miles East of Zoutkamp and about half a mile apart. He raises a question about teal as one Decoy catches great numbers whilst the other never catches any. The conundrum he raised relates to why the teal are never seen on the coastal punting grounds, although they are caught in large numbers in the Ameland Island Decoy. He speculates that there is a perpetual autumn migration over the island and the resident call birds on the decoy make the migratory birds, "short stop". He laments that the teal do not find their way to the punting grounds and puts this down to the extent of sandbanks which attract low water roosting wigeon but are not close enough to the rather muddier habitat preferred by the teal.

1898. RPG visits Anglesey, Malltraeth and the Inland Sea

Perhaps it was Gould's letter that inspired RPG to make his October trip to Malltraeth. On 26 October the whole punting outfit was once again shipped from Belan Fort to Malltreath and RPG joined Croutear and his assistant at Captain Owen's shore side home.

Their first day afloat started at 7am on 27 October, and they did not return to the launch site until 3pm. Prospects looked good as they saw between four and five hundred ducks, some of which were thought to be mallard and pintail. The weather deteriorated and although nearly getting a heavy shot they eventually took a long shot only picking up 11 wild duck, (mallard). The next day it blew hard and at dawn they took a long shot at two Bewick swans but did not bag either of them. The diary records; "Afloat all day till 5pm in a continual deluge and a south west gale. Came home with boots full of water and myself soaked to the skin. Got no shot at ducks but saw many birds. An enjoyable day as we saw numerous varieties of wildfowl."

Four Mile Bridge and sluice into the Salt Lake (Inland Sea).

At the weekend RPG travelled to Holyhead to assess the punting opportunities on the 'Inland Sea'. He also visited The Valley Hotel meeting Mr. Price the proprietor. On Sunday he returned to Glynllifon where he stayed as a guest of Frederick Wynn.

On 31 October they were afloat at dawn; the birds, though numerous were very wild. On returning to the launch they spied a small sitting of 9 wigeon which rose at long range, "to save a blank day, they rose a long way off and flew very high over me. I pulled the trigger and 6 out of the 9 came down dead and fell all around the punt. A very artistic shot." They remained for two more days but the weather was against them and no further shot was made.

On 25 November instructions were given to move the punting outfit from Malltraeth Bay to Valley, a distance of 15 miles. On arrival RPG took up residence at The Valley Hotel and the punt was moored within a 10 minute walk from the hotel. Hopes were high that 'The Pool,' a tidal area between the main road to Holyhead and the road to the south leading to Rhoscolyn would hold a good number of duck. RPG describes the new punting ground in his diary; "This Pool is about two miles long and about a mile wide in places. The only entrance and exit for the tide in 'The Pool' is the sluice (an awful boiling cataract) under the N. W. Railway and Holyhead main road and another sluice at Four Mile Bridge at the other extremity of 'The Pool'. The result is that with spring tides 'The Pool' has not time to empty sufficiently for the mud banks to show for shooting at low water. The water from the main sea rushes into 'The Pool' through two small entrances for no less than 2 hours after it is high water outside, and it runs out of 'The Pool' into the sea for 4 hours after it is low water outside. In fact on spring tides 'The Pool' is kept full and does not have time to empty. The neap tides will show plenty of mud banks with every prospect of birds coming to the banks but these are spring tides!"

This trip was clearly about exploring the area so it is not surprising that RPG was anxious and all did not go quite as intended; "We paddled down comfortably with the last of the ebb tide and back with the first of the flood. Or so we thought, the 'local idiots' swore low water was at 3pm but when we got to the sea at Cymyran Bay I was told that low water was not until 7pm!"

"Mark Owen (acting as his puntsman) and I started back at 4 pm and had to fight our way inch by inch against a furious spring run in the tidal area below the 'Four Mile Bridge' and south to Cymyran Bay." They set off against the ebb in the dark for almost 4 miles, "slip slopping about in holes and rocks towing the punt as no power living could have rowed or poled against the ebb; It took 3 hours of slaving at the tow rope. Saw no fowl to speak of. A grand wild bay, Cymyran is strewn with wrecks and wreckage and a figure of a great gigantic man, (an old figure head of a wrecked ship) on the headland looking out to sea, also a little fort manned with old guns and cannon from wrecks."

The following day they were still exploring but this time they went through the sluice to the north into Beddmanarch Bay and on to Penrhos Point where they saw a good number of wigeon and picked up a shot of 9 pochard.

Weather and tides were against them on 30 November so they spent the day working out a plan for the future when punting below the sluice. Notes in the diary were made for future reference;

"1. Pass through the sluice at 8 am.

2. Shoot down to low water at 12 noon.

3. Pass through the sluice back into The Pool at 4pm

4. Note. A boat can only pass through the sluice during the 10 minutes for which it is motionless once in every tide of 6 hours!"

On 1 December, Mark Owen and RPG were afloat at daybreak on 'The Pool'; " We saw a mass of wigeon on the water. Set to them. They rose out of shot and flew towards me. I fired a longish shot at one end of the flock as they passed me high. Down came a shower of birds.

The Salt Pool (Inland Sea).

The gale being offshore, I should have been swamped had I followed a number of birds to the open water, we gathered 27. A splendid shot."

Bad weather and the fear of further loss of birds deterred a shot the next day but a small shot of 3 wigeon was made on 3 December, "A long silly flying shot." He immediately wrote to George Gould, who was aboard his yacht at Zoutkamp, to tell him of his success but complained about his puntsman's lack of skill. He asked Gould to send Walter Pope's address as he intended to write to him and invite him to Valley.

After enjoying the weekend at Glynllifon RPG returned to Valley on 5 December. Once again a gale of wind and rain ruined any chance of getting a decent shot although they battled every day with the elements from dawn to dusk. Finally on 9 December RPG decided to return to Thirkleby. The family were to join him for Christmas and some big pheasant days were planned at the Hall.

Gould wrote to RPG from Zoutkamp Holland on 6 December 1898;

"My Dear Gallwey

You seem to have got among the widgeon at Valley and I hope to hear soon of your getting a century, but it is not possible over 60 yards and there are a good many 'ifs' in the way besides. I had no idea that there was any place in England (in fact Wales!) with widgeon as you describe them at Valley.

Why don't you work them yourself and what do you want a 'clever' punter for when you can have the sport yourself? Pope's address is 2, Hanover Terrace – Weymouth, but I think he is going to shoot in France - he told me he was when I saw him not long ago. He is certainly a 'clever' punter and has few if any equals, but whether you would like him is another matter. He is very opinionated and likes to have his own way in everything. But, I dare-say if he were shooting with you these peculiarities would not appear. He wanted me to shoot in France with him, but I don't care to, for various reasons.

I came here last Friday. Saturday and Monday it blew a gale and I could only look at them from the Dyke (I kept walking backwards and forwards off and on during the day to see if they were still there) but this misery, I could not stand any longer and went out although it was blowing still very hard. I got two shots (50 and 45) in the main channel down from here, in places where I had never seen a bird before- both shots were on a lee shore and in very shallow water. I was in a constant shower of small waves coming aboard, as I went up to them. I was back at 10.20am but it was about the severest work I have ever had in sport.

The tides here are right this week so I shall shoot up to Saturday and leave for home on Sunday. As these are the last wigeon going South I shall now lay up for the season. I have got about 1350, but if I am not stopped by wind during the next four days I may easily get another 200 duck, now it is blowing half a gale.

Yours sincerely,
G.J. Gould.

1899. Anglesey after Christmas

RPG had high hopes of making a very good shot at Valley. The reconnaissance work had been completed before Christmas and on 16 January 1899 he returned to stay at the Valley Hotel, accompanied by his valet Whitfield, Sam Croutear, and a local boatman, to man a hired following boat. All was set to take advantage of the knowledge he now had about the movement of fowl on 'The Pool' and foreshore to the north and south. But with wildfowling not all goes according to plan! Travelling on the train from Chester he observed the damage done by the tide and a gale of wind; "Part of the seawall (just at the entrance to the Penmaenmawr tunnel) 3 miles from Conwy along the Holyhead line was washed away. I saw today, as I passed, the smashed up luggage train and its engine lying in a heap on the sea shore, where it had run into the sea. The line had been washed away!"

17 January saw them afloat at dawn and making a small shot of 7 wigeon. The birds were on the water and Croutear sculled RPG up to them and he remarks, "I ought to have killed a score but the birds being so near I fired, I imagine too much over them." The following day they did not get afloat due to severe weather. The next few days resulted in a beautiful shot of 27 wigeon but more frustration created by wind and rain.

An interesting note in the diary reads; "The charm of this place, the fascination of it, is there are always plenty of fowl to be seen and tried for, so that hope ever urges one on with the visionary phantom of success before the mind and it would not be very visionary either if suitable weather set in. Splendid sport would then be certain, as the hundreds of mallard that frequent the numerous freshwater lakes nearby would, if they were frozen come down to visit me on the coast!"

RPG decided to give punting a break and went snipe shooting at Bodfuan recording 17 couple over the two days he was away. A note records that he bagged 18 snipe to his own gun and if the other guns had performed as well as he did the bag would have been 50 couple! Meanwhile Croutear was afloat, shooting 12 wigeon on 24 January and 18 wigeon the following morning, there are no details where he got the shots. Three days followed when they were afloat for most of the day, frost and calm fine weather saw all the fowl at sea. There followed a weekend at Glynllifon and a chance to rest from the toil of fowling in congenial surroundings.

Returning to Valley on 30 January they were afloat again at dawn and made a poor flying shot in rough water picking up 9 wigeon. 31 January was unproductive and on 1 February weather was mild again but they got a small shot of 7 wigeon.

On 2 February RPG fired a shot while it was still dark in the morning, he records, "many wigeon piping all round some shelduck, fired in the dark and as luck would have it picked up 4 shelduck." From time to time the diary contains clues of frustration and even despair, "Fowling with the big gun is one list of sad monumental failures, surely undeserved ones too, considering the great toil hardship, expense and continual perseverance I undergo in the quest of success in this sport."

There was some small reward for their effort on 3 February when they punted to the north around Penrhyn Point opposite the Holyhead breakwater, again, it was a shot at wigeon on choppy water, "I took the shot as the nearest birds heaved up and knocked over 18. If the water had been quite calm I should easily have got 50-60 as there were 500 sitting close together."

On 4 February it was to be the final day for RPG's wildfowling season as he had to catch the Holyhead train at 11am. Despite the travelling arrangements they rose early and managed to get two shots at daybreak, one of 14 wigeon and finally a small shot of 6 wigeon and 2 shelduck. Then it was farewell to Anglesey and back to Thirkleby.

RPG summarised his thoughts about Valley; "I did fairly well considering: and now that I know the place intimately should do better another visit. I have no doubt that a very heavy shot is to be got here under suitable conditions."

Photographs of RPG often showed him smoking a cigarette. He writes;" My average has been rather over than under 18 per day for 20 years. This equates to 18 cigarettes per day = 6570 per year. Or 131,400 in 20 years. Take each cigarette as 3 inches and their total length is 394200 inches; or 6 miles 390 yards. That is to say that I have smoked a cigarette over 6 miles in length. This quite accounts for a chronic sore throat!"

1899-1900. RPG revisits Valley, Anglesey

Twenty eight days game shooting occupied RPG's time prior to returning to Valley on 7 December 1899. Once again he stayed in the Valley Hotel and the first day was spent putting the punt in the water and glassing 'The Pool' and the punting grounds to the north and south.

RPG wearing his game shooting attire

He went afloat at dawn on 9 December, a dry cold day and saw many wigeon feeding on Zostera in 'The Pool'. The day went really well and they had three shots. The first 7 wigeon and 3 teal followed by a second of 24 wigeon and 4 teal. Finally a shot as they were coming home in the evening of 14 wigeon. The day was not without incident; RPG's 12 bore broke and Ralph Wingfield, acting boatman did not have a shoulder gun in the following boat. All this frustrated RPG as he lost a number of birds. However, it was a good start and the following day was equally good. Their first shot in the morning producing 25 wigeon, 3 teal and 11 wild duck (mallard). There followed shots of 12 wigeon and a shot of 13 wigeon. RPG writes, "the best two days of sport with punt and gun by far I ever had excepting in Ireland or abroad as I have killed 116 in two days."

It is unusual for Anglesey to get a lot of snow, but inland the snow covered the ground and this perhaps was the reason why there were so many fowl on 'The Pool'. RPG counted 2000 on the morning of 12 December. He was just setting up to a fine shot of wigeon, "thick as bees" when a man fired a gun at a pheasant or a rabbit and put them all up, RPG writes, "may the common hangman wring his neck!" Frank Payne-Gallwey had come to stay the previous evening and after the disappointment of not getting to the shot earlier in the day RPG changed places with Frank in the following boat allowing him to get a small shot of 11 wigeon.

13/14 December saw them going north to Penrhos Point. There was a hard frost and the birds sat well enabling them to get a shot of 24 wigeon on the 13th and another of 11 wigeon in the

The Valley Hotel same place on the 14th. 15 December saw them afloat at 7am but they did not get the heavy shot they had hoped for. RPG writes, "immense numbers of ducks about but could only get a small shot of 4 wild duck (mallard) and 9 wigeon. Afterwards went down the bay when Frank made a mess of a fine shot. He ought to have got 30 or 40 at least but only got 8 wigeon. I afterwards made a very pretty shot at a bunch of 30 birds and bagged 15, by moonlight."

RPG summarised, "my six days afloat at Valley was an unusually successful expedition."

Success at Valley must have been telegraphed to George Gould who was at home in Dublin, having returned from Germany where he had only been allowed to shoot for seven days. The German Government had banned punt gunning in 1884 but up until now no action had been taken to stop fowling afloat with punt and gun. The story of how he was stopped punting remains unknown.

Christmas and the New Year of 1900 were celebrated at Thirkleby. RPG returned to Valley inviting Gould to join him for a few days. They met up at the Valley Hotel on 14 January. RPG was accompanied by his valet and Sam Croutear, and Croutear's son once again joined them from Lymington.

RPG would have been keen to show his friend 'The Pool' where he had enjoyed such good sport before Christmas. They were afloat at dawn the next morning with Gould behind the 2 inch Bentley and Playfair gun, "at dawn Gould fired a shot and killed 14 wigeon and 3 mallard, 2nd shot I killed 8 wigeon, a long flying shot. We spent the afternoon in the Bay (north) and saw fully 1,000 wigeon about Penhros Point but could not manage a shot. I set up to two splendid lots. I picked up one wigeon to a long shot."

The weather was against them for the next two days, calm and warm and consequently the birds were out to sea. RPG got a small shot of 8 wigeon on 18 January, Gould got a nice shot of 12 wigeon and 4 shelduck and by the 19th a gale set in. This did not deter them from an early start and RPG writes; "Afloat at 7.30am. Blowing a hard gale with heavy squalls and rain from the south. Nearly got a splendid shot into 300-400 wigeon closely packed on the mud but wind and water so rough I had to take what I could get which was 22. Came home to breakfast at 11am wet to the skin, teeth chattering, hands numbed, boots full of water."

On 20 January RPG returned to Thirkleby, the journey taking him 11 hours. He missed the train at Manchester by one minute and then the Leeds train broke down near Harrogate! In the meantime Gould had a final day afloat with Croutear and had a long flying shot picking up 4 wigeon. After laying up the punt and gun Gould went back to Dublin with plans to return again on 30 January. Croutear was instructed to stay on but not to go afloat until their return.

1900. The Mersey Estuary explored

RPG knew a Mr. Leonard Brooks who punted the Dee Estuary, near Chester. Brooks sent RPG reports from time to time and he had heard that the Mersey estuary, just north of the Dee might be worth investigating as a future punting ground. On 29 January, RPG decided to break his journey en route to Valley with a view to inspecting the Mersey; "The train stopped at Frodsham and then I drove (by carriage) three miles to Weston to inspect the Mersey Estuary. It was too misty to see through my telescope, but the place looked very well for punting." He then caught the next train and arrived at Valley at 9.30pm.

Gould joined him the following day. The weather and tides were against them so they went to inspect a bay 6 miles away on the coast round Penrhyn point and beyond to Llanfawr close to the Nimrod rocks. There they found hundreds of duck and wigeon," swarming round some low rocks and not far from the shore."

1 February saw them up early and afloat by 7am, and heading for the Nimrod rocks where they had seen the duck the day before. Conditions were not good; "A heavy snow storm and a nasty rolling sea, over 4 miles to the bay and difficult conditions." After a battle with the sea, on arrival they found there were fewer birds than the day before and they did not get a shot. Such is punt gunning.

On 2 February, an early start and a good shot in 'The Pool' as dawn broke rewarded their effort with 14 mallard and 1 wigeon. The ducks that RPG had seen on the Mersey were clearly on his mind as that afternoon he and Gould left by train to spend the night in Chester. The next day they rose early, hired a carriage and drove 8 miles to Ince, overlooking the Mersey; "We calculated we saw from 2500-3000 wild ducks, (no wigeon or teal), in a walk we took along the shore from Ince to Stanley Point. A marvellous and unexpected sight of wildfowl. Back to Chester by 12.30pm and onto Thirkleby by 8pm; "My men left Valley for Lymington today." The season was over, gun and belongings were all returned to Thirkleby and the punt stored at Belan Fort.

Then, quite unexpectedly, the weather turned really cold. RPG writes; "The weather has been more severe than any we have had since 1895. From 15 to 20 degrees of frost every night, deep snow and easterly gales and blizzards. In fact glorious weather for fowling. Flesh and blood could stand it no longer so I brought Croutear back to Valley from Lymington, and self and servant arrived there on Thursday 16 February, gun gear and ammunition all back again."

What happened? Well, of course, a complete soaking thaw with a deluge of rain, and a southerly gale of wind set in the very day he returned to North Wales. "A few days ago, deep snow, hard frost, now not a vestige of either. Infernal bad luck." But, as we shall see, he made the most of what sport was to be had.

On 17 February, instead of going to the 'The Pool' they decided to go south to the bay below the sluice where they had seen a large number of wigeon; "Afloat soon after daybreak and made a fine shot at a mass of wigeon. Blowing very hard off shore so that I lost a number of birds. Anyhow, we picked up 46 wigeon. A grand shot and the best I have made in home waters since my shot at Queenstown Harbour in 1886. I also added to the bag, a rabbit which I found in a trap and killed to have for my dinner."

Sunday was spent at the Valley Hotel resting and chatting to other visiting sportsman who reported excellent shoulder gunning sport on the coast.

Monday dawned and proved to be a day when disaster nearly struck. RPG and Croutear were up early and had decided to go through the sluice but their timing was not good. He writes first about the shot that they got; "Set to a splendid lot of wigeon below the sluice. I was just coming nicely in range when they flew off the mud and pitched in the water. They at once started swimming again into the mud but I was by then too near to them and they saw me. I had then to take a rather long flying shot bagging 15 wigeon. Three minutes earlier or later I should have got 30 or 40, such is luck." Excitement over he reflects, "we came in at 11.30am for breakfast soaked to the skin despite all precautions in the way of oilskins and long boots. Had rather a narrow escape of being capsized going through the sluice with a roaring sea and tide. A case of touch and go this time that was too near to be pleasant!"

On 20 February RPG decided that there were insufficient birds to warrant staying at Valley any longer so all was packed up again and he went off to London. Croutear was sent back to Lymington.

On the train he added some notes of interest about this fowling headquarters; "The Valley Hotel where I put up for punting in the Salt Lake and in Holyhead Bay is 3 miles from Holyhead. It is large and comfortable and offers very good plain cuisine. It is within 3 minutes' walk of the railway Station, post and telegraph office. Mr and Mrs Price, the proprietors, have lived here for some 30 years. They own and hire from 14,000 to 16,000 acres of land on which the guests, who stay at the hotel, can go out shooting. There is a great deal of duck and snipe shooting. Mr Price pays £800 a year for the shooting which is scattered all round the hotel, near and far. The sport obtained is very good in a small way generally, and in suitable weather conditions excellent. For instance during the recent 10 days of severe weather the 6 or 7 shooters staying in the house have each brought in on an average daily some 5 or 6 couple of snipe 6-10 wild duck (a few partridge before the season closed) beside, plover, curlew and other shore birds. The bag of partridge in a season here is usually from 1200-1400 brace, and a good many wild pheasants. Last Friday one shooter killed 17 snipe-10 ducks and 5 woodcock! I have known one of the hotel guests kill 18 duck in an evening flight and 81 ducks in 5 days, all with a shoulder gun. The guests who come to Valley usually come in separate parties of 2 or 3 and go shooting together. All I have talked to seem pleased with the sport they get at Valley and are quite satisfied – a very good sign."

1900. RPG's crossbow feat

RPG was invited to Glynllifon estate to shoot game with Frederick Wynn. He was then planning to go punting at Valley but on 25 November 1900 he went to Belan Fort to undertake a friendly challenge. RPG was an expert on all matters related to crossbows and at this time was planning an extensive new book covering the history and use of bows and arrows, crossbows and ancient siege projectile engines. 'The Crossbow' was published on 18 April 1903.

RPG tells the story of his challenge as follows; "On Monday 25 November 1900 I went with my large steel crossbow to Belan Fort, and shot from the battery of the fort several bolts right over the strip of water at the entrance of the Menai Straits, to Aber Menai Point (a distance in O.S. of 400 yards) in the presence of many witnesses. I brought the crossbow on purpose from home to do this feat which it was said was an impossible one to achieve, that it never had been done and never could be done save by the aid of gunpowder. It certainly never has been done before and it is never likely to be done again with either a long bow or a crossbow. Previous to making the attempt I had carefully measured the distance across at low water and I found I could do it with some 20 yards to spare. As I had a slight wind in my favour I did it with 33 yards to spare. Another first to be recorded in the annals of history."

RPG with Crossbow

1900. The Inland Sea, Anglesey revisited

The next day RPG returned to the Valley Hotel and asked his cousin to join him for five days. On arrival Frank seems to have gone in pursuit of snipe for most of the weekend and did little punting although he did get a shot on the last day of his visit.

RPG was afloat early on 27 November and made a disappointing shot of 20 wigeon. He thought the birds were on the mud but it turned out that the distance deceived him and they were on the water. The next day he went north to Penrhos Point in the morning and did not get a shot. In the afternoon he went through the sluice into the Salt Lake and writes, "I wantonly and mischievously blew off the gun at a few birds flying. A reckless and useless shot. I picked up one." Frank did rather better and had a great day snipe shooting. His bag was 9 snipe and 1 green plover. RPG adds a short note, "Frank thinks that we might have got 14-15 couple if I had been with him."

The 29 November turned out to be another bad day, "made a rank bad shot, got up so unusually close I think I fired over them. Result 5 wigeon." 30 November saw them going north to Penrhos Point again and getting a flying shot of 11 wigeon among the rocks. In the afternoon RPG joined Frank and they went snipe shooting together. He writes, "in good snipe weather we might have got many more." The bag was 17 snipe (three of which were jack snipe), and a hare.

Frank had his day afloat on 1 December firing, as RPG reported, "a wild random shot." He picked up 2 wigeon. He then went home! RPG spent the afternoon afloat and although there were no wigeon to be seen he had a shot of 36 green plover.

Sunday 2 December was a day to relax at the hotel and Monday heralded a deluge of rain and a hurricane of wind which led to another day at the hotel. The next day RPG managed to get out and take a small flying shot of 6 wigeon, "to save a blank day". He then left Valley for several serious days covert shooting at Norton Priory near Runcorn.

RPG's sporting notes are sometimes interspersed with amusing stories. A mixed bag is always welcome and RPG mentions the most unique bag he ever heard of as being made by an Eton boy who succeeded in peppering three Chief Constables from Nottinghamshire, Derby, and Worcestershire all in one day!

On 10 December RPG was back at Valley encouraged by Croutear's report of good numbers of fowl. In fact that day he set about the plover, two shots, the first rewarding him with 24 golden plover and the second 14 golden plover and 6 green plover. A short lament suggests that had his Bentley and Playfair been loaded with number 1 shot he would have bagged many more.

A blank day was saved on 11 December with a small shot of 7 wigeon. The weather then deteriorated and a south westerly gale set in. This confined operations to the sheltered waters of 'The Pool' and further shots of plover resulted, as the wigeon were all in the bay to the north. 12 December records two shots resulting in 40 green plover and 1 golden plover then, on the 13th a further 31 green plover were added. Frustrated by the weather RPG writes, "weather and tides unsuitable and wigeon as wild as hawks." He returned to Thirkleby on 15 December.

Christmas at Thirkleby Park seems to have been a rather quieter event than usual. RPG's son Willie, now aged 19 was at home. They enjoyed three days shooting together on the estate and clearly Willie was becoming a very proficient shot.

After the New Year of 1901 Croutear reported seeing large numbers of wigeon on 'The Pool' and RPG was eager to go after them. But the ducks that RPG had seen on the Mersey were still at the back of his mind. On 5 January he went to stay at Norton Priory, an estate where he had often shot as a guest of Sir Richard Brooke. The next two days were spent searching for a launch site for the punt and seeking suitable local accommodation. The diary records, "saw great number of ducks so made all arrangements for a visit to Hale later on." He then went on to Valley arriving on the evening of 7 January.

The next morning he and Croutear were afloat at dawn in 'The Pool', conditions were calm but they got a small shot of 16 wigeon. They spotted 3 brent geese which was unusual for the area at that time.

The following day they were again afloat in the Bay at dawn and at low water they went through the sluice into 'The Pool' and made a fine shot of 26 wigeon. This day was to prove to be the most remarkable and memorable occasion in RPG's punting career. We will let him recount the events that unfolded.

1901. 10 January, RPG's personal record shot at Valley, Anglesey

"One o'clock. Just come in for breakfast having made, soon after daybreak this morning, a really glorious shot at last! Croutear and I brought in 68 wigeon as a result of one grand shot. I had fully eighty birds down, but it was blowing very hard and as my following boat was not with me, I of course lost some birds but I was determined to pick them up later on.

This is the best shot I ever saw or ever made either at home or abroad (I got 62 once in Holland). I have been working very hard at Valley for two winters to obtain such a shot as this, and I have at length succeeded, and even better than I ever hoped for! All comes sooner or later to the man who never gives in. I fired across the line of birds. There were 1500 of them, packed liked bees all along the edge of the sand that is on the west side of the 'The Pool'. If I could have taken the birds in line I should have killed about double! This is the sort of shot that makes one feel drunk with joy at the moment after seeing the result of pulling the trigger. It is a record for Wales and has been very seldom done in England or in Scotland."

The following day RPG instructed four men to search all around 'The Pool' to look for any birds that might have been lost. Two were found to RPG's great delight making his great shot 70 wigeon. He records, "I should have been miserable else!"

Although he adds a final note, "I shall probably not go to Valley again now that I have, at length obtained the shot I have slaved for night and day, for two years." Later he does decide to return.

1901. Punting the Mersey estuary with George Gould

RPG now focussed on other plans. Croutear was instructed to transport punt and gun and all the gear on the punt carriage to Hale and await his arrival. His intention was to get on terms with the immense number of ducks he had seen on the Mersey Estuary and he invited Gould to join him on this new punting adventure.

"Gould and I arrived at Hale on Monday 21 January. We went afloat on the Mersey Estuary from Hale every day for the next five days and never brought home a duck or fired a shot at one! We saw every day at least 2000 wild duck (no wigeon) on the Dungeon sands, back of Hale. But could not get any chance at them! The tides were too terrific in their violence to make any chance of getting at the birds possible! The sand bank on which the birds sat used to cover in less than an hour, and the piece of it on which one would naturally expect to obtain a shot at the ducks as they crowded in a great mass together was covered by the roaring tide in a few minutes! The birds being swept off their legs would then fly off to the open water and scatter in

Sam Croutear

all directions. The tide rises in 'springs' over 20 feet in 3 hours, and at a rate of an inch a minute. The flood does not commence till 3 hours before high water, then it rages in like a mill race, and is very dangerous! A slight wind makes a heavy sea for any boat in the channel. There are no creeks or outlets to the main channel at low water or even at half-tide. In fact this infernal river is the very worst and most risky place for punting I ever saw. There is not one place all round its miles and miles of shore where a punt can be kept safely and with a chance of going afloat to work the tides. At the same time, if a man did not mind 30 blank days or so he might eventually kill 100 mallard at one shot."

This proved to be the last outing of the season. Gould returned to Ireland and RPG to Thirkleby Hall. As luck would have it, no sooner had he arrived home with carriage punt and gun a spell of ideal fowling weather set in, "the hard weather commenced on 28 January and lasted without a break until 18 February. Horrible luck."

Mr Thomas Mayer Pike recounts his adventure of fowling in Holland with Mr Hugh Leyborne-Popham in the winter of 1901/02

George Gould was not punting abroad this season but a fellow puntsman Mr T.M.Pike gives a vivid account of shooting in Walcheren, Holland that year. Pike wrote regularly to RPG and his wildfowling career spanned twenty four years many of which were spent with Hugh Leyborne-Popham punting in Holland.

"The state of the weather during the past autumn and winter when continuous strong westerly winds prevailed with high temperatures, rendered the successful pursuit of wildfowl in Walcheren almost out of the question. Geese, wigeon and ducks were on the ground which we rent in numbers, and could easily be seen with the assistance of the glass, but any attempt at launching a punt to go after them was perpetually frustrated by the strength and unfavourable direction of the prevailing winds. We had therefore to be content with an occasional shot at ducks at flight time and with tramping over the somewhat extensive, but not very productive area of sand dunes and rough shooting, which is there available. In this way we managed to bag some 350 head, the most noteworthy item being sixty two woodcock. At Christmas we retired from the unequal contest and went to Bournemouth for a change of scene, leaving the geese and ducks very much masters of the situation.

It was not until the beginning of February that an opportunity occurred of coming to terms with them. A friend, Mr Hugh Leyborne-Popham, who was shooting with me, had just returned to London to fulfil an engagement, when a sudden change to North East wind and frost set in and on 4 February I rowed down the Veere Gat hoping to make up a little for lost time. There were a considerable number of wigeon, a few wild ducks among them, pitched on the edge of the channel in a favourable position; but unfortunately, the sands were alive with waders of all sorts, oyster-catchers, bar-tailed godwits, knots, dunlin together with a few scattered sheldrakes. Many hundreds of these were between the punt and the wigeon, and the incessant flying up and pitching finally proved too much for the nerves of the wildfowl; they also rose in a body and pitched again some half mile out in the tideway. Imagining that they would return to the sheltered bight as soon as the punt was out of the way, I rowed off some three miles down to the end of the Veere Gat sands and returned just as the sun, like a copper globe in the frosted air, was going down in the west. From under the shelter of a sandbank, a glance with the telescope showed the wigeon back in their old place, half of them already landed, the rest swimming close by in the water. It was evidently a case of waiting until they were all landed, so there was time for a pipe, the boat being well sheltered from view. At this juncture a great seal reared his head and shoulders out of the water within twenty yards of us and, had a good stare and then dived with a splash. Seals are very inquisitive.

Thomas Pike rowing his punt down the Veere Gat

After the shot. Hugh Leyborne-Popham's steam yacht 'Toso' is beyond

One of my Dutch keepers accompanied us in another punt, so to pass time, I asked him about the seals in the Veere Gat and surrounding area. He said they existed in considerable numbers especially on the great sandbanks of the Roompot channel of the East Schelde. The Dutch Government offers a reward for their destruction for they naturally do much damage to the salmon and other fishing industries in The Netherlands. The fishermen from the village of Burgsluis, on the south-west side of Schouen Island, capture them in numbers by aid of nets, a somewhat unusual method. The nets are purposely made of great strength and with an extra-large mesh. A considerable length of net is required and it is shot from a boat in such a position, that it is carried down by a strong ebb tide right on to the bank where the seals are resting, the ends and the middle of the net being, of course well buoyed. When it is sufficiently near the seals, another crew of men make their appearance from the far side of the bank, and by firing a gun or shouting drive the seals off the bank into the water when they immediately dive, get caught in the net and are soon exhausted and die.

It was now time to peep over the bank again to look at the fowl. They were in a good position, all ashore, with their heads down and apparently asleep, some thirty duck and mallard on the near side and at least one hundred wigeon in a nice line beyond them. An off-shore wind left the water white along the edge of the bank, whilst the last rays of the sun directly astern helped as a disguise and the young flood running up the water way rendered any but the slightest movement of the setting pole unnecessary. In a short time the punt glided up unnoticed within sixty yards of the fowl. Not a head stirred, the birds being evidently unaware of the danger. As, however, firing a punt gun at birds on the ground is a poor and unproductive way of making a shot it was decided to move them. My head and shoulders cautiously raised, had an instantaneous effect. The necks of the mallard shot up, as wings opened a band of space was visible between the ducks and the sand upon which they had been resting. That is the moment to fire; they will all be in the air by the time the shot reaches them. The smoke clears and twenty eight dead ducks can be seen in a line on the sand. A neat effective shot that rewards our patience.

The frost and north east wind continued and my friend Hugh returned from England and together we enjoyed fowling together until the middle of March I hardly remember during my punting career such pleasant climatic conditions although on returning to England I found my friends there hardly so enthusiastic on the subject.

We made many successful shots and the most productive one resulted in fifty-eight birds, namely fifty-one wigeon and seven teal. The best shot however, was made at grey geese, in weight at least if not in number. The lower part of the estuary is most frequented by geese. On this occasion we made our shot just after low-water which resulted in fifteen pink-footed geese being picked up.

In this way the time slipped pleasantly away, and six weeks shooting, with our two punts on occasion firing together resulted in a combined bag of some seven hundred and forty two fowl. Of these five hundred were wigeon, one hundred duck and mallard and eighty grey geese, the remainder were a mixed lot of teal, shoveler, and pintail.

Owing to the rough weather we lost the best chances for coming to terms with the geese during the early part of the season. In addition frosts so late in February are rarely productive as the sun begins to negate to a great extent, the frosts by night. Wildfowl do not migrate to the same extent on account of cold at that time of year, though an exception to this was experienced in February 1895, when the cold was altogether exceptional. It is only in an estuary that has been comparatively undisturbed by shooting in the early part of the season when the fowl that have arrived in autumn are induced to remain in the vicinity, that much sport can be expected at so late a period in the winter. However, with the three hundred and fifty head above mentioned at the beginning of our visit this brought our grand total to over one thousand head, a bag which a well preserved English estate can easily show for a single day's sport with half a dozen guns. To us it meant some three months' hard work, long tramps over sand dunes through thick scrub, continued labour with our oars and setting poles, getting up often hours before dawn and exposure to wind, frost and fog, and other disagreeable experiences in a way of weather. An ordinary gunner is usually of the opinion that a punt-shooter is necessarily of a sanguinary disposition; as a matter of fact, he is willing to work hard for a moderate result. The fascination of his pursuit consists in its difficulty, and if some element of personal danger arises from the adverse conditions of wind and tide the charm, it may be said, is all the greater."

Hugh Francis Arthur Leyborne-Popham M.A., M.B.O.U. (1864-1943) was educated at Charterhouse and Brasenose College, Oxford and a landowner at Hunstrete, Somerset. He made three expeditions down the river Yenisei in Siberia in 1895, 1897 and 1900 where he made extensive collections of bird skins and eggs. These collections can be found at the Ornithology and Rothschild Libraries of the Natural History Museum at Tring. Hugh Leybourne-Popham bankrupted his estate by attempting to establish a trade route, by sea, round northern Russia. He lost nine ships in one year through ice and rough seas. His obsession with shooting in Holland was also said to have contributed to his financial downfall. He died during the Second World War and the latter part of his life was spent in a cottage on the Huntstrete estate.

RPG's diary continues

1902. Belan Fort. RPG's favourite retreat

Returning now to the pages of Payne-Gallwey diaries, RPG evidently had great affection for Belan Fort as he writes in January 1902, "here I am again, at this delightful retreat, by the sea once more - It is two years since I was here. I gave it up as showing no sport when I was here in November 1900 (at the time when I shot the bolt from the crossbow across the Menai Straits), I saw several hundred ducks. On the strength of this I at once determined to give Belan another try with punt and gun."

"Croutear and his son arrived last Saturday, self, valet and cook arrived today. Went afloat this afternoon for a short cruise. Croutear saw 600 ducks about this morning and general report has it there are plenty of fowl about here this year. We shall see. Welsh men are all such terrific liars; or to put it more kindly, they cannot tell the difference between 100 birds and 500 birds." The first three days afloat were totally unproductive, the tides were wrong and it was blowing a gale. However, the prospects looked promising as there were plenty of wigeon to be seen in the Voryd Bay.

Sunday's entry in the diary reads, "Belan Fort. Ate, drank, smoked and wrote letters and wished for Monday!" As luck would have it Monday proved to be an exciting day. They made a beautiful shot of 33 wigeon at dawn. There were two lots in a creek in the Voryd and the smaller lot would have had to be passed to get to the better shot so they decided not to risk trying this as they would have disturbed the other birds. The shot was taken in rough water and the swell hid the birds somewhat from the charge, however, this shot proved to be the highlight of the 20 days spent at Belan as RPG did not get another chance at wigeon. He comments, "I only had one shot at the ducks and then they vanished, whether the reason was because they were fired at, or because of strong northerly gales I cannot say, probably from the latter cause. We experienced very hard and suitable weather for fowling but the real fact is there is little food here for the ducks this late in the season."

Frank joined RPG on 29 January and they then seem to have decided, in the absence of duck, to set about the plover and knots! 18 golden plover on 31 January, an extraordinary shot of 1 mallard and 92 knots on 3 February. Then RPG records on 10 February, "had a fine day's sport at the plover today firing 4 shots, 47, 30, 44, 19. A total of 140 made up of 34 golden plover and 106 green plover, my record for plover," he proudly states.

One concludes that the ducks must have become weary of Voryd Bay and this is confirmed when on 12 February RPG was able to cross the Menai Straits to the Anglesey shore and make a flying shot of 9 mallard.

George Gould did not join RPG this season and remained in Ireland punting the Shannon estuary. His bag was 308 ducks and 306 plover. His best shot was 68 teal on 5 November in Clonderalaw Bay, River Shannon.

1902/03. RPG RETURNS TO VALLEY, ANGLESEY

Gould was not punting during the 1902/03 season, having gone to Morocco. For RPG, five days grouse shooting had not been as good as usual and the partridges at Thirkleby were a disaster; "The worst bag of partridges and the worst season at Thirkleby Park I have ever known, a bitter cold spring and summer. Not half as many birds now on the estate as were left last season!"

Early December 1902 saw RPG back at Valley; "Here I am at my old quarters again. Sam Croutear and son arrived yesterday and my valet and cook arrived this evening."

This season RPG hired 'The Bungalow' for £20 securing the house for the months of December and January. The new fowling headquarters was within 50 yards of the 'The Pool'. Punt and gun could be moored close by. The Bungalow overlooked where the wigeon tended to sit. He also hoped by living here it would deter shoulder gunners spoiling the chances of him getting a shot!

The 11 December was spent preparing the punt and breeching the gun. All was ready to go afloat at 2 pm. By 2.30 pm they had made a shot of 5 brent geese. There were only 9 in the sitting and he remarks, "a happy start. The first brent I have killed since 1896. Brent are rare on this coast and I have only seen two or three before."

12/13/14 December were uneventful and then by RPG's own admission, two wild shots on the 15th and 16th produced 6 mallard and 5 wigeon. Weather permitting they went afloat each day at 7.40am and, according to the tide, either stayed in the shelter of the Salt Pool or went through the sluice punting around Penrhos Point. A shot of 10 wigeon followed on 17 December in the Salt Lake.

Bad luck struck on 18 December; "Afloat in the bay at 7.40am. A hurricane from the west. Blue lights and rockets flying up in all directions from the coast in reply to the signals of a large vessel in distress. Finally just at the moment I was drawing in shot of a fine lot of wigeon, a signal gun fired from Holyhead and put all my birds up. One of the few instances I ever knew of real bad luck out punting, as it was not in my power to prevent the mishap to my possible chance of a good shot." Better luck followed on 19 December. RPG caught up with the brent geese again; "Went through the sluice at 10.30am and found the remaining four brent geese, I shot these remaining four geese dead, so I have got the 9!"

RPG returned to Thirkleby on 20 December and summarised this visit, "I have been afloat 8 days, always out at 7.30 am. Nothing but gales from south-west and west, rain and very mild. Large numbers of fowl about but mild weather and gales and spring tides, showing no banks at low water in the Salt Pool, made sport most impossible."

At the beginning of January 1903 RPG and his son Willie went back to 'The Bungalow' at Valley, a place which he describes as, "delightfully warm house having comfortable beds and rooms situated on the very verge of the water." In his absence Croutear and his son had shot 3 mallard and 15 wigeon.

Frank Payne-Gallwey arrived on 8 January. Willie and Frank were encouraged to go rough shooting while RPG went out in the punt with Croutear. RPG got a shot of 9 wigeon. Willie and Frank brought home 6 snipe, 1 water rail and 1 rabbit. Much to RPG's frustration three days of gale force winds then set in. Willie and Frank continued rough shooting each day getting a nice mixed bag. Willie had never had a shot in the punt and RPG was naturally anxious to get him afloat. His chance came on 12 January when he went out with Croutear under a bright moon. There were plenty of duck about but they did not get a shot. A northerly wind had set in and this brought a very hard frost. Willie was out under the moon on 13th and RPG rejoices in his success; "Wind north. Glass higher than I ever saw it (halfway between 30 and 31) and 15 degrees of frost. Willie fired his first shot with the big gun and got 6 wigeon."

Then, glorious Arctic weather set in and 'The Pool' nearly froze over. RPG records 15 degrees of frost at night which froze the milk and water in the house. Chances of a shot at wigeon came and went without success. He does mention a bag of 11 green plover, 2 golden plover and 8 wigeon but he does not say how they were acquired.

Frank and Willie left early on 15 January and RPG laments his lack of success, despite going afloat all day and every day; "During the past week I have only shot 17 wigeon. One of the worst and most cruelly disappointing experiences I have ever had." A final note refers to a dramatic change in the weather; "A complete thaw, no frost seems to last nowadays more than 3 or 4 days."

Croutear finished off the season by going out at night on 20 January and returning with 3 wigeon. RPG departed to Norton Priory where he had arranged to stay with Sir Richard Brooke and show him how to net plover. Punt and gun were dispatched back to Thirkleby and Croutear back to Lymington. RPG estimated the total cost of wildfowling this season to be £85.

1903/04. RPG RETURNS TO THE HUMBER ESTUARY STAYING AT PATRINGTON VILLAGE

From 15 September 1903 until 9 October RPG and Lady Edith were staying with their old friends Lord and Lady Dunraven at Adare Manor where they enjoyed playing golf. Thoughts of wildfowling did not occur until after Christmas when RPG decided to return to the Humber with a view to punting the lower part of the estuary. He describes the area, "Croutear is with me and the punt is moored in a very safe position in a creek close to the sluice which is the outlet for the drainage water of this part of Sunk Island and Holderness.

The sluice is 3½ miles from Patrington and 2 miles from Patrington Haven village to which place vessels used to come up about 60 years ago, before Sunk Island was entirely reclaimed and joined to the main land. Sunk Island now comprises about 10,000 acres of good land chiefly growing mustard. There are thirteen large farms on it. It is quite flat as far as the eye can see on all sides and not a tree or hedge for miles. Some of the fields are 80 to 100 acres in size bounded by deep dykes like Holland. Wild and weird countryside, swarming with plover.

Croutear lodges at Newlands Farm (the last land reclaimed) about ½ mile from the sluice, and I Lodge at the Holderness Arms in Patrington Village just opposite the magnificent old church, the steeple of which is 200 ft. high and is a plain mark for vessels at sea many miles distant. An old fisherman with a small punt and rusty old gun lives every winter on board a very small smack (about 2 tons) all alone in the creek below the sluice. I envy him! I at once engaged him to attend me with a following boat."

On 5 January it was RPG's intention to meet Croutear and go afloat with him on the Humber but en route he felt unwell and returned to Thirkleby. He sent John, his valet to tell Croutear that he would join him as soon as possible.

Recovery was swift and on 11 January RPG arrived at Patrington and went afloat that afternoon. He did not get a shot but commented, "since I was last in this district a fine new lighthouse has been built at Spurn (1895). I saw it today in the distance. The fowler I used to employ at Spurn (Walter Arnes) was, I hear, drowned, together with his son through having his sheet made fast in a gale when fishing in his boat off Spurn."

The next three days were unsuitable for punting, the weather was warm and windy and RPG decided to return to Thirkleby. On 20 January he was back with Croutear but once again the weather prevented him from going afloat. Croutear did get one shot of 16 wild ducks while RPG was away.

Summarising the season he writes; "Not really a season at all as I was only out in the punt on four occasions which I was glad not to have missed doing as I have now done so for 28 years, though this is the first year in 28 in succession that I have not fired off the big gun. Splendid sport could be obtained without the slightest doubt from Patrington off the shores of Sunk Island if the weather was cold; and the wind from the north-west, north or north-east. There are many hundreds of wild duck about and some wigeon always about. At low water and 2 hours before or after a punt can be worked safely in almost any wind. The creeks, channels and flats, are most suitable for poling to birds; about a foot of water in them and hard ground for poling. There is also unlimited space in every direction for cruising about in search of sport."

An interesting note follows setting out the cost of fowling this past season.

Cost of killing (by Proxy) 16 ducks.

Self and valet to Patrington and back (3 times)	£3.0.0
Croutear's journey from Lymington and return	£3.0.0
Croutear's wages and board for 3 weeks	£7.0.0
New boots and mop for Croutear	£1.13.0
Account at Holderness Arms	£5.07.0
Paid for horse and trap and man	£2.11.0
Paid extra for boatman	£1.16.0
Transit of punt and gun back and to Patrington	£4.14.0
Total	£29.1.0

Footnote. Was this the time RPG met Stanley Duncan and discussed the Wildfowlers' Association of Great Britain and Ireland (WAGBI)? See Graham Downing's book on WAGBI history, 'A Sporting Century.' We are indebted to John Marchington who when writing his excellent book, "The History of Wildfowling" in 1980 received information from one of Stanley Duncan's sons ; "In 1903 RPG was at Patrington Channel, Sunk Island on a wildfowling trip, Duncan approached him on the subject of forming a Wildfowlers' Association and RPG told him that an Association had already been formed but had failed due to lack of support."

RPG's failing health

In February 1905 RPG lamented that during the past season he never went afloat in his gunning punt. Health issues were arising with RPG who was now 57. We first detected these in his diary notes in January 1904 when he became unwell en route to Patrington. Clearly frustrated he writes; "The first year punting I have missed in 30 years. The cause was that I had been unwell during the summer of 1904 under Doctor Thorne the famous specialist for more or less imaginary heart disease." In reality RPG knew that his malaise was chiefly due to smoking thirty cigarettes every day for thirty years together with cigars, port, wine and champagne, all of which he was not about to give up.

Determined as ever he writes, "I was however ready to go anywhere if the short spells of frost had lasted but they never did last more than a week or so. A mild winter on the whole, thousands of duck on the river Humber, but no use going to them in mild weather."

1905. Wildfowling regulations introduced in Holland

News from George Gould would not have helped RPG's frustration. Gould was moored off the north Holland coast and had been fowling for 6 weeks from his yacht, near Holwerd, a place that RPG knew well. He had brought to hand 1133 ducks from 28 shots, an average of 40 birds per shot. But even Gould, now aged 59 was suffering from ill health and the following season he was also unable to go afloat due to a broken hip. He did return to Holland for the 1906 season. Then, from notes in RPG's diary, it appears that 1907 was the last season when Gould went afloat.

We speculate here why Gould gave up punting. He lived to the ripe old age of 89. His health might have been part of the reason but we believe we have uncovered another important fact. Our research suggests that from the late 1890s the Dutch decoy owners were putting increased pressure on the Dutch Government to prohibit punt gunning. In August 1899 Hugh Leyborne-Popham records receiving a letter from Mr de Bruyne the British Vice-Consul at Middelburg stating that, no 'big gun' shooting was now permitted on any unleased waters. The interpretation of the term 'big gun' referred to a gun larger than 4 bore. This was a consequence of a 'Motion' brought forward by Mr. Rink in the second chamber of the Dutch Parliament which was carried by a large majority. A press cutting stated that Holland was now closed to 'English Wildfowlers.' Despite the ban on punt gunning in Holland we know Gould was amongst a number of well-known wealthy gentlemen wildfowlers who continued to punt in Holland until 1907. It seems most unlikely that they simply broke the law. The ban that the Government introduced referred to Public Waters. But, the gentlemen punt gunners were not punting Public Water. From the evidence we have seen it seems that in certain areas secure leases existed permitting them to continue to pursue their sport for the duration of the lease. We know that Leyborne-Popham owned an estate bordering the Veere Gat

Hugh Leyborne-Popham in his punt with double Bland Magnum 4 bore amongst the sands of the Veere Gat

where he and Pike had together improved the shooting. Tom Pike certainly punted from Terneuzen between 1883/84 until 1907 having held a lease on the Veere Gat since 1894 granted to him by the Dutch Government.

We speculate that by 1908 the leases that they held would have expired and this spelt the end of punt gunning in Holland. Some of the gentlemen fowlers including Leyborne-Popham did move their operation or resorted to using 4 bore punt guns which were still legal; but we believe that when Gould's lease expired at Holward he decided that if he was unable to sail to Holland to live on his yacht and use his Holland and Holland punt gun, then he would give up punt gunning.

Gould loved to travel and with the coming of the motor car we find him later in life spending much of his time in Morocco and travelling widely abroad. His enjoyment of punting was clearly not forgotten as we find that in his Will he left Michael Grimes his friend and respected Irish puntsman, the sum of twenty five pounds.

Holwerd and Lauwers Zee were the main wigeon grounds that George Gould punted when living aboard his yacht. The Dollart was the most easterly of the Dutch estuaries and lay on the boundary with Germany. Wigeon were rare visitors to the Dollart but teal and mallard were in large numbers.

In the autumn of 1897 George Gould was afloat in the Dollart for twenty three days and shot 951 teal. He then moved his anchorage to the Lauwers Zee, fowling for a further twenty days. In total he fired 67 shots for the total bag for the season of 1808 fowl. The best shot was 121 wigeon on 4 November in the Lauwers Zee.

The following season 1898-99 the total fowl shot numbered 1478. It was at this time he achieved three of the most remarkable shots ever achieved with punt and gun.

1898	11 October	Lauwers Zee	One shot of 149 wigeon
1898	11 November	Lauwers Zee	One shot of 105 wigeon & 17 teal
1898	29 November	Dollart	One shot of 132 teal

Records from Captain George Gould's wildfowling diary

	Country or place	Fowl	Green plover / curlew
1877-78	Cork Harbour, S. Ireland	56	-
1878-79	Cork Harbour	223	14
1879-80	Cork Harbour	231	64
1880-81	Cork Harbour	187	106
1881-82	Shannon Estuary	399	176
1882-83	Shannon	370	65
1883	Germany	1350 up until 31 December	-
1884	Holland	464 to 7 November	-
1885	Holland	284 up to 2 December.	-
1886	Holland	420 up to 23 October.	-
1887	Holland	742 up to end of October	-
1888	I was not punting	-	-
1889	Holland	1004 up until 11 November	-
1890	I was in Morocco	-	-
1891-92	Holland/Shannon	698	58
1892-93	Shannon	613	324
1893-94	France	535	41
1894	Holland	1453	-
1895	Holland	109	-
1896	I was not punting	-	-
1897	Holland	1808	-
1898	Holland	1478	-
1899	Germany	232	-
1900	I was not punting	-	-
1901-02	Shannon	308	306
1902-03	I was in Morocco	-	-
1903	Holland	1511	-
1904	Holland	1133	-
1905	I was not punting, laid up with broken hip	-	-
1906	Holland	774	-
1907	Holland	132	-
	TOTAL	16514	1154

A curious coincidence

A short article written by Tom Pike appeared in 'The Field' magazine on 15 February 1908. In it he summarises his wildfowling career spanning 24 years punting most of which was done in southern Holland, often with his friend Leyborne-Popham at Veere.

The article starts by describing the winter weather experienced during the 1906-07 season. A relatively mild winter with several spells of frost which proved ideal conditions for going afloat. He contrasts this weather with that of the 1890-91 and 1894-95 seasons when severe weather rendered the waterways in Holland impassable as a result of pack ice.

29 October 1907 was to be his last ever punting trip and it proved to be a memorable day. Snow had fallen on the evening of the 28th and there was a severe frost that night. Tom was out single handed punting and his total bag for the day amounted to 56 ducks (mallard), 33 wigeon, 8 teal, 5 pintail and 1 shoveler. The best shot with his punt gun was 47 or in reality 50 as 3 wigeon were picked up the following day. His big shot consisted of 25 wigeon, 7 teal, 5 pintail and 13 mallard.

This was the best bag he had ever made in his whole life.

Tom Pike's bag records

Year	Place	Wildfowl	Year	Place	Wildfowl
1883-84	Terneuzen	218	1895-96	Veere	250
1884-85	Veere	296	1896-97	Veere	660
1885-86	Zierikzee	1135	1897-98	Veere	156
1886-87	Findhorne	208	1898-99	Veere	171
1887-88	Bonawe	105	1899-1900	Veere	241
1888-89	Zierikzee	556	1900-01	Veere	530
1889-90	Veere	630	1901-02	Veere	742
1890-91	Veere	459	1902-03	Veere	483
1891-92	Veere	475	1903-04	Veere	598
1892-93	Veere	424	1904-05	Veere	642
1893-94	Veere	---	1905-06	Veere	266
1894-95	Veere	650	1906-07	Veere	1258

He writes, "this was certainly a splendid day's sport and a very agreeable finale to a career of punt shooting extending as it does from the year 1869, when as a boy at Rugby, to the present day, most of the time being spent in Holland, where I have passed some of the happiest years and far the best sport was had there though I was in Scotland for a few years."

Tom Pike shared a ten year lease over the Veere with his friend Hugh Leyborne-Popham, they often shot and punted together. Remarkably Tom died on 5 February 1908 the same day as he sent the article to 'The Field'. He is buried in Epsom cemetery, Surrey.

1908/09. RPG AT BELAN FORT AND THE ROAD TO RECOVERING HIS HEALTH

RPG may have lamented losing the company of George Gould, his punting partner and friend but he certainly had not lost his enthusiasm to go afloat. It was almost four years to the day on 16 January 1908 that RPG rejoiced in being fit enough to go punting again. He chose not to return to Patrington on the Humber Estuary but instead arranged to return to North Wales and set up his fowling H.Q. at the Caernarvon Bay Hotel three miles from Belan Fort where he had hitherto stayed, courtesy of Frederick Wynn. Perhaps this was because he was mindful of his health as he describes the hotel, "the resort of Caernarvon fashionable in the summer; now in mid-winter deserted and lonely, a few yards only from the breaking surf of the Irish sea and shook and swept by every wind that blows from land or sea." Doubtless he would have had the whole hotel to himself and the staff would have looked after his every need.

His old friend and puntsman Croutear was billeted in the buildings at Belan Fort and by the 17 January 1908 the double punt, breeched with the 2 inch Bentley and Playfair, was moored in the dock ready for RPG's arrival at 7am. Croutear had glassed the Voryd Bay the day previous and reported optimistically he had sighted, "a nice lot of wigeon in the Bay."

Reading RPG's diary, you can sense his delight at the prospect of going afloat again and his eager anticipation of being out in the Voryd Bay with Croutear and amongst the fowl; "A south-west gale, and a grand lot of wigeon in the Voryd! Watched them for hours with ecstasy of delight; as soon as the tide suited off we went. We had to go through rough water which almost filled the punt and drenched us to the skin as we lay down to the birds. At least 600-700 birds within three gunshots of us for half an hour, but what with strong ebb and furious wind and shallows, we could not get to them! At last we blundered up within about 85 yards, and I fired, and only gathered 11 wigeon. A very bad shot indeed, as the birds were so tame that I believe we could have got far nearer and then bagged 50 or 60. They were so tame by reason, I imagine, of the strong gale and not having been previously shot at this season."

The Caernarvon Bay Hotel (and staff) 1908

It is unclear whether RPG blamed Croutear or himself. In setting to the wigeon, conditions were clearly very severe and when they ran aground within 200 yards of the wigeon Croutear had to sit up and work the punt into open water. At this point the birds rose, which would have undoubtedly unnerved the gunner! But, such was the weather they then dropped back in and settled in what was an even better sitting. RPG laments, "I should have waited for them to rise and drop back again when we were in range instead of firing at long range." Hindsight is a wonderful thing but the anticipation of what might have been is very compelling!

Following the miserable pick up and an uncomfortable wet trip back to Belan Fort RPG writes; "My first shot for four years has thus been one of the worst ones for judgement and execution possible."

The next day, following breakfast at the hotel at 6.30 am RPG was determined to try and get a better shot. Once again all did not go according to his plan, "saw about 400 duck and wigeon and did not fire at them as they were all swimming and scattered. When the tide suited, at about 2 o'clock went after the birds, but just as we were going for them they rose and flew across the Straits to Abermenai Bay. Followed the birds and found quite 700-800. Weather calm, warm and bright, birds scattered all over. Set to one nice lot but a man on shore digging bait put them up. As I saw no chance of a good shot I took a small bunch and bagged seven wigeon."

The 19 January was a Sunday and RPG walked to Glynllivon and joined Sir Fredrick Wynn for lunch. To his delight Fredrick suggested that he saw no reason for him to stay at the Caernarvon Bay Hotel and Belan Fort might be more convenient as a wildfowling HQ.

The diary entry on Monday 20 January records a move of all bags and baggage and RPG's manservant from the hotel to Fort Belan, "Belan, as when I was last here, a fascinating retreat, all just as before. Big cannon and small cannon on the battery and ramparts-armoury, rooms in the house crowded with pictures and curios and models all to do with the sea and ships. I now have far more chance of success as I can almost step out of bed into my gunning punt."

Sam Croutear with RPG, Belan Fort dock. The John Pickett punt and the 2" Bentley and Playfair gun

On 21 January the weather was dry, bright and fine; "Afloat at 7.30 am, very nearly got a splendid shot at 100 mallard with 100 wigeon on Abermenai side of Straits but ran aground on a shallow bank just out of range. Then crossed the Straits to Voryd and found a couple of hundred wigeon on the water and was foolish enough to disturb them by firing a long wild shot in rough water for only three birds." One cannot help but wonder at RPG's judgement which time and time again is called into question. On this occasion, by his own admission he writes; "If I had only had the sense and patience to leave them quiet I might have had a fine chance of a better shot at low water this evening."

Patience is a virtue when out in a gunning punt as events on 22 January illustrate. RPG was afloat at dawn, crossing the Straits and looking for a shot on the River Briant as daylight broke. He remarks the weather was fine and flat calm with no chance of a shot although many birds were seen. From the watch tower at the Fort he could observe the movement of fowl on the Abermenai banks at low water. He writes, "I saw 16 wigeon swimming near the point of the great Abermenai Sand, I waited for an hour on the mere chance of them going up on the sand, which at length they did do. They clustered close together. I made a capital shot into them 'bullseye' and killed and gathered 12 and one teal." He rejoices, "it is always a good shot to gather every bird one kills, and to, besides, kill nearly all the birds fired at."

On 25 January; "Out at 6 am to catch the dawn; birds scattered and no chance of a shot. A very strong wind all day and a raging boiling sea in the Straits. All I did today was to walk up and down the battlements of the Fort, and up and down its towers viewing some fine lots of duck and wigeon splendidly packed for shooting across the Straits where I had no chance of getting to 'em!" A joyous footnote is added to this entry. "What greater joy or excitement is there than to make a good shot with the big gun, and to see, after the smoke of the gun has cleared, the birds lying on the sand."

The 23 January, "found hundreds of birds in Abermenai bay. In the evening I could not get to the big lot but had a pretty little shot of 12 wigeon." By 24 January the birds had become

RPG's poem about Belan, Ann was Frederick's formidable housekeeper

> Oh! Belan thou art beautiful as everybody knows.
> The Straits so full of fish and fowl right past thy fortress flows
> Tis not the fish nor yet the fowl that prey upon my mind
> My joy would be too great for words if Ann were less unkind
>
> R.T.P-G. Jan: 23. 1905.

very wary and although RPG was afloat at dawn there were no wigeon in their usual haunts. Returning to Belan he spied the wigeon all drifting about in a calm sea well away from any danger. With that he had breakfast and then went to the nearby marshland snipe shooting. He returned by 4 o'clock whereupon Croutear had the punt ready to go across the Straits to Abermenai. There they saw a nice sitting of teal on the sand, "I took a flying shot and bagged 20, very satisfactory as only one was lost in the rushing tide."

Sunday's entry stated; "The telescope was all I amused myself with today!" In this part of North Wales there was no shooting on a Sunday. An entry in the diary sums up how RPG spent this day, "An idle day- Writing-Reading-Eating-Smoking and devoutly wishing for Monday. A gale of wind and occasional deluges of rain all night. The wind has roared, hummed and squealed incessantly round the battlements, chimneys and windows of this old sea fortress, but it stands like a rock on the verge of the tide. Great waves, and a racing sea of 7 knots current beat and boil round its walls to no effect. The windows so thickly covered with salt I could not see through them. A grand lot of birds sheltering in the creeks this afternoon. Glass still falling fast."

Belan Fort, the hall

By Monday the gale had abated and RPG was afloat at dawn. Despite being out all day, he was unsuccessful in getting a shot. In the evening the wind veered from south west to north-west, a much better quarter, which would improve his chances for a shot the following day. On this day RPG tells of an interesting encounter which gives the reader a further insight into his personality.

"I saw today on the Abermenai Sands the poor man who is crippled in both legs and who hobbles on crutches a mile across the sand to sit behind a rock with an old single muzzle-loader for the chance of a duck drifting on the tide past his shelter. He is an old friend of mine of former days here and I regard him as a splendid and true sportsman. Today, I anchored my punt well away from him as I would not for fifty ducks run the risk of preventing him getting a shot at just one. His joy at seeing me again (after 6 years) was most pleasurable. We had a long yarn about wildfowl and their ways and habits, of which he knows as much, if not more, than I do. A piteous ragged cripple to look at, but a brother sportsman every inch of his poor attenuated body. He had fitted to the ends of his crutches a kind of expanding foot, like a ducks', to enable him to pass over the soft ground."

By 28 January the promising light north-west wind had turned in to a raging gale! There was no chance of going afloat. The following day they were able to cross the Straits where they had no luck, but in the evening, to save a blank day, took a small shot of 4 wigeon and a shelduck at the mouth of the Voryd creek. That evening the wind veered again, this time to the north-east and snow appeared on the Snowdonia mountain range.

On the 29th they were afloat at 7.30 am and into the Voryd Bay. They observed a fine lot of wigeon, but on an ebb tide there was no way to get to them, so they took a long flying shot of 4 wigeon, rather than return with none. In the evening, the following day they saw 10 grey geese in the Voryd bay which was regarded as unusual.

30 January was a day of great excitement, the tides were ideal, the wind held in the north. In the morning they were out at dawn, pushing into the Voryd on a rising tide and then in the evening seeking a shot on the great sandbanks at Abermenai, "I all but got a shot of 40 duck and wigeon in the morning and I all but got a shot of at least 40 in the evening. In both cases I was a little late on the front of the flood tide, and the flood had just washed the birds off the sand so they were swimming and scattered. I could have got a dozen or so but did not disturb them on the chance of getting a good smack into them at close quarters on another occasion."

"Oh for tomorrow! A long while, a whole night, dinner, breakfast etc. until I can have another chance! But hope supports me to exist!" Reflecting that evening RPG writes, "my only companion at Belan, at meals, in my sitting room and bedroom has been a very handsome, charming dog

Belan Fort, the study

of foreign breed, like a great sheep dog. One wild night he was found crying round the walls of the Fort soaked to the skin and covered with seaweed. He had evidently come across the sands of Caernarvon Bar. He had either been washed overboard from a ship, or perhaps a wreck."

On 1 February they went afloat as dawn broke and had a small shot of 6 wigeon, "just to save a blank outing." So much for thoughts of not taking a small shot for fear of spoiling, 'the big occasion.'

Sometimes wildfowling afloat can become a risky adventure and more often than not it is the lure of the perceived opportunity of a good shot that can cloud the mind. Sound judgement and common sense go out of the window. One such occasion happened to RPG and Croutear on the afternoon of the 1 February.

"In the afternoon went all over Abermenai, but saw nothing. North-East wind allows birds to sit out at sea. Came in at 4 o'clock, changed wet clothes, gear taken out of punt, Croutear just going into Caernarvon by boat to buy provisions for himself. BUT! I chanced to look through the large telescope in the lookout tower of the fort. I saw about 300-400 wigeon 'massed' in a dense crowd on a sandbank about two miles from Belan. The sea breaking heavily on the seaward side of the bank. The question was, could we get to the birds before the sea broke over the bank and rushed in big waves up the straits? In three minutes I was in the punt again, just as I was, white shirt, thin lounging suit and light shoes! Off we went, about one and a quarter miles beyond the Perch marker seaward. A strong tide was running and water very rough, at least for a duck punt. The birds, mallard, wigeon and teal crowded together, a lump. I could have killed 100 if I could have got within 70 yards, but we could not float nearer than 150-180 yards and there we left them in security. We could not wait a moment longer, as the tide and the sea not to mention the wind were increasing every moment, and we had some two miles to cover in the dusk to reach Belan dock in safety. I cannot say what would have happened to us if we had got the shot and had a large number of birds to pick up."

The following day was a Sunday and RPG appeared to be none the worse for wear and was searching for a really good shot before the end of the season. To this end he and Croutear took a six mile walk along the Dinas Dinlle shoreline in search of a small inlet where he had received reports that there were, "large numbers of fowl" in this sheltered bay. They successfully found the inlet and estimated they had seen at least 600 birds. To quote Sam Croutear, "less than a 100 could not be got if the shot was a proper one!"

Nothing is simple when it comes to making such a shot. In discussion with a local man they were warned that an old woman walked along the shore every day collecting drift wood. On a spring tide this pushed the birds off their low water secure roost and out to sea. Croutear and RPG made a plan; "This old woman must be arranged for by posting a man, as a sentry, with half a crown in his hand, half a mile on either side of where the ducks sit, one man on one side along the shore and one on the other side." All the necessary arrangements were made and the punt and gun prepared for an early start on Monday morning.

At midnight RPG took a stroll along the Fort battery contemplating the prospects of an exciting day afloat. He observed, "Sea and Straits as smooth as glass, every star reflected as in a mirror. A grand chance of a big shot to look forward to." Alas, he was woken in the small hours by a roaring wind baying and trumpeting down the chimney, and by sheets of hail drumming against the window panes. Of course, this was the end of the possibility of making any shot, let alone a big one.

They did go afloat but, in the circumstances, the sheltered Voryd Bay was the only option. They did not get a shot on the flood but returning to Belan, in the late morning, they chanced upon a sitting of birds, "150 wigeon, sat as close as bees in a hive, but in rough water and punt rolling heavily, and gun jerking from side to side and up and down. As I got to within 60 yards of the birds, and didn't want a blank, I took a chance flying shot and bagged 8, (if it had been calm I would have bagged 30)."

The afternoon foray to Abermenai was frustrated by cocklers who had come out from Caernarvon and followed the ebbing tide back as the cockle beds uncovered. This, of course, disturbed the birds and made it impossible to get a shot. Homeward bound at dusk RPG writes, "I can see a magnificent and densely packed lot of 500 duck and wigeon on the same bank of sand where I saw them last Saturday. I hope to manage a shot here at these birds but it needs be very calm to go out to sea."

You cannot help but admire RPG's turn of phrase at times. 4 February is described as, "an offensively fine calm warm sun shining day." He went afloat at 7am only to find all the birds flew out to sea where they remained in big packs all day, "I could see them with the glass but could not follow them with the punt and gun. Saved a blank day by killing a couple of snipe for dinner in the marsh near the Fort. Saw about 20 but all got up too wild to kill."

The next day records a nice bunch of wigeon at dawn on the Anglesey side of the Straits. He should have picked a score but ended up with 11 blaming some shelduck rising making the birds lift their heads, so he had to take them without delay and they were a little too far off.

By 6 February RPG's visit to Belan Fort was almost at an end. He proposed to return to Thirkleby the next day. But his determination to try for a really big shot took him outside the entrance to the Menai Straits and towards the Caernarvon Bar. Such a trip in a gunning punt could only be done in flat calm conditions; "Found about 100 wigeon drifting, but could not get near enough to make a good shot, so took a long flying chance and killed 5." Following the pick-up they headed into Abermenai Bay where they spotted a great northern diver stranded on a sand bank; "We landed and walked up to him and caught him quite uninjured. He could not rise off the ground, only flap along. I had often heard this of these divers (great northern, red throated and black throated) and now it is proved beyond question. Brought him ashore and put him in a large tank in which he lived and washed and eats raw meat and is quite tame; so I hope to keep him alive. After breakfast I saw a small bunch of wigeon drifting up the Straits on the tide. Croutear and I flew to the punt and edged up along the shore under the shadow of the land till we got above them. We then sculled out from the shore to them, but there was rather a swell coming in with the tide from seaward! However, took a flying shot and bagged 3. In the afternoon went after snipe in the marsh near the fort. Saw at least forty; but all rose so wild I did not even get one for my dinner, as I had hoped."

Until now there is no mention, during RPG's visit of punting at night but on the last evening it is clear that Croutear decided to try and get a final shot on his own under the cover of darkness.

Not an uncommon ploy for a man that hails from Lymington. RPG reports, "Croutear afloat most of the night but too dark and could not see to get a shot though birds all round him and as he says almost aboard him!"

On 7 February, they were out again at dawn and went down the coast along the Newborough shore to near Llanddwyn Island, a distance of 3 miles. The weather was calm, and they saw few birds, returning to the Fort empty handed.

In the afternoon RPG writes, "All packed up, with punt and gun and all gear stored safely at Belan. By boat to Caernarvon at 6.30 tomorrow morning. I leave Belan and its many charms of sea, shore, and Straits and wonderful birdlife with the greatest regret. Not to speak of it as a treasure house of curiosities and interest to do with all who love the sea and shipping – I have done fairly well, I have had two chances of killing 50 ducks at a shot and I have had many exciting moments and several nice shots."

The days spent at Belan Fort were like a tonic for RPG. A gap of four years between punting on the Humber in 1904 and his detailed accounts of days afloat since 16 January 1908 seemed hugely important to a man who had experienced the finest sport on the most famous estates throughout the country. The challenge of the pursuit of fowl in their own special environment is unique, and we are sure it was this that he really missed. It is a very compelling force as every true wildfowler will know. He must also have missed the company of his old friend Sam Croutear, a man without pretentions whose knowledge of wildfowl and ability to handle a gunning punt he much respected.

1909/10/11 seasons. RPG feels his age

Belan Fort held a fascination for RPG: it was a place he loved to visit and where he was completely at ease with life. His punt and gun were stored in the dockside buildings and this place was to become the focus of his wildfowling adventures for the rest of his life. But, health issues once again plagued him. The diary notes lack detail for the 1909/10 season and right up until 1912 RPG's usual enthusiasm is missing.

One has to search the pages of his Game Book to find clues of what was troubling RPG. Here we found references to his enlarged heart and smoking but such matters appeared to be under medical control and of little trouble to him as can be seen from the previous seasons' vigorous activities. However, hidden in the notes we found an almost indecipherable reference which caused us to refer to a medical dictionary. He complained of suffering as a result of a drainage tube inserted in a 'antrum (cavity) between his jawbone and the cavity under his eye. The tube had broken off and despite the attention of surgeons and a dentist, 'trying to fish it out' they could not find it and it caused unpleasant abscesses inside his face! The tube was eventually retrieved in October 1909 but it had clearly caused RPG great pain and suffering. However, his main complaint was the cost of surgery. The treatment was estimated to cost, "no less than £120."

On the 26 November 1909 RPG was staying at Glynllivon, shooting game as a guest of his friend Frederick Wynn. He was not feeling sufficiently well to ask Croutear to come up from Lymington but he could not resist the temptation of arranging a few days afloat. After all, everything was stored at Belan and he could quickly get the punt and gun afloat. To this end he recruited old Richard Roberts to assist him. Richard was the boatman and caretaker of Belan Fort. (Ref. A Maritime Fortress by Michael Stammers 2001)

27 November; "Down at Belan at daybreak. Fired two shots, got 10 wigeon. A fine lot about but old Richard no good as a puntsman." Two more days afloat with Richard proved unproductive and then it was time to go home.

There follows a short note, "The last week of January 1910, very hard frost and deep snow. Made all preparation for going to Belan but a complete thaw set in, so did not go." No more entries appeared for the year 1910 and we found only a brief entry referring to 1911. In November there is one short note when RPG was staying at Glynllivon and he went afloat taking with him The Hon. T. Wynn. There was none of the usual enthusiasm and it seems likely he only went afloat to entertain Wynn as they had no puntsman.

Contrasting the later entries in RPG's diary with the 1904/05 season it clearly shows that health issues were now occupying his mind. However, by Christmas he was feeling better and made plans to return to North Wales.

1912. RPG's recovery

In early January 1912 RPG travelled from Thirkleby to Glynllivon where he was to stay for two weeks. The old determination and his love of wildfowling had clearly returned, "My old friend and most excellent man and puntsman (who has been with me in many waters, off and on, for 18 years) Samuel Croutear, arrived at Belan Fort from Lymington."

" I drove down to Belan five and a half miles every day for a fortnight, arriving usually so as to be afloat a little before daybreak, then drive or walked up to Glynllivon on or about dusk. I worked like a galley slave to obtain sport. A fine lot of duck and wigeon about (perhaps 1200 or more) I made a number of small shots, 2 wigeon on 8th, 7 wigeon on 9th and 3 wigeon on 11th."

On 13 January he described a miserable heart breaking experience, " I set up within 65 yards of 300 duck and wigeon in a narrow creek, the birds densely packed, smooth water and many of them on the edge of the sand but, had a misfire, the only one for 10 years. I should otherwise have killed 70 birds at least."

The weather remained mild and most unfavourable but there was just one day of frost and snow and this brought new fortune, "We got a fine shot of 65 golden plover and the same day a small shot of 6 wigeon."

On 22 January RPG went home as the weather was not conducive for fowling. In early February the weather turned very cold with 20 degrees of frost. He writes on 5 February, "I could stand it no longer and rushed off to Belan today where Sam Croutear joined me."

He records that by the time they had both reached Belan all the frost had gone! "Just my luck, heavy rain and south-west winds. No frost last night, summer weather. Afloat at 7am, went across Straits to Abermenai. A grand lot of wigeon about and very tame. They are very hungry after 10 days of hard frost, walking up the sand banks all over seeking weed for food. I should have had a fine shot as the tide made but some rascal on shore fired a quick double shot and put the birds up just as I was paddling nicely in range of them. I thought this shooting might have been an accident. The birds, however pitched again, when 'bang bang' from the shore shooter once more. A low dirty mean jealous scoundrel, may he burn in Hell. I would have given him every bird I killed if only he had let me knock them over. In the evening a fine shot at wigeon showed in the Voryd but the tide was ebbing strongly I could not get up to them. Today in order to get up to a big shot I at one time paddled through scores of scattered fowl within 30 yards of my punt, a thing I have not seen for years and which shows what might have been done punting in a real hard prolonged frost."

Sam Croutear at Belan Dock

Sport continued until 9 February but the weather turned mild. Punt and gun were laid up. Croutear returned to Lymington and RPG made his way back to Thirkleby.

A footnote is added to the end of season note; "If I had been at Belan during the frost I should assuredly have had some fine sport, as fowl were there in great numbers, but I was shooting instead a lot of stupid pheasants, instead of revelling in glorious sport with wild birds on the coast- ALAS!"

1913. Belan Fort with Evan Roberts as puntsman

RPG did not go afloat before Christmas and it was the middle of January 1913 before he could make plans to travel to North Wales. He arrived at Glynllivon on 18 January and stayed with Frederick Wynn until the 22nd whereupon he moved to Belan where his punt and gun were stored. He writes, "my puntsman this year is Evan, son of Richard Roberts of Belan." Sam Croutear did not come up from Lymington to join him this year, no reason was given.

On the evening of 22 January RPG was joined by his daughter Dorothy and her servant. RPG was anxious to show Dorothy the Fort as she was interested in places she had heard her father talk about when he had been away fowling and, moreover Dorothy was to provide RPG with excellent company during long winter evenings in this lonely place.

On 23 January all was ready to go afloat but a southerly gale blew up and the ebb tide made it difficult to punt in the Voryd from Belan Fort. As they did not go afloat RPG decided to have a medical check before submitting himself to the rigours of a fortnight of wildfowling! He writes; "Doctor Lloyd Evans (a clever medico from Caernarvon) examined me today and gave me a good report of my enlarged heart, enlarged through hard straining at shooting bows, and other violent exertions."

The next day they were once again plagued by a gale of wind and a deluge of rain, the tide ebbed slowly and was kept up by a southerly gale. In the afternoon they were almost successful in getting a shot. RPG writes; "We set up to about 100 wigeon nicely placed for a shot and tame, but wind, rough water and a rushing ebb tide prevented us from coming near enough to them though we nearly did so after a great struggle."

By 25 January the wind had gone round to the north which was a better wind for punting into the Voryd Bay. At dawn they found the birds scattered but matters improved; "We suddenly sighted some 500 wigeon thick as bees, but I could not set near enough to them for a good shot. However, I fired rather than get none and picked up 10. On my way back to Belan I saw 3 brent geese (a very rare bird here) fired and killed all three."

The 27th was an altogether better and more productive day: one small shot at dawn in Abermenai Bay brought him 6 wigeon. They then returned over the dangerous straits to the Voryd Bay where they made a nice shot of 20 wigeon. RPG describes the shot, "a grand lot of birds all swimming up to and landing on a low point of sand. I dared not wait till they all got together, as some of them saw me (the few swimming in the water). Next I fired a small foolish shot at dusk and picked up only three wigeon."

A diary note about this day is interesting, when they fired the final shot at dusk the gun went up in the air crashing down on the deck and the legs of the gun rest went clean through the foredeck of the punt and the gun almost went overboard! The excess recoil was blamed on a fine grain black powder they had been forced to use as Messrs' Holland and Holland could not supply the usual coarse grain punt gun blackpowder.

There followed two days of fine weather and calm seas. They were afloat on both days from dawn to dusk but the birds were out at sea after the previous days disturbance. On 29th they again fired one shot to save a blank day, picking up 4 wigeon.

A change in the weather brought wind and rain but it did not deter them from going afloat. Needless to say punting was not easy; "Fired at about 25 wigeon on a sandbank half awash. I might have perhaps killed a dozen but it was blowing very hard in heavy squalls, in the Voryd, with driving hail in my face and spray lashing high over us and the punt and gun. I did well to get 8 wigeon." There is no mention of young Evan, his trusty puntsman, who must have found handling the punt a little difficult. 31 January is notable for a hurricane and hail squalls and a wild flying shot.

The 3 and 4 February brought no addition to the bag but on 5 February there was the opportunity to make a good shot; "Afloat at daybreak and nearly got up to a fine lot of wigeon in the Voryd, but just at the wrong moment for me a shepherd walked along a bank on the shore, not far off, and put all the birds up."

For the next three days a raging gale made going afloat in a gunning punt a perilous event and they often found themselves running for shelter. On the night of 7 February RPG writes, "a most furious hurricane from the south-west all last night, even the strong old fort of Belan shook. Up at daybreak and found that the storm of last night had actually blown the punt upside down with the gun in her even though she was snugly secured in the dock with the other boats. She and the gun now at the bottom of the dock in several feet of water." It took most of the day to get things right again. Meantime the wind abated and it became fine and calm, ideal conditions for a shot and the best chance of a shot all week. Such is the luck of punt gunning. Ducks sitting about quite tame after being exhausted by the great storm and simply asking to be shot!"

The 10 February was their last day at Fort Belan and before laying up the punt and gun RPG and Evan Roberts had one more try for a shot, bagging 4 wigeon, no doubt to save another blank day!

As we have seen elsewhere in RPG's diary he has not always been complimentary about his puntsman but on this occasion he praises Evan, "My puntsman this year Evan, son of Richard Roberts of Belan. He is an excellent puntsman and a fine willing keen and gallant young sailor lad of 22. A short time ago he saw a small yacht go aground on the awful Caernarvon Bar near Belan. On looking through a glass he saw also the crew (two gentlemen) walking hopelessly cut off by the tide on a small sandbank in the middle of the Bar. A heavy sea and a fast rising tide flowing. Without help they were drowned men. Evan rushed to his little dinghy. He pulled like a madman through the sea and breakers for it was blowing hard. When he came up to the two men they had been washed off the sandbank by the rising tide and had been swimming in heavy clothes for a quarter of an hour, were both exhausted and were caught in a racing tideway drifting them from the land. He rescued first one of the men and then the other, dragging them into the dinghy and doing all this at the risk of his own life. The rescue took three hours and when the men were landed they were too ill to speak or walk. They were taken to Fort Belan and well cared for and put to bed. A Pilot Boat with four men from Llanddwyn Lighthouse saw the accident but declined to go out to the rescue. However, Evan said, "if I drown myself I cannot see these men drown without trying, at all events, to save them." And he did save them, but only just in time. His hands were so raw from pulling with desperate energy that he could not even button his clothes for a week. Evan, his father and brother also rescued the small yacht which had drifted waterlogged up the Straits towards Caernarvon. The men Evan rescued were Mr. Rathbone of Liverpool, and Mr. Vaughan, an Eton Master.

For rescuing them and their yacht Evan was given £10. These people apparently valued their lives at £5 each and their yacht at nothing."

A diary note in November 1913 indicates that RPG bought a Studebaker motor car. There is no indication that the car was used to go on his wildfowling adventures. It seems more likely that his preferred method of travel was by train and this would certainly have been the case where long distance travel was involved and not least when his punt and other equipment need to be moved.

1914. Back to Belan Fort

RPG was back in North Wales on 3 January 1914. Initially he was the guest of Frederick Wynn at Glynllivon, but on 5 January he was joined by his daughter Dorothy and they took up residence at the Caernarvon Bay Hotel at Dinas Dinlle. There had been a hard frost at Thirkleby when he left but it did not turn cold on the Anglesey coast until 6 January when a gale of west wind set in and then went north resulting in a covering of snow on the nearby high mountains of the Snowdonia range.

There were a good number of fowl about and RPG remarks, "saw more duck, wigeon and teal than I ever saw here before, quite 2000." He again asked Evan Roberts to act as puntsman and Evan had prepared the punt and gun for RPG's arrival. Two blank days were followed by a small flying shot of 3 wigeon and although there were plenty of birds they were extremely wild and difficult to set to.

On 7 January they went afloat soon after dawn. There were no birds in the Voryd so they crossed the Straits to Abermenai bay. Here there were great numbers of wigeon, but so wild that they could not come within a quarter of a mile of them; "Some splendid shots in view but they would not let me scarce within a telescope range of them. Gave them up on their rising and pitching in the water. Left one fine shot behind me without trying after much deliberation as to pros and cons." The pack of wigeon was on a sandbank two miles off in a very exposed place and with a rising tide and wind the frightful Straits were beginning to look nasty for the re-crossing to Belan. This element of discretion may have saved their lives since many people lost their lives crossing the turbulent water of the Menai Straits.

The next day the inclement weather continued, "The usual, too usual, to report! Afloat at Belan at 8 am, a tearing southerly gale and a deluge of rain. Set up to about 500 wigeon closely packed at the top of the Voryd. But, rough water slopping over us in bucket fulls every moment, and the punt dancing up and down like a rocking horse resulted in getting within shot of the birds, (on a lee shore), I could not aim the gun so did not fire."

There followed seven days fowling without a feather and even two despairing shots at long range which would normally save a blank day produced nothing. Tides and weather were against them and it was not until 17 January that success came, "Across the Straits before dawn, set up to a few birds on a sandbank, but made a bad shot of 2 duck and 8 wigeon. I fired over them as shown by the pellet marks in the sand. I should have had double the number picked up."

By 19 January RPG was frustrated by the lack of success. He writes; "having frittered through a dull Sunday waiting for Monday still no luck. Thousands of fowl sitting at sea in front of the Hotel, only 300 yards away, and where they are they know they are safe from me. I look at them continually through my powerful telescope and see mallard, wigeon, teal in large and small bunches mostly fast asleep one lot of quite 1000 wigeon appearing like a small black island."

"Afloat this morning at Belan before daybreak, and weather just as it has been for days, calm and fine. I went in the punt 3 miles along the north shore of the Straits towards the open sea and the Bar. Saw nothing. Then back again and all over Abermenai bay following a nice pack of birds with gun at full cock for fully two miles. But they kept rising and pitching again just out of shot. Then all over the Voryd in the afternoon and saw nothing."

On Tuesday morning they were hopeful of finding a shot at golden plover as much of the land behind the seawall was frozen. But there were no golden plover about in their usual haunts. Even the wigeon were wild and kept pitching and rising just out of shot.

During the next two days they went afloat at dawn and crossed the Straits on each occasion. They found wigeon present in large numbers but they were hopelessly wild. They did however get a small shot at mallard and then a very long shot at wigeon which RPG admits was fired rather in despair. The birds were straggled along the edge of a sandbank and to his surprise they picked up 5 wigeon and 1 mallard.

The 23 January was more productive. RPG writes, "afloat at day break on the Voryd, quite 1500 wigeon with mallard and teal. Frost and calm, birds very restless. Rather than return home to breakfast empty handed I took a shot at 6 teal asleep on some floating seaweed and killed them all. Then across the Straits in the afternoon and in Abermenai Bay set up to 14-15 mallard sitting on a sandbank and killed 12, a nice shot."

It was almost time to return home to Thirkleby and this was to be their last day afloat. Amusingly RPG writes; "Afloat at day break but could not leave the shore. All I did was to look through my glasses at 1000 duck, wigeon and teal sitting on a sandbank which I might have had a try at except for the raging gale that was blowing.

So ends three weeks of bad luck owing almost entirely to the weather as birds were in great numbers. I stayed this visit at the Caernarvon Bay Hotel, my daughter Dorothy with me. We were the only guests in the hotel. A wild lonely place on the verge of the sea, scarce 20 yards away. The scenery lovely. The sea, once this visit, flooded the hotel cellars."

Punt and gun were stored safely in the Belan dockside buildings and they returned to Thirkleby on 26 January.

It must have played on RPG's mind that, despite there being more fowl than he had seen for many years around the punting grounds that surround Belan; he really had not met with much success. He blamed the weather so when, in February, a severe frost set in and a biting northerly wind he immediately thought of returning to North Wales. As luck would have it Frederick Wynn extended an invitation to him, in the middle of February, to visit Glynllivon enticing RPG to return on the chance of getting a punt shot and perhaps some snipe shooting.

On 17 February he reports, "afloat at Belan 8am and for most of the day. I engaged Mark Owen (as Evan had been ill and was weak). Mark was with me as a puntsman for several seasons some years ago. But, he has, I hear taken to drink and been in hospital for 6 weeks. I kept him for only a few days, until Evan came to attend me. No chance of a shot as I saw very few birds in the estuaries even though it was blowing a gale from the sea. All mostly left for the North I expect."

The following day there was a strong onshore wind and most of the wigeon were out roosting on the water off Dinas Dinlle beach. RPG walked the small marsh at the back of the hotel and shot 4 snipe, (two rights and lefts). He also spotted about 100 duck and teal rise from a pond in the marsh. Determined to try and get on terms with them he waited 3 hours till dusk but they did not come back.

The 19 February, "On the marshes north of Dinas Dinlle at 8.30 this morning and walked hard till 2 pm over all likely spots. Shot 3 snipe, 2 mallard and 1 teal." In the afternoon RPG went afloat but as there was no chance of a shot he decided to walk from the punt to the shore three quarters of a mile over the ooze in the hope of shooting a few snipe. Just as he got to the shore he saw a dozen wigeon pitch not far from the punt so he walked all the way back over the mud to the punt, set to the birds and killed 6. With the punt safely back at Belan he decided to walk back to the hotel. An amusing entry follows, "On the way home when seeking snipe I was chased by a small Welsh Black bull, and simply flew over a very deep and wide drain I had never risked crossing before but had always gone some way to a plank bridge instead. I got 4 snipe on the way home and lost one owing to the bull driving me away."

The 20 February diary entry indicates that the weather continued to cause frustration, "I went to Belan this afternoon when the tide suited but a gale and rough sea kept me ashore. I walked home along the Voryd estuary almost at times within shoulder gun shot of several lots of scattered wigeon which were feeding on the short grass of the shore bank. This shows these birds were migrants to summer quarters in the far north as they knew not signs of danger as did the former inhabitants of the place. They had evidently come a long way as they were feeding greedily and were very tame."

The next four days were a mixture of wild weather and wild birds. When the wind abated they tried for a shot in the punt but most of the time they had to settle for a walk in the saltmarsh and amongst the dune pools for either snipe or the occasional mallard or teal.

On 26 February, Vaughan Wynn and RPG went early to the famous, but dangerous, floating bog Pant-Glass, 10 miles from Glynllivon. More bad luck prevailed as they found that it was too flooded for sport; "We killed 13 snipe, 4 mallard. Home to lunch." In the afternoon RPG and Vaughan went to Bodfuan Hall. Frederick Wynn owned Bodfuan Hall on the Llyn Peninsula, 20 miles from Glynllivon. A wonderful 600 acre marsh formed part of the estate. For the next two days RPG and Vaughan stayed at the Hall, and spent the days walking the marsh for snipe and fowl. The marsh was flooded and the snipe were wild with few rising within range. Sport was brisk and RPG writes; "Snipe were there in hundreds and there was scarcely a moment in the day that some were not to be seen on the wing. Enough birds to kill 70 couple if they had laid for us." Their bag was 37 snipe, 9 mallard and 8 teal. (RPG noted that Vaughan accounted for 10 of the snipe.)

Joy at last on 2 March, "went afloat in the punt mostly because it was the last day of the season, (It was in fact already legally closed). Saw 200 wigeon on the Voryd estuary but could not come close to them. Then set up to a little lot on a bank and gathered 11. A quite unexpected pleasure. Walked home across the marshes."

On his way home to Glynllivon the previous night RPG found, in a lonely place, a small 30 yards square pond edged with reeds. He writes, "I noticed mallard feathers floating about on the surface. So this morning I breakfasted at 5.30am and arrived at the pond at 6.20am, (over in the dark bogs, ditches and barbed wire) But, I was 10 minutes late as dawn was breaking as I arrived, and quite 50 ducks flew away. Only a few came back though I waited 3 hours. I killed 2 teal, 1 mallard and 2 snipe."

A short 'reminder note' referred to a new tip he had received from a friend to see a gun barrel when you go out duck shooting in the dark or dusk, "smear it with grease or tallow before you go out."

The season was over and it was time to return to Thirkleby. Most of January and February had been spent staying as a guest at Glynllivon and he had clearly enjoyed his stay, "shooting from Glynllivon and then to Belan Fort is hard work as it is six miles distance to the fort. This entails very early starting in the morning and late arrival home at night. Though my bags have been small I have had some six weeks of most enjoyable fowling."

1914. Death of William, RPG's only son

Captain William Thomas Frankland Payne-Gallwey M.V.O. was born in 1881. He was educated at Eton where he showed devotion to all forms of sport. At 19 he was selected to play cricket for his school against Harrow and later for Yorkshire second eleven in the same year. He attended the Royal Military College and was gazetted to the Grenadier Guards. In January 1902 he went to South Africa (Boer War) serving there with distinction for ten months. It was here that he was awarded the South African Medal and gazetted a Member of the Victorian Order.

A keen dry-fly fisherman and in 1906 a member of the Driffield Beck Fishing Club, he was of the opinion that salmon fishing was the finest of all sports and his favourite river was the Helmsdale. However, we discovered a telling entry in his Game Book which reflects his love of fowling.

22 January 1910, Holkham Marshes.;

> "Heavy blizzards from North West. I got two right and lefts at grey geese (Pinkfeet) close to the Station facing south. Then one out of a small lot. Alex Napier and I, in blinding snow, went to Marsh Farm . He got three grey geese and I another. Saw over 3000 grey geese within 150 yards. The edge of the company came over me. I downed one, never thought of picking him up as more geese were coming and he seemed dead. More did not come . My goose got up and flew away. Hot soup at the station with Tom Coke who had a brace of Egyptians. Suddenly saw large flock of geese coming from the North. Another right and left. Waited at Marsh Farm in a blizzard all afternoon till 5.30. (Terrible hail stones.) So endeth the BEST DAYS SPORT recorded in this game book. Anything more splendid than those 3000 geese I have never seen rising shrieking, a solid mass and disappearing into the blizzard."

William's Game Book contained fourteen years of sport on many of the finest estates in the country so he had certainly inherited his father's love of field-sports. How sad it is that a cruel war claimed his life just weeks after Britain declared war on Germany on 4 August 1914. A memorial at La Ferte-sous-Jouarre bears his name. His final resting place is unknown.

1915. Repairs to the punt before going afloat

In 1914 RPG did not go afloat before Christmas and it was not until 11 January 1915 that he returned to North Wales to stay with Frederick Wynn at Glynllivon. On arrival he arranged for the double punt to be sent from Belan Fort to Glynllivon where he instructed the estate workshop staff to undertake repairs that had not been attended to at the end of the previous season. The punt was now 18 years old; routine maintenance had ensured that it was always seaworthy but it was time for a complete overhaul with special attention to the damage to the foredeck caused by the gun crashing onto the deck when fine grain powder was used to load the cartridges. A fresh coat of paint and the replacement of the hemp breeching rope followed. All this took until 15 January. While the work was undertaken RPG enjoyed rough shooting with friends, staying at Glynillivon where he shot 6 woodcock.

William Payne-Gallwey

While the work on the punt progressed RPG walked down to the Voryd Bay to assess the number of duck about and, from the watchtower at the Fort, he could also observe the sandbanks in the Abermenai Bay. The prospects were excellent and he estimated there were, "quite as many as last season and I have seen at least 2000 wigeon."

Everything was made ready to go afloat at dawn on 16 January. There is no mention of who was acting as puntsman: it certainly was not Sam Croutear and one must assume it was most likely young Evan Roberts who was with him the previous season.

As dawn broke we find them fighting a strong ebb tide pushing in to the Voryd Bay and adding to their difficulty, there was a gale of wind from the north-west. "Went up the Voryd at one o'clock on the ebb tide. Found lots of birds well packed and tame but water near them very rough. Set to one very nice lot and bagged 16. Lost 2 or 3. Then set to a really splendid lot of 300 as thick as bees. Could not come near enough to fire as water too shallow and tide ebbing fast. Then set up to another fine lot also on the sand and very tame. But could not work the punt up to them owing to the strong wind and tide driving the punt in all directions but the right one. Though we were nearly in shot of them, after one hour of struggling, they were still too far. Returned to Glynllivon (6 miles) soaked to the skin."

The weather deteriorated over the weekend which RPG regarded as excellent news, recording that "sleet and hail and mountains covered with snow."

On Monday they got a good shot of 11 wigeon out of about 12 that were sat on a sandbank. In the afternoon RPG made what he regarded as a silly wild water shot of 5 wigeon. He writes; "This was an act which I have always preached and written against."

On Tuesday morning they tried for several small lots in the Voryd without success. Then on the way home they came upon a fine lot of wigeon (about 200), well placed on a sandbank. RPG writes, "made a proper mess of the shot and only got 6. I ought to have had 30 at least." Late in the evening they crossed the Straits to Abermenai Bay and found 1500 wigeon, 500 of which offered a magnificent chance well placed on a sandbank. They rose and pitched several times but they could not get the punt up to them.

On Wednesday the weather was calmer which allowed them to cross the dangerous mouth of the Straits to Abermenai Bay. They set to a very fine lot of birds on the sands but could not get near them. Then a gale came on and they had to re-cross the Straits without delay. They then went up in to the Voryd bay on the flood but had no shot all day.

Thursday was uneventful and a strong north-west wind and squalls prevented them from crossing the Straits. Instead they went into the Voryd and bagged one small shot of 7 wigeon.

The next day they again crossed the Straits to Abermenai Bay. It was a calm fine morning, birds were all very wild and they had no chance of a shot. RPG writes, "I got one wigeon without firing a shot! A magnificent peregrine falcon dashed it down on to the sand close to me. She sailed round and round me within a few yards as I landed and walked ashore to pick it up. I felt I was a thief!"

About Saturday he writes; "Another blank though I worked hard all day. In the early morning I crossed the Straits to Abermenai Bay. I hate those awful Straits, a sea can get up in them in a few minutes which is enough to swamp a ship's boat let alone a gunning punt. I found two splendid packs of wigeon there on the sandbanks, quite 300 in each pack. As usual, in this calm bright weather, they would not let me near them. Then a gale came and I had to hurry back across the Straits. In the Voryd bay all afternoon but saw nothing."

Sunday was spent at Glynllivon looking forward to Monday.

When Monday dawned there was a slight frost but the weather was against them, "A bright calm day like summer. Went all over Abermenai Bay in the morning and into the Voryd Bay in the afternoon. Plenty of birds about but so wild, on such a day, no chance of a shot."

The next day was equally frustrating with the weather like summer, "Birds as a result of the weather quite hopelessly wild. I set up to one glorious lot of wigeon in Abermenai Bay. They would not let me within three gun shots of them. I should have killed 60 if I could only have come in shot of them."

RPG was now nearing the end of his stay at Belan and this was to be his last day afloat. He writes; "Another foul summer day. Birds, if possible, wilder than ever. I set up to a grand lot asleep on a sand bank in Abermenai Bay. I really did think at last I was going to make up for all my failures by just one glorious shot on my last day. But no, they rose a gun shot and a half off me, even though I came down the wake of a dazzling sun behind me."

The next day punt and gun were put into store at Belan Dock and RPG returned to Thirkleby. RPG summarised his visit to North Wales, "This trip a failure, though full of incident and excitement. As usual I several times came very near making a splendid shot or two, but just didn't do so. Very unfavourable weather and one week of extra low neap tides that did not cover the sandbanks at High Water, always a great drawback here when this occurs. I saw no golden plover, teal and only very few mallard."

1915/16. RPG returns to the Caernarvon Bay Hotel

On 8 December 1915 RPG returned to North Wales to stay at the Caernarvon Bay Hotel. On this occasion the hotel was to be his wildfowling headquarters and he was accompanied by Bullock, his valet. Sam Croutear had arrived on 6 December and spent two days preparing for RPG's arrival by launching the double punt in Belan Dock and breeching the Bentley and Playfair gun.

On arrival at the hotel after a 9 hour journey from Thirkleby, RPG writes a sad note in his diary; "It is nineteen years since I first shot at Belan. How different it is since I was here last with Dorothy in 1914. A fearful war showing no sign of ending and my dear and only son gone. 10 pm. the rain beating furiously, like drums, against the windows, the wind howling and raging and the sea roaring just beneath the house gives me hope of sport for tomorrow as without wild weather I seldom do much good here."

On the first morning afloat the flooding tide already covered the favoured banks where the wigeon roost at low water. The weather was fine and calm. They saw in the Voryd quite 400 wigeon and they appeared to be undisturbed by the punt. RPG decided not to molest them as they were all swimming up on the flood tide and he professed never to fire water shots if he could help it. The decision was made to leave the birds quiet and look forward to a better chance when they were on the mud or sandbanks and where a far heavier shot could be made. The following diary entry makes short work of his sentiment; "However, on my way home I came upon a lovely cluster of wigeon, very tame and well positioned for a shot in shallow water. The temptation was irresistible. I set up to them within 60-65 yards and bagged 25."

The 10 December, "wind flew into the south, south west last night and today a hard gale and a deluge of rain all morning. A very high tide and a heavy sea. Afloat on the Voryd at 8.15 am. Set up to a fine lot of wigeon just inside the Voryd but mostly afloat in shallow water. I chanced a flying shot, but the pitch and toss of the waves caused me to shoot clean over them and I only bagged two. With a little luck I should have bagged 20. We then fought our way to the top of the Voryd where we set to a nice lot of wigeon along the edge of a bank of rocks and seaweed and I gathered 21 of them. A small rise of mud partly between us and the birds prevented the shot charge taking full effect or I should have bagged many more. I afterwards shot a long-tailed duck (very rare on this coast) with the shoulder gun. Came into Belan soaked."

After all the disturbance it was not surprising to read that the next day Croutear saw a large number of wigeon fly out of the Voryd and across the Abermenai Bay at daybreak. That day they did not see a worthwhile shot. There was a strong north-westerly gale all day and heavy sea on shore and although they waited for 3 hours hoping a lot of wigeon would come from the outer sandbanks driven by the weather. But they clearly had been disturbed enough and preferred to flight in to feed under the cover of darkness.

Sunday was spent relaxing in the Caernarvon Bay Hotel. It was a glorious day with a brisk north wind and the mountains covered in snow.

Monday dawned and they went across the Straits to Abermenai Bay. Here they saw about 1200 wigeon and fully 150-200 mallard driven down to the tide edge by frost and snow in the mountains. RPG writes, "birds very wild and although I set to several fine lots I never came nearly near enough to pull on them. Went up the Voryd in the afternoon, lots of wigeon there but too wild to come near. Wind north-west and too calm and fine."

There followed five blank days in succession RPG comments; "So much for the sport of fowling with punt and gun. I have worked hard on every one of these five blank days. Plenty of fowl in view but this stinking mild weather with filthy soft south-west winds spoils everything."

The summer weather continued until 21 December but there was some consolation when they made a beautiful shot of 62 golden plover on 20 December. As Christmas was fast approaching it was time to lay up the punt and gun and put all the gear safely into store at Belan Dock. This done Croutear departed for his home near Lymington.

RPG remained for one more day which he spent walking up snipe on the Bodfuan estate where he bagged 12 snipe and one mallard. This concluded his visit to North Wales on which he comments, "So ends an unsuccessful expedition, but a very happy time all the same."

Cost of this expedition	Railway fares, self and valet.	£4.16.0
	Croutear wages and journey	£10.16.0
	Caernarvon Bay Hotel	£11.0.0
	Cheques and Traps	£6.10.0
	Total	**£33.02.0**

1916. RPG visits Laughton Lodge, Lincolnshire

Many of RPG's friends were now fighting a terrible war abroad and one such person, serving in France, was Mr. F. Meynell who owned Laughton Lodge, near Gainsborough, Lincolnshire. Over Christmas RPG had received a letter inviting him, as a guest to three days duck shooting.

He was very excited about the invitation as he knew that the record duck shooting bag for the British Isles was made on Mr Meynell's estate in November 1913. Five guns had enjoyed a morning flight starting at 5.30am and shooting until 11am. The bag was 74 mallard, 396 teal, 15 wigeon, 5 shoveler plus one various. Grand total 491.

RPG writes, "I went there full of enthusiasm, but the one thing I wanted I did not get, i.e. plenty of wind. Instead the weather was calm, bright and frosty. (Several times I got out of bed to look out of the window hoping I might find the weather was changing)."

"The 'duck ground' which during the last two years has in parts, where it borders the river Trent, been much spoilt by reclamation (warping). It is part of an estate of 5-6000 acres and is about 1200 acres in extent consisting of a great wild houseless, treeless common of sandy moorland interspersed with marsh and shallow pools and rush fringed meres of 12-15 acres. The various pools and meres are scattered over the common, one or two miles apart."

"The system of shooting is for five or six guns to be in shelters of reed, one on each mere, before daybreak. They shoot the birds on morning flight and as they come back afterwards as driven birds, driven by the guns from one mere to another. The shooting usually terminates at 11am by which time the birds are driven away."

The weather was hopeless for flighting. RPG writes, "the first morning I should have killed 100 duck and teal if I had a good wind. As it was I shot 20 mallard and 8 teal." The second morning the weather was equally bad and the birds were becoming wary, his bag was only 4 mallard and 2 teal. Finally on the last day, 14 January he picked up 2 mallard and 3 teal.

Bodfuan Hall snipe shooting on the famous bog

From Lincolnshire RPG lost no time in travelling to Bodfuan Hall, the estate in North Wales owned by Frederick Wynn where he had been invited to shoot the great snipe marsh. On arrival he found the marsh flooded and although there were large numbers of snipe, they rose in wisps of 50 and 60. Where the marsh was dry, the snipe were wild and he could not get near them. On 18 January he walked all day, up to his knees most of the time and picked up 1 teal and 7 snipe. The next day, determined not to be beaten he writes, "I shot the whole marsh today. Very wet. Started shooting at 8.30am and left off at 4.30 pm with only 15 minutes interval for lunch." The bag was 3 mallard and 9 snipe. Then on the final day he walked for two hours and picked up 2 mallard and 4 snipe.

RPG returned to his host's house at Glynllivon and decided to arrange two days afloat in the Voryd bay before the end of the season. Croutear had not been called to North Wales from his home in Lymington so one must assume he was relying again on young Evan Roberts as his puntsman.

The first day afloat drew a blank but on the final day he writes, "afloat at 8.30am. Made a nice shot, but there was a fine lot of birds and if I had Sam Croutear to punt for me I should have got 40." However, it was not a bad shot and they picked up 14. We know this was the last punt shot that RPG ever made. There followed several days of pheasant shooting at Glynllivon he then returned to Thirkleby Hall on 29 January 1916.

Death of RPG

Sir Ralph Payne-Gallwey Bart passed away peacefully on 24 November 1916 and this was the last wildfowling adventure recorded in his diary.

His punt and 2 inch Bentley and Playfair gun were already gifted in 1907 to Frederick Wynn and left stored in the Belan Fort dockside buildings. They remained there until 1986 when they were acquired by the Merseyside Maritime Museum as part of a large collection of nautical and historically important artefacts which formed the Wynn Family Collection. For a number of years the punt gun and carriage were placed on display at Liverpool Museum. Today they remain in safe storage at the museum.

Sir Ralph Payne-Gallwey was laid to rest outside the main entrance of All Saints Church, Great Thirkleby. Inside the Church a wall tablet was erected by his widow; on it is engraved; "In memory of Ralph William Frankland Payne-Gallwey third Baronet of Thirkleby. Born August 19th 1848. Died November 24th 1916. "He nothing common did nor mean."

Epitaph

"But time, tho'sweet, is strong in flight,

And years roll swiftly by,

And Autumn's falling leaf proclaim'd

The old man - He must die!"

Old English Gentleman

As we bid farewell to Sir Ralph Payne-Gallwey it would seem an appropriate moment to look more closely at his personality and try to understand why such an eminent wealthy Victorian gentleman should have had a lifelong passion for punt gunning.

His old friend William Speight must have a lot to answer for: it was at Derry Castle at the age of 19 where he first met Mike Considine, Speight's puntsman, and went afloat on the upper reaches of the Shannon estuary. We know from our own experience that whatever you enjoy in your formative years is most likely to become a lifelong interest.

We are all influenced by what we read, and, as a young man, RPG would have been reading the Sporting Magazine, a splendid publication which boasted the patronage of H.R.H Prince Albert. It contained much on hunting, yachting and the turf but it is here you can find articles written by Hoary Frost under the regular chapter heading of, 'Days and Nights of Wild-Fowl Shooting'. The author was Henry Coleman Folkard a barrister-at-law who wrote 'The Wild-Fowler' in 1859. It is known that Folkard's articles were enjoyed by RPG as he praises them in his books. Folkard even lays claim to inventing the name Wildfowler, the term we all now commonly use. Moreover, he was particularly offended when Lewis Clement adopted the pen name Wildfowler when writing for 'The Field' and subsequently publishing 'Modern Wildfowling' in 1880.

Folkard recognised that the sport of wildfowling was changing and the writing of Colonel Hawker in 'Instructions to Young Sportsmen' was becoming out of date. Although we can only speculate, here is our theory; Hawker's book had remained unrivalled for fifty years as a manual for guns and shooting, especially to all that related to fowling. Hawker died in 1853 when his book was in the ninth edition and although two further editions were published after his death, much of the content must have been regarded by RPG as out of date. RPG was a young man with all the enthusiasm of youth and many of Hawker's characteristics; wealthy, an inventive mind and with all the confidence that the army would have given him as an officer. Why should he not become the modern exponent in the art of wildfowling? After all, he had by now been fowling for over ten years and probably thought there was little else to be learnt so why not pass his knowledge to a new generation of fowlers? Surely this is what Hawker had also thought but it was now time for a new authority on the sport.

We have seen that RPG had remarkable drive, commitment and a compulsion to succeed, borne out by his tireless daily exertion in pursuit of fowl, in all weather conditions and on every possible occasion. He started writing his first book, 'The Fowler in Ireland' when living aboard the yacht '*Gipsy*' on the Shannon estuary during the winter of 1881/1882. The book was published in 1882. A sub-title states the book contains notes on the haunts and habits of wildfowl and seafowl including instructions in the art of shooting and capturing them. The new book received excellent reviews with the effect of immediately raising RPG's sporting profile.

By August 1884 there is an entry in the Game Book which showed that he enjoyed three days grouse shooting on Blubberhouse Moor as a guest of Lord Walsingham. A short note confirms Walsingham's prowess with the gun when RPG writes, "I saw Walsingham kill today 120 grouse in one drive of 20 minutes." Interestingly, during the three days only Walsingham and RPG were shooting. Based on the bag that day, there is no doubt that RPG acquitted himself satisfactorily. Perhaps it was at this time that he was asked to consider contributing to the two Shooting Volumes in the proposed new Badminton Series which were later to be published in 1886. Acceptance of this invitation might have come when RPG reciprocated the shooting invitation, inviting Lord Walsingham to shoot partridges at Thirkleby in September of the same year.

RPG's memorial tablet

At this stage we might have speculated that RPG would desert his Irish wildfowling roots. He was certainly now a part of 'the smart country house shooting set' and regarded by many as an authority on all matters related to shooting. He was also a very good game shot. Why else would Walsingham have approached him? But, far from abandoning punt gunning it is evident that it was becoming even more of an obsession: he had already commissioned Holland and Holland to build the double breech-loading punt gun. This serves to support our theory that RPG, whilst admiring Hawker, he wanted to show how Hawker's original idea of a double flint and percussion punt gun could, with careful thought, be improved and developed to accommodate the modern breech-loading action.

Between 1890 and 1896 RPG published a series of three more books under the heading of 'Letters to Young Shooters'. The first of the series embraced the subject of the use of gun and was dedicated to Lord Walsingham; the second 'Game Shooting' and the third in the series is devoted to ' Wildfowl and Wildfowl Shooting'. The similarity to Colonel Hawker's book 'Instruction to Young Sportsmen' is striking.

When Walsingham learnt RPG was to dedicate the first series of "Letters to Young Shooters" to him he wrote the following letter to RPG.

36 Lownder Street
13 Nov 1890

My dear Ralph

The compliment you propose to pay me in dedicating to me your "Letters to Young Shooters" is one which I value more highly as coming from yourself than if it came from any other quarter – moreover the flattering terms in which you, a past master in the art of Venerie, have thought fit to express yourself in regard to my own claims to the title of "true sportsman" are very grateful to me, although I can only accept them as describing the ideal at which I aim, rather than the actual effect of my theory or practice.

Believe me

Your affectionate cousin

Walsingham

RPG's notoriety as a wildfowler lives on to this day. Reading his diary it is clear that his exploits have not always been without criticism and his behaviour on occasion questionable. It has also been suggested that he lacked the intellectual literary skills and ornithological knowledge which Lord Walsingham certainly possessed. This may well be true but we have a feeling that he would have brushed such comments aside with the wave of a hand, pointing to the weakness of his critics whom he would adjudge as having left little more than a smudge on the pages of history of wildfowling. Even today there are critics of RPG who fail to recognise the inadequacies of their own writing. Their books will not be used as cornerstones for the sport in one hundred years. As the first President of WAGBI, RPG inspired Stanley Duncan to form a strong Association which has fought for wildfowlers and fowling for over one hundred years, which is not a bad legacy for our sport.

We have established that RPG was the Victorian authority on wildfowling but we suspect he may have felt inwardly disappointed that his own results with punt and gun never matched those obtained by George Gould and Walter Pope. Shuttler and Croutear were his excellent puntsmen but neither of them would have ever thought to question an instruction given by RPG. In reality they were servants, and they would not have contemplated verbal criticism of their master's tactics. One must therefore conclude that RPG's successes and failures were of his own making and patience was not his strongest virtue.

In contrast, evidence suggests Gould's relationship with Shuttler was more relaxed and measured. Together they worked as a team to obtain the best possible result even if on occasion it meant going without a shot for several days. In Pope's case he acted as puntsman and gave the order when the gunner should fire. Gould commented that Pope was a 'clever' puntsman but he found him to be self-opinionated, a characteristic which, we know, annoyed him.

Gun room; Thirkleby Hall.

We believe that RPG went punt gunning right up until the end of his life because he loved the wild estuaries he visited and the birds that he observed at close quarters. He loved being afloat in pursuit of truly wild birds that always provided him with a challenge. We sense he became bored with the formality of covert shooting on the grand estates and instead he sought the solitude of true friendship offered by trusted and respected companions with whom he could relax and share amusing stories. In a telling diary entry, following illness, in January 1912 he writes about the joy of returning to Glynllivon in North Wales and meeting up with Sam Croutear again, referring to him as; "my old friend and excellent puntsman." Throughout his life, when wildfowling, he complained about his ill-luck and the weather which was his constant enemy. He was, however a realist, admitting that much of the ill-luck he complained about was brought about by his lack of patience and his own stupidity.

Sir Ralph Payne-Gallwey, we conclude, was a man of his time with all the characteristics of an eccentric English Victorian gentleman. He was a happily married man, devoted to his dear wife Edith who bore him five children; four daughters, Margaret, Winifred, Dorothy and Geraldine, and their only son William, killed in action on 14 September 1914 was a loss that the family never came to terms with. In her sorrow we understand Edith destroyed nearly all the photographs of her son following her husband's death in November 1916.

RPG freely admitted that largely as a result of his many excesses, not least his smoking habit, and enjoyment of fine wine his health was affected. If we had met him we think we would have found him witty and no doubt, in conversation he would have commanded our utmost respect when talking about a lifetime's experience of sport and in particular punt gunning. We regret that such a meeting was never a possibility but we have both enjoyed every moment of researching his life and we salute him for the indelible mark he has left on the history of wildfowling.

Painting by Anthony de Bree 1914. The gun room Thirkleby Hall.

Analysis of Wildfowl Shooting extracted from a previous Volume.

Winter	Place	Birds	Totals
1869-70	Lough Derg	My first winter with punt gun. No records	0
1876-77	Lough Derg R. Shannon	55 Duck. 20 Teal. 65 Golden Plover. (Married Ap: 25. 1877.)	150
1877-78	Lough Derg	40 Duck. 18 Teal. 50 Golden Plover	108
1878-79	Queenstown Ireland	25 Ducks. 140 Wigeon. 21 Teal. 6 Shovellers. 8 Pochard. 120 Golden Plover	320
1879-80	Queenstown	33 Ducks. 120 Wigeon. 114 Teal. 3 R.B. Merganser. 80 Golden Plover. 7 Golden Eye. 5 Tufted Duck	262
1880-81	Tidal Shannon	41 Ducks. 750 Wigeon. 12 Pintail. 23 Teal. 6 Grey Lag Geese. 40 Golden Plover. (My record.)	872
1881-82	Tralee & Dingle Bays	3 Ducks. 68 Wigeon 10 Pochard 7 Brent Geese.	88
1882-83	Tidal Shannon	57 Wigeon 9 Ducks 17 Teal	83

Continued on page 158.
From 1883-84 to 1899-00, and then on page following (231) down to 1915-16

"Records of 35 Winters fowling

Various extracts from RPG's wildfowling diaries

Continued from page 158. Analysis of

Winter	Place	Birds killed	Totals
1900.01	Valley Anglesey	164 Wigeon. 39 Golden. & 114 Green Plover	317
1901.02	Belan N W	10 Duck. 41 Wigeon. 2 Teal. 11 Snipe 92 Knot. 64 Golden & 133 Green Plover	353
1902.03	Valley	9 Duck. 59 Wigeon. 22 Snipe 9 Brent Geese. 2 Golden. 44 Green Plover	145
1903.04	R. Humber	16 Duck. Not well. Only afloat on 4 days.	16
1904.05	✓	Did not go afloat once this season	0
1906.07	✓	Did not go afloat once this season	0
1907.08	Belan	1 Duck. 92 Wigeon. 21 Teal. 3 Snipe. 1 Shell duck	118
1909.10	Belan	10 Wigeon. Only went afloat 3 times	10
1910.11	✓	Did not go afloat	0
1911.12	Belan	2 Duck. 53 Wigeon. 1 Shell duck. 68 golden plover.	124
1912.13	Belan	57 Wigeon. 3 Brent Geese. 2 Godwit	62
1913.14	Belan	39 Duck. 33 Wigeon. 19 Teal. 60 Snipe	151
1914.15	Belan	45 Wigeon	45
1915.16	Belan	8 Duck. 70 Wigeon. 1 Teal. 29 Snipe. 1 Long Tailed Duck. 62 Green Plover.	179
"	16 Laughton	26 Duck. 13 Teal. (Shoulder gun).	39

RPG's totals of ducks shot

Best Shots

Date	Place		Total
Nov 1878	Lucanstown	80 Golden plover	80
Dec 1880	Shannon	52. 47. 46 Wigeon (on tidal water)	52. 47. 46.
Oct 1883	Husum	38. 40. 47. 40. Wigeon	38. 40. 47. 40.
Jan 8 1886	Lucanstown	46 Wigeon	46
Oct 12 1887	Holwerd	46 Wigeon	46
Oct 22 1889	Holwerd	40. 45 Wigeon	40. 45.
Oct 24 1889	Holwerd	60 Wigeon & 2 duck	62
Nov 2 1889	Zoutkamp	47 Wigeon	47
Dec 11 1899	Valley	25 Wigeon 11 Ducks 3 Teal	39
Feb 17 1900	Valley	46 Wigeon	46
Jan 10 1901	Valley	70 Wigeon (my record shot)	70.

= Shots of less than 40. omitted =

Records of Best days at Duck, and Best Shots { with punt & big gun.

= Best days =

Date	Place		Totals
Dec 17. 1880	Shannon	119 Wigeon (166 in 4 consecutive days)	119
Jan 1881	Shannon	80 Wigeon (This and above on tide.)	80
Oct 4 1883	Husum	70 Wigeon and duck (Holland)	70
Oct 8 1883	Husum	78 Wigeon (Holland)	78
Oct 22 1889	Holwerd	132 Wigeon (Holland)	132
Nov 2 1889	Zoutkamp	121 Wigeon and duck (Holland)	121
Dec 11 1899	Valley	64 Wigeon and duck (N Wales)	64
Jan 10 1901	Valley	70 Wigeon (one shot)	70

= Days of less than 60 omitted =

14

The history of Sir Ralph Payne–Gallwey's punt gun collection

"The wandering flocks, expelled from northern shores,

In varied forms pursue their trackless way,

Courting the genial aspect of the south,

Whilst iron winter holds his despot sway."

T. Hughes

Colonel Hawker's Double Punt Gun

Following the Colonel's death on 7 August 1853 an advertisement appeared on 21 January 1855 in 'Bell's Life in London and Sporting Chronicle' and 'The Field' over the name of Charles Heath who was a tenant and shooting companion on Hawker's estate at Longparish, Hampshire. Heath's advertisement read, "To dispose of some punts and punt guns belonging to the late Colonel Hawker." It was at this time that Colonel Birch Reynardson (born November 1809) bought the Hawker flint and percussion ignition double-barrelled punt gun. In April 1889 Reynardson died and the gun was put into an auction at which time Sir Ralph Payne-Gallwey purchased it for £12.

Hawker's double gun was made in 1824 with Damascus barrels 8ft 3½ inches in length and a muzzle diameter of 1$\frac{9}{16}$ inches. Fullerd was responsible for making the beautiful forged iron twist skelp barrels whilst the action and stock involved the craftsmanship of Durs Egg and Joseph Manton. The gun's overall weight of almost 200lbs included the under-barrel spring recoil breeching mechanism which was made by Westley Richards to the Colonel's design. This mechanism was later adopted by many punt gun makers and is still regarded today as the finest way of managing the recoil of a heavy punt gun. Additional work was undertaken by Daniel Long of Andover and Thomas Parsons of Salisbury.

Following RPG's death a number of his guns were sold by his widow. William, their only son had died in action and there was now no-one in the family to carry on the fowling tradition.

Lady Edith Payne-Gallwey made the decision to contact Stanley Duncan, founder of the Wildfowlers' Association of Great Britain and Ireland (WAGBI) who, on formation of the Association, had asked RPG to be the first President. Duncan had become a trusted friend and now was a partner with his brother in their gun shop in Hull. He was therefore well placed to give advice on how best to dispose of the valuable collection of RPG's guns.

Duncan arranged the sale of the Hawker gun to Doctor Charles Heath F.R.C.S. a leading Harley Street specialist and authority on ear, nose and throat matters and certainly no relation to his namesake Charles Heath who had sold the gun in 1855 to Birch Reynardson. Heath was later to succeed RPG as President of WAGBI in 1918. In November 1916, Heath bought the gun for £100 and it remained in his ownership until his death on 13 July 1934. Subsequently the gun was generously gifted to WAGBI by Rachael Heath and her sister in September 1934. This gift was conditional that it remained the property of 'The Richards Memorial Fund'. Dr Richards was Heath's dearest friend in all matters related to fieldsports and Heath set up this Fund to pay tribute to his friend. The Richards Memorial Fund was to be used for the relief of professional wildfowlers in hardship or other purposes that may arise. In 1984 it was decided to liquidate investments to reduce the Associations considerable overdraft. By this time there were no longer any professional wildfowlers.

Colonel Hawker's double punt gun

Dr Charles Heath was born in Totnes in Devon on 25 December 1856, the youngest son of Mr John Heath. Heath lost hearing in his right ear at a young age, brought about by a severe chill which affected him whilst salmon fishing and as a result much of his distinguished medical career was focused on resolving problems associated with deafness. His success in this field of work gained great acclaim. Throughout his life he was a keen wildfowler and salmon fisherman. He owned a house in Southern Ireland, punted the Shannon Estuary and fished in Galway. He was a great exponent of chamberless guns maintaining that they shot much harder than chambered guns. He designed and built, with the assistance of his gunmaker Mr F.T. Baker, a double $1\frac{1}{8}$ inch chamberless punt gun.

What perhaps is less well known is that in the early 1960s WAGBI was under severe financial pressure and John Anderton (Director) was instructed by the WAGBI Executive to have the gun valued as it seemed likely that for the Association to survive and prosper it might be necessary to sell the Colonel Hawker double punt gun. Keith Neal a renowned gun collector valued the gun at £1000 and at this price there seems little doubt he would have welcomed adding the gun to his extensive collection. The Executive Committee were split on the decision to sell the gun but after considerable debate finally decided to keep the punt gun.

It seems most likely that the photo of Hawker's gun outside Duncan's shop (Page 55 in the book, 'Through the Lens with Stanley Duncan' compiled by Jean Skinner in 1988) was taken after Heath died and before the gun went on display at various venues around the country. We know that through the efforts of Mr H.W. Robinson, Museum Caretaker at the local natural history museum associated with the Lancaster Royal Grammar School, the gun was placed on display there, and then, in 1946, moved to the York Philosophical Society's Museum in York. Thereafter it went on display at the Wildfowl Research Institute in Tring, followed by various gun shops including Bland's famous London Strand shop. The Dee Wildfowlers borrowed it for an exhibition and eventually it went on display at the Birmingham Proof House. Today it enjoys its rightful place in history on display at the British Association for Shooting and Conservation Headquarters at Marford Mill.

There is an untold story relating to the Hawker gun. At around lunchtime on Friday, 8 January 1982 BASC Headquarters went on fire. The account given in Graham Downing's book, 'A Sporting Century' has one small omission. As Downing states in his book John Richards detected the fire and the building was evacuated promptly with no danger to human life. John's concern at the time was to ensure that there was no loss of valuable irreplaceable artefacts. Unfortunately the fire had taken hold in the library so it was here that the battle was centred on control of the fire. Richards phoned Anthony McEntyre, who had an office in Ellesmere Port and asked him if he could, 'hot foot it' to Marford Mill. There was just one irreplaceable item that they both wanted to save and that was locked in a glass case in the Mill reception. While the Wrexham Fire Brigade turned all its attention to the fire and onlookers gazed in despair Anthony and John found the key to the glass cabinet and carried the Hawker gun to safety, placing it on the grass by the duck pond! No one really noticed the two of them struggling with the weight of the gun, carrying it out of the smoke filled building and ignoring all the rules of 'health and safety'. As it turned out the building did not burn to the ground but at the time it seemed a real possibility. John and Anthony had the satisfaction of watching the fire slowly coming under control knowing that at least the Hawker gun was safe, whatever else happened.

RPG's 1⅞ inch Bentley and Playfair after it had been converted to a breech-loader

1½ inch double muzzle-loading punt gun by Clayton

Stanley Duncan's photograph of Payne-Gallweys' double gun

Below; Duncan's photograph shows the two single punt guns after conversion; the left hand half is the gun on the right.

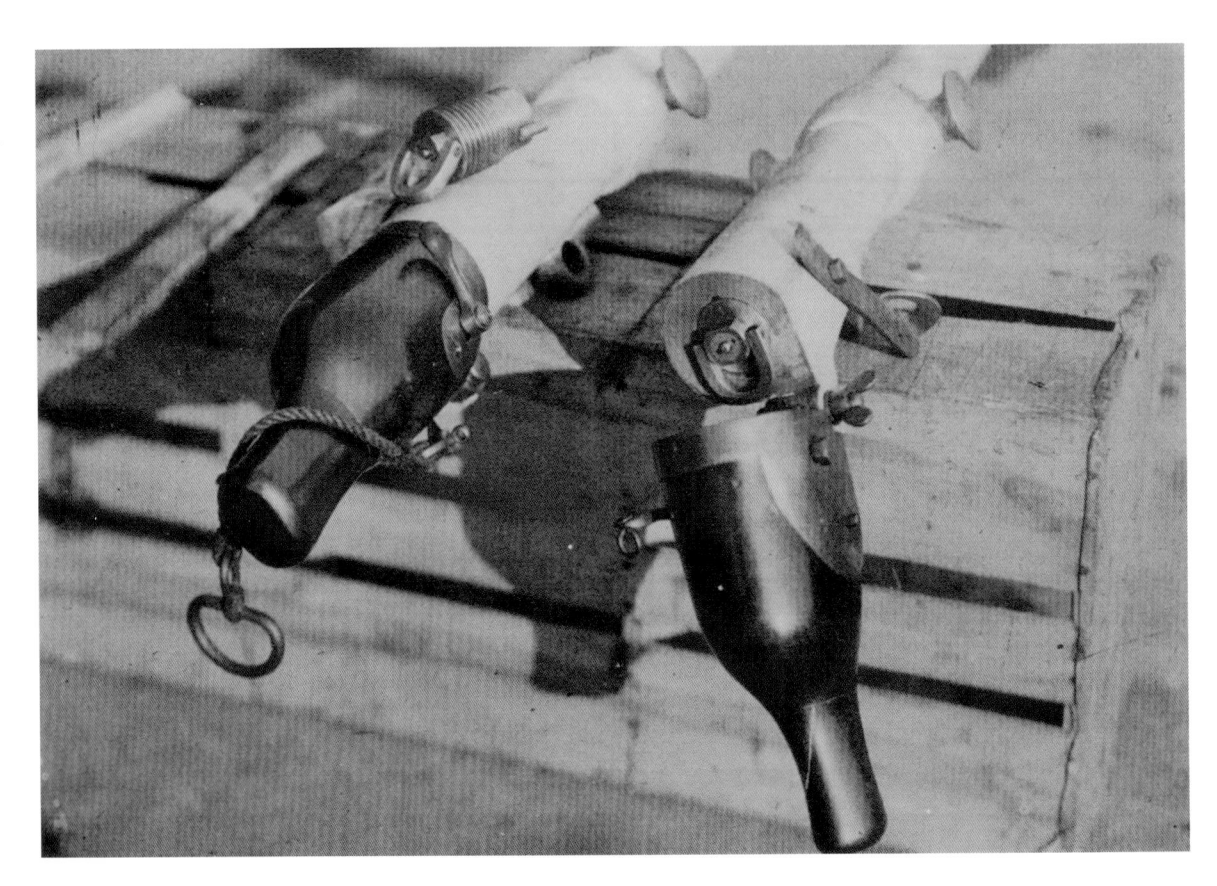

The Bentley and Playfair and Clayton punt guns

It seems essential that the history of three equally important historic punt guns is also fully told. We have already written about the design, construction, shooting trials and ten seasons of use of the Payne-Gallwey double gun. The last season of use was in 1894/5 and the last shot was fired at Fenham on 16 February 1895.

In 1895 the double Holland and Holland punt gun was taken back to Thirkleby Hall and placed, along with RPG's other punt guns in the gunroom rack where as far as anybody knows it remained until RPG's death. It can be seen in the oil painting of RPG in his gunroom, painted by Anthony de Bree in 1914 along with Colonel Hawker's double and a double muzzle-loading Alfred Clayton punt gun which he bought from Holland and Holland in 1893 for £100.

The 1⅞ inch Bentley and Playfair, converted to a breech-loader, had already been gifted to the Wynn family and lay at Belan Fort. This left the double Holland and Holland breech-loader and the double muzzle-loading Alfred Clayton both of which Duncan purchased. We suspect Duncan was very interested in how the Holland and Holland had been made. Later he even went as far as proposing improvements to the design in his book 'The Complete Wildfowler Ashore and Afloat.'

The Clayton was most certainly another important gun, in historical terms, as it was one of two very early double punt guns made by this company. This muzzle-loader 1½ inch double probably came from Ireland. It appears in a photograph of RPG's gunroom in 1914 and we also know that Duncan sold the gun to Mr Ronald Armstrong-Jones prior to 1947. A lengthy discussion took place at this time regarding converting this gun to a breech-loader. However the gun remained unmolested and was never used by Armstrong-Jones, because in 1950, he was able to purchase George Long's breech-loading double 1½ inch Holland and Holland, a gun that George had regularly used at Blakeney, Norfolk. The story has a happy ending as in 2014 the Clayton, which was by now in a very poor state of repair, was sympathetically restored by Ronald's son Peregrine Armstrong-Jones, with the help of Emrys Heard and Jim Spalding (See The Field article, 'Armstrong-Jones' Big Boomer' 2015).

The 'Gallwey' double Holland and Holland punt gun

Duncan decided to buy RPG's 'Gallwey' double gun from Edith, RPG's widow. He may have gone afloat with the gun as he mentioned, when discussing the design of double punt guns, in his book 'The Complete Wildfowler', "the design here depicted is necessarily copied from existing double swivel-guns some of which we have had the good fortune and pleasure to personally use." However, Duncan regarded the Holland and Holland double gun as impractical for use on home waters and best suited for use overseas where the fowl might be more numerous. But, by this time the fowling grounds abroad were restricted and punt gunning with large bore size prohibited. He decided that the best way to sell it would be to convert it into two single guns which he felt confident he could sell. In 1920 he writes that he contacted H&H as there was doubt, in his own mind, as to how the barrels were joined together at the breech and he did not want to damage the barrel tubes . Duncan writes, "It was upwards of thirty five years ago that the gun was made and the makers were unable to say how the barrels were attached. H&H would not undertake the conversion work needed." It therefore fell to Duncan to carefully undertake the work and interestingly the whole process is well documented in Stanley Duncan and Guy Thornes' book 'The Complete Wildfowler' 1950s second edition (illustrations opposite page 32). The engineering work is credited to Duncan, Wade and Gower (Stanley Duncan was an engineer on the L.N.E. Railway for practically his whole working life and did not retire until 1943). An advertisement in the 'Shooting Times and British Sportsman' suggests that it was in fact Cyril Duncan who was involved with the engineering work as Duncan Wade and Gower were listed as agents for, amongst other things, the letting of shooting and fishing with offices at 44, De la Pole Avenue , Hull. Cyril, with his brother 'Young Stanley' opened and ran Duncan's gun shop on Anlaby Road Hull which was opened in 1932. Duncan Wade and Gower were not solely an engineering company as we first suspected, but Duncan's son Cyril must have been a partner in this business. Stanley Duncan does confirm in his 'Shooting Times' article in 1920 that, "he had no alternative but to rely on small engineering firms to undertake the making of gunmetal trunnions for rope breeching which were shrunk on 13 inches from the breech and eyes for the safety ropes fitted below the barrels." He also said, "It was particularly pleasing to relate that none of the high-class shooting of these big tubes has been impaired by the alterations."

Stanley Duncan with the left hand half of the Payne-Gallwey double on his punt

When the conversion was completed the only record of the separate guns being used was in an unpublished article written by the late Trevor Field in the mid-1930s.

Trevor was a lifelong friend of Duncan and he tells the story of George Butt (a wealthy trawler owner) asking Stanley Duncan to join him for a few days fowling at Tetney Lock on the south side of the Humber, nearly opposite Duncan's fowling headquarters at Patrington. George had two single punts and Duncan took along two single punt guns which Trevor Field clearly remembers had originally been the RPG double gun. Each of George's punts was breeched with a gun and they set out together before dawn to try for a big shot at a stand of curlew roosting on the estuary mud banks. Trevor was instructed to remain behind the seawall and as day broke he observed two orange flashes followed by a double boom. They returned triumphant with 20 curlew. Duncan must have used both of the single guns on other occasions as he took photographs of punts breeched with one or other of the guns which can be positively identified by the fact that the cocking lever on the left barrel was on the left side. ("Through the Lens with Stanley Duncan" by Jean Skinner, 1988 page 42). Duncan may have wanted to sell the guns. On 17 June 1933, an advertisement appeared in the 'Shooting Times', over his name, offering three 1½ inch Holland and Holland breech-loading punt guns. He had by 1933 promised to sell one gun to an Irish gentleman, Captain Harvey, a well know punt gunner at Wexford. His plan may have been to keep one barrel and sell the other one. In fact the sale to Captain Harvey was never completed but by this time Duncan had already decided to sell the other barrel. Captain Leonard Scott Briggs MC, (1895-1974) of Melkington House, Cornhill bought the gun for his use at Holy Island. Following this sale Scott Briggs was later offered the other half of the double gun which he then bought. The story does not end there with the two barrels in one man's ownership. Scott Briggs, we are told by Duncan, sold the Harvey half 'to a gentleman in the South' in early 1933.

We believe Duncan decided to sell the two halves of the Payne-Gallwey gun in order to finance the purchase a large muzzle-loading punt gun which was offered for sale in July 1933 by Captain Gilbert Bradish of Strandfield, Wexford, on behalf of the widow of Mr Graves, (from Limerick) who formerly owned the gun. Duncan later converted this gun into a breech-loader.

By 1934 one half of RPG's double gun was somewhere in the south of England, and the other half was with Captain Scott Briggs in Northumbria. At some stage they must have been re-united, although the trail now gets more difficult to follow. The two were eventually found in the ownership of Major Tommy Foley who lived in Herefordshire and punted in Pembrokeshire around Pembroke Dock and Lawreney. His puntsman was a local man called Tom Davies but sadly there are few records of their fowling adventures. One letter, written to a friend in February 1947, mentioned an excellent shot of 47 (26 wigeon and 21 teal) and another of 40 teal in 1933. These shots were made with a single Holland and Holland 16oz gun which he must have owned prior to buying the two halves of the Payne-Gallwey gun. Foley, it seems, had a large collection of punt guns as he also owned a double 1½ inch Holland and Holland. Tommy Foley died on 13 December 1959 and, as there was no family interest in punt gunning, all his guns and punts were sold.

In 1965 Mr David Bassett of Portiscliff, Ferryside owned some of the Foley guns. Bassett, apparently was not a punt gunner and we speculate the guns had been purchased cheaply at a sale due to a vague interest in wildfowling. The guns remained in his ownership for almost 30 years but had been left to rust with no attention to routine maintenance.

The next person to be linked to the Payne-Gallwey double gun was James Stephen Dorrington an avid and knowledgable Essex punt gunner. He already owned a number of important guns including a 2 inch Gilbert and Kellett Ltd. of Barrow-in-Furness, which he bought from Alexander Dalgety (Christopher Dalgety's son) in March 1991. This wonderful gun was delivered to Michael Bratby and used for the first time on 6 November 1937 when Peter Scott was puntsman and 'The Baron' was gunner. The first shot was 13 teal. Thereafter the gun was used on many occasions by Scott, Bratby and also Dalgety. Dalgety eventually owned the gun, acquired from Peter Scott in the late 1940s and, much to Christopher's annoyance, 2 inch guns were then banned in 1954 by the Protection of Birds Act! By this time Peter Scott was no longer punting.

James Stephen Dorrington

James Dorrington also owned an early Holland and Holland 1½ inch 'London' gun number 7003, made in 1881 with the Clayton's Bar Action closing mechanism. James was well acquainted with Holland and Holland punt guns. He also had friends in the gun trade and he always urged them to give him first refusal should they come across a punt gun. On 12 August 1995 he received a call from a Cambridgeshire gun dealer who had an unnamed 1½ inch punt gun in poor condition. The gun had come from a London auction house and having failed to sell, it was put into storage. The auction house wished to redeem the storage charges it was owed and sold the gun to the gun dealer. James called to see him and was shown the gun. He immediately noticed something very odd about it. The cocking lever was on the left hand side. The gun had no maker's name but the breech plug was of the patent Holland and Holland design. James knew quality when he saw it.

James negotiated an acceptable price for the gun and on arrival home quickly realised that he had located one half of the famous Payne-Gallwey double punt gun number 8155. What confirmed his suspicion was a small hole drilled through the cocking lever. This was described by RPG to enable him to add a small metal ring to the cocking lever and a floating pin. The pin could be passed through the ring and engaged into a hole in the stock to act as a safety catch thus preventing the left hand barrel from discharging. In addition the right hand side of the barrel, at the breech end had a flat where it had been faced to the right hand barrel. A photograph in Stanley Duncan's book confirmed these facts

The left hand half showing Holland & Holland patent breech plug and cocking lever with the hole that RPG had for his safety catch

With half of RPG's gun in James's possession, he recalled being told about the possible existence of the other half of the gun. This apparently had been seen in very poor condition with no breech plug and eighteen inches of the barrel missing and described as scrap! With help, James, eventually found the gun, and established it was indeed the other half of the RPG gun.

James was a very talented engineer and with both halves of RPG's gun in his possession he vowed he would rebuild the double gun. His first job was to strip the locks. They were found to be in a very poor state but made, as you would expect, by the finest lock maker of the day, engraved with the name Chilton. James found a retired spring maker who had made Chilton locks and immediately commissioned him to remake all the worn parts. Meanwhile James pressed on with other restoration work.

James was a stickler for detail and before carrying out further work he wanted to see how Holland and Holland had originally constructed the gun. There were no plans he could consult so the only answer was to trace the owners of two other Payne-Gallwey double guns and to go and look at them. In 1996 he inspected both guns and John Richards allowed James to borrow his gun and gave him permission to disassemble this gun. James then took photographs and measured every component related to its construction. The gun was then reassembled, but in doing so, as a mark of appreciation, James totally restored the barrels, the breeching mechanism, the walnut stock, the action and the lock work. Parts of the wooden stock were soft due to gun oil, the passage of time and wear and tear. James cut out these parts as screws would no longer hold, and he then let in new seasoned walnut to complete a perfect restoration. It was then returned to John in 1997 in an, 'as new' condition. Such was the skill that James possessed.

Chilton Lock

To James the most important thing was to know how the Holland and Holland guns were made so that he could commence the major task of rebuilding Payne-Gallwey's double gun.

James started work on the two guns, first removing Stanley Duncan's additions made during the conversion to two single guns. Off came the trunnions and loops for the check rope. Then he drilled out the lead filled screw holes in the walls of the barrels at the breech end that located the old rib and purchased a fine baulk of seasoned walnut which he proposed to use for the stock. A new hexagonal trigger cam was made to operate the single trigger allowing the offset cam to fire the right barrel followed by a small delay before the left barrel discharged, in fact just as Holland and Holland had designed it in 1884.

James was now aged 45, shooting hard, and running his own bakery business but it was about this time that close friends recognised that all was not well with his health. There followed a slow but progressive deterioration over a number of years which effectively brought the restoration of the gun to a standstill. Tragically, from the hugely dynamic person that we all knew, James became dependent on care assistance and it was soon evident that he would be unable to finish the project that had become his lifetime ambition.

By 2009 it was clear that James's collection of guns was a liability to the family and they decided that they had to be sold. Fortunately the usable guns were quickly sold to James's friends and the money from the sale went into a Trust for his children. The only remaining gun was the disassembled RPG double gun, the locks, and breech of which were stored in a large box. Alongside lay two sad lengths of Damascus skelp twist barrels, one of which was missing 18 inches from the muzzle end.

Close friends of James discussed at length what should be done with RPG's gun. Nothing would have thrilled James more than to have seen the gun reassembled in full working order. To do this would have necessitated the making of new barrels, and had James not become ill there is no doubt that, he would have commissioned new barrels, and indeed he had already made an inquiry with a Birmingham company skilled in the manufacturing process of deep boring steel tubes.

However, it was concluded that the priority must now be to reassemble the famous gun and if agreement could be reached, to exhibit it, alongside Colonel Hawker's double gun at the British Association for Shooting and Conservation (BASC) Headquarters. To this end Julian Novorol

Julian Novorol, Jim Spalding and David Conway inspecting the stock of the double gun

Stock work carried out by James Dorrington on John's double H&H puntgun

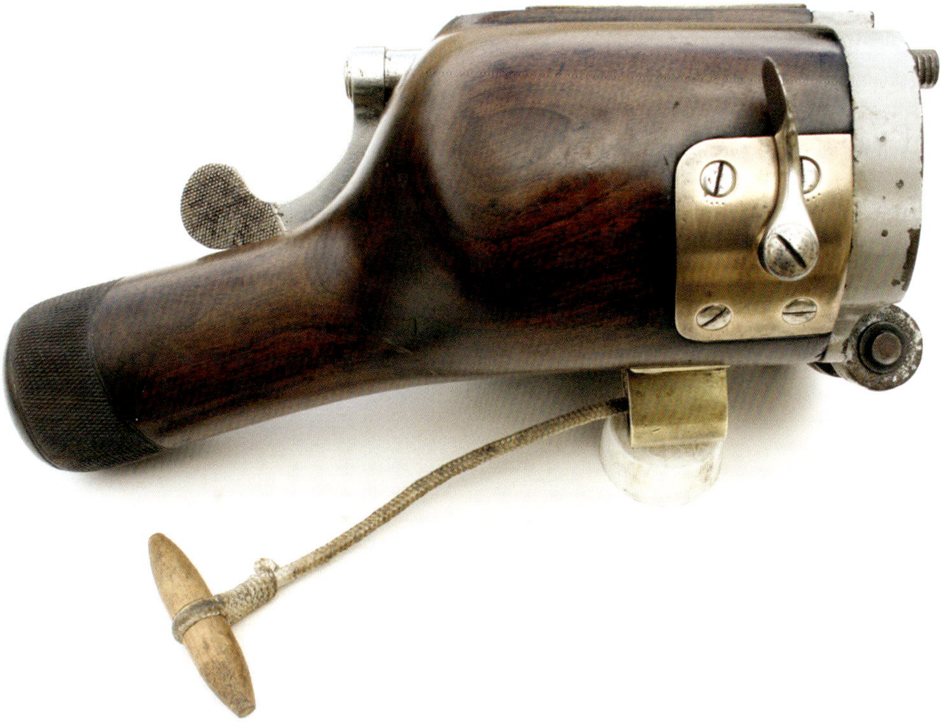

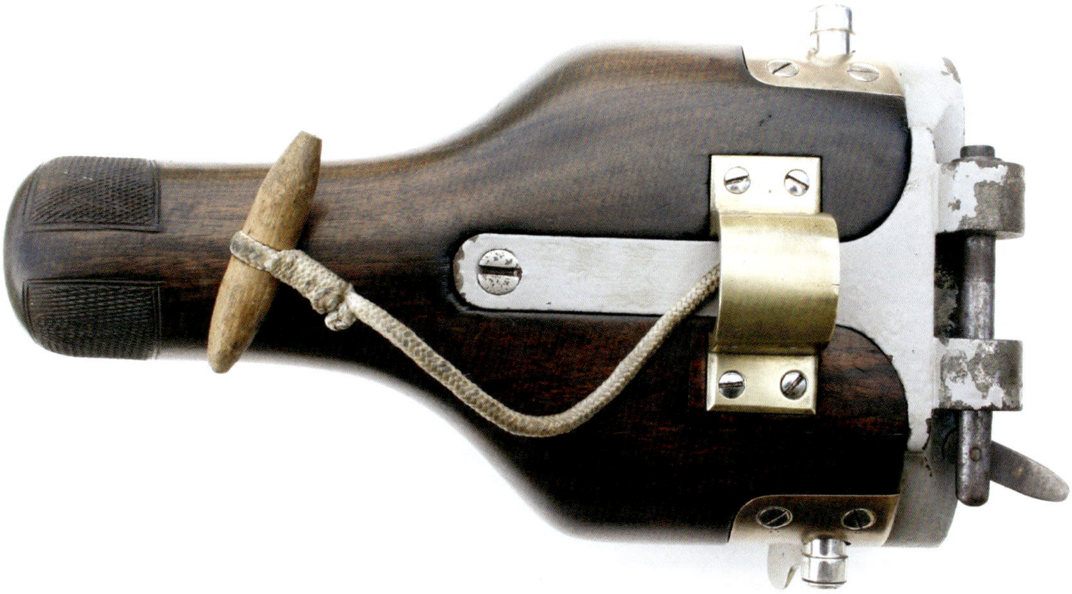

Underside of the breech end after removal of trunions and loops that Duncan had attached

Top of barrels at breech end showing threaded holes in the barrel walls to secure top rib

Following James' work on the two guns, here are the original components; two breech faces plus locks, hexagonal cam, one breech plug and a block of walnut

One complete barrel and the right with eighteen inches missing

spoke to James's father George Dorrington and suggested that if the gun was gifted to the Punt Gunner's Group, they would make every effort to see that the gun was restored. George liked this idea, especially if a display could be set up dedicated to James when the work was complete. This, then, was the agreed plan and it was up to a small team of James' friends to make the idea work. Julian contacted David Conway, a fellow punt gunner and accomplished engineer who lived on Mersea Island, Essex, who had already expressed his willingness to help. The next person Julian contacted was Jim Spalding, a professional stock maker who also lived on Mersea Island. It was at that time that Archie Moore came forward with a magnificent piece of walnut that was ideal for the stock and of much better quality than the piece James had found. Jim then started work on the stock; he had a long association with punt guns and had previously made the stock for Irish Tom, the largest punt gun ever made, when Allen Owens restored the gun in 1983. Meanwhile, John Richards contacted John Swift, BASC's Chief Executive at that time, to see if the Association was prepared to put the gun on display. As the gun was of such historic importance he suggested that it would be appropriate to ask Lord Home, President of BASC to unveil the gun when it went on display, as it was the gun owned by the first President of the Association.

David Conway who rebuilt the gun

Everyone contacted agreed to contribute their work as a labour of love, but there was a need to meet the cost of materials and other incidental costs which would undoubtedly arise.

Most generously a wonderful picture was painted by Julian Novorol which was raffled at the 2009 Punt Gunners' meeting at Marford Mill. The painting depicted Payne-Gallwey and Steven

The history of Sir Ralph Payne–Gallwey's punt gun collection

Top; Assembled gun with breech open

Assembled gun with breech closed and before the new stock was fitted

Shuttler on the Holy Island slakes after the shot they made at brent geese using the double Holland and Holland on 18 January 1893 (The bag was 14 pale-bellied brent geese). Also included in the raffle was a copy of 'Stanley Duncan Wildfowler', a bottle of whisky from Paul Upton and two boxes of steel cartridges donated by David Upton. The sale of tickets raised the sum of £1065 which was a great result and provided the financial backbone for the project.

During the ensuing two years everyone honoured their individual commitment to the project and quite remarkable work was done, in particular by Jim Spalding and David Conway.

Jim Spalding at work on the stock

The finishing touch came in April 2012 when Ginger Blaney, another punt gunner had the top rib engraved with the original wording on RPG's gun, 'Holland & Holland 98, New Bond Street'.

Painting of RPG and Shuttler by Julian Novorol

The finished stock

To complete the restoration the manufacture of two new breech plugs was completed by Clive Cooper, a skilled engineer and keen punt gunner, the latter work, not being finished until 2014.

The gun was then transported to BASC Headquarters at Marford Mill by Julian Novorol and Jack Hoy. Jack had also been working tirelessly behind the scenes throughout the project. On arrival Bill Harriman (BASC staff member) arranged for the gun, plaque and framed photographic history, to be displayed in preparation for unveiling at a meeting on 26 May 2012 attended by many punt gunners.

A special invitation was designed by the late Trevor Stokes (WAGBI member and former printer of the WAGBI magazine) and this went out to all who had helped with the project. The meeting was honoured by the attendance of the BASC President Lord Home. Following a presentation by Julian Novorol explaining the history of the Payne-Gallwey gun, Lord Home performed the unveiling ceremony. Lord Home then presented David Conway and Jim Spalding with individual paintings by Julian in recognition of the wonderful work they had done.

As a final tribute to Jim's and David's skill they were invited to attend the 2013 BASC Annual General Meeting where they were presented with BASC awards for rebuilding the gun.

A project which was started by James Dorrington in 1995 has ended as a tribute to him. James sadly died on 7 August 2013. The Payne-Gallwey double punt gun is now on permanent loan from the Punt Gunners' Group and can be seen on display at BASC Headquarters.

Jim Spalding and David Conway holding paintings and decanters which were awarded to them at the BASC AGM in 2013

The Payne-Gallwey Holland and Holland on display at Marford Mill. Above, the Anthony De Bree painting of RPG with Shuttler at Holy Island.

David Conway receiving his painting from the Lord Home

15

The historical importance of The Wildfowlers' Association of Great Britain and Ireland

"There is a rapture on the lonely shore,

There is a society where none intrudes,

By the deep sea and music in its roar,

I love not man the less, but nature more."

Byron

It is not our intention to write extensively on the subject of all the legislation that has influenced wildfowling but this book would not be complete without mention of a number of landmark events which forged the legal framework on which wildfowling can be conducted to this day.

For readers who are interested in the wider historical background of current legislation we would refer you to the various editions of the excellent and comprehensive book, 'The New Wildfowler', first published by Herbert Jenkins in 1961, with a cautionary note that even the third edition published by Stanley Paul under the auspices of BASC in 1989 must be regarded as somewhat out of date.

We take for granted that current wild bird protection permits wildfowling, but this authority hides the historical determination of a small resolute group of wildfowlers, many of whom went afloat in their gunning punts.

The story starts with the formation of The Wildfowlers' Association of Great Britain and Ireland (WAGBI) in 1908 by Stanley Duncan (1878-1954), a Humber Estuary wildfowler who invited Sir Ralph Payne-Gallwey Bart. to become the Association's first President. The way in which Duncan championed professionals, who were often punt gunners, and the amateur wildfowlers' sport for more than 30 years, marks the first major landmark in the history of fowling. His contribution is legendary and for a full account Graham Downing's book, 'A Sporting Century' published by Quiller Press in 2007 is essential reading. The book details the history of WAGBI progressing to the development of the British Association for Shooting and Conservation (BASC), as it is known today.

Footnote: In May 1911 at a meeting of WAGBI at the Imperial Hotel, Hull Doctor Charles Heath F.R.C.S. presented Stanley Duncan with a gold watch and Mrs Duncan a gold brooch in recognition of Duncan's work as Honorary Secretary of a now successful and vibrant Association. Heath referred to WAGBI as, "a living force and Duncan as its wise organiser."

Stanley Duncan

Less well documented are events immediately prior to the outbreak of the Second World War in 1939. At this time the control of the wildfowling season in England and Wales lay substantially in the hands of County Councils and differed from area to area. Unsurprisingly the British Section of the International Committee of Bird Preservation felt that there should be a minimum national closed season. This was eventually agreed and came into force on ratification of the Wild Birds (Ducks and Geese) Protection Act on 1 August 1939. This Act protected wildfowl from 1 February to 11 August with a proviso that, on the coast, an 'Order in Council' could be made to permit shooting on the tidal shore up to and including the 20 February.

Criticism of wildfowling was not confined to just the length of the season. A growing number of people thought that the law as it applied to shooting was not fit for purpose and there was a need to look more closely at the cause of a diminishing number of wildfowl both inland and around the coast of Britain. A special Wildfowl Inquiry Sub-Committee of the British Section of the International Committee for Bird Preservation had been established and in 1941 their report, 'Factors Affecting the General Status of Wild Geese and Wild Duck' was published. We have already made reference to their findings in respect of duck decoys at home and abroad but it is here we also find the first comprehensive investigation of punt gunning. The findings were made by C.T. Dalgety assisted by R.A. Coombs, H.A. Gilbert, H. Leyborne-Popham and T. Russell-Goddard. It is particularly interesting to note that at this time there were no less than 105 working punts but no more than 150 in England and Wales, with a further estimate of 20 in Scotland. Professional wildfowlers, in the strict sense of the term, had ceased to exist, although there were of course a number of paid wildfowling guides.

The full Report was to be the logical foundation on which further revision of the law might be based. However, by this time there were far more pressing issues. Britain went to war in September 1939. No doubt in places where fowling continued, ducks, geese and waders would have been a welcome addition to a wartime diet. In fact Rex Irvine, a Solway/Holy Island punt gunner received a petrol allowance to allow him to continue to go punting to help ease the food rationing crisis! Wildfowlers were amongst the troops who risked their lives defending their country. Sadly, many did not return, but those who were more fortunate and did, may have looked forward to a winter chasing ducks and geese.

Post war Labour promised new found prosperity but this was not always what wildfowlers found when they returned home. Coastal villages were becoming ever more popular with bird watchers and amongst them were a growing number of hobbyist-conservationists who were against shooting. The foreshore, once a remote area known only to the fishermen/fowlers had become the focus of those championing the cause of conservation. Suddenly wildfowling was on the 'back foot'. Labour pressed on with discussions surrounding 'The National Parks and Access to the

New Year, January 1909.
1. Mr. Thos. Waddington, Vice-President
2. Mr. Guy Thorne, Vice-President
3. Mr. Chas. F. Proctor, Chairman
4. Mr. T. Straker, Vice-Chairman
5. Mr. W. Lancaster, Hon. Treasurer
6. Mr. Arthur Waddington
7. Mr. Thos. B. Gower, Hon. Sec. for Ireland
8. Mr. Norman K. Duncan
9. Mr. Sydney H. Smith
10. Mr. W.A. Nicholson, Hon. Sec. for Scotland
11. Mr. Bernard Pye
12. Mr. Percey G. Timms
13. Mr. J. Barehard
14. Mr. J.C. Hepworth
15. Mr. W. Crowe

Countryside Act 1949' (1948 Hobhouse Committee) and the Huxley Committee (chaired by Dr. S. J. Huxley) was looking at the idea of creating coastal reserves which were certain to curtail some wildfowling. Adding to the situation, the Wild Birds' Advisory Committee was discussing draft proposals for a new Protection of Birds Bill and taking advice from the Wildfowl Inquiry Committee. Gone from the Committees were many of the old guard who had some sympathy for wildfowling. Stanley Duncan was now in his seventies; health problems and advancing years appear to have taken a toll on his resolve to defend every aspect of fowling. He desperately needed support to counter the growing criticism of the sport of wildfowling. Help was on hand, James W. Johnson a north Lincolnshire wildfowler serving on the WAGBI Executive Committee (affectionately named Judge Johnson owing to his reputation for fairness) took over Duncan's position on Wild Birds' Advisory Committee.

In May 1950 WAGBI representatives, led by Judge Johnson, were invited to attend the Wildfowl Inquiry Committee chaired by Sir Norman Kinnear, former President of the British Ornithologists' Union. Discussions focused on the reasons for an apparent decrease in wildfowl at home and across Europe. This meeting broke up acrimoniously, the Committee Members appearing to the wildfowlers to be short on facts and long on blame. Stalemate had been reached and it was not until September 1952 that a further meeting was arranged, this time with Colonel H.J. Cator, a wildfowler/conservationist, taking the Chair. Peter Scott had been very vocal about the behaviour of some wildfowlers and was now viewed with great suspicion. He attended the meeting welcoming the wildfowlers saying he was not against wildfowling and still spent a considerable amount of time fowling each winter. The aim of the Committee was to maintain stocks

James W. Johnson, known as Judge Johnson.

of wildfowl and, by so doing, this would enable wildfowlers to enjoy their sport with as few restrictions as possible. Achieving this would involve discussion and possible compromise on both sides. The meeting served to clear the air and members of the Wildfowl Inquiry Committee now respected the views of the WAGBI representatives. The meeting also served to alert WAGBI to many changes to the Protection of Birds Act that were in the pipeline.

Judge Johnson reported back to the WAGBI Executive that Committee recommendations had already been made to the Home Office, who were tasked with drafting the new Bill. He understood that the recommendations included an increase to the close season, a ban on Sunday shooting across all Councils and the placing of some restrictions on punt gunning and semi-automatic shotguns. There were additional proposals to reduce the number of species of ducks, geese and waders that could be shot. Wildfowling was on the verge of a major crisis at a time when WAGBI was at a low ebb in terms of membership support and finance. To the bird protection lobby new legislation seemed to be a "done deal". How wrong they would prove to be.

What happened next is quite remarkable. WAGBI, led by the then Chairman Mr Edward L. Parish MBE., M.B.O.U. (a wildfowler/puntgunner living in Esher, Surrey) ably assisted by Dr Geoffrey W. Storey, Honorary Secretary, mounted a major campaign motivating members to join forces and write to, and visit their M.P.s pointing out that wildfowling was a working man's sport followed by people of modest means and who appreciated their responsibility for wildlife and the countryside. In addition the sporting press rallied to the call to support the wildfowlers' cause.

Sixty years later on reviewing the correspondence that took place between Eddie Parish and Lady Tweedsmuir (whose responsibility it was to steer the Bill through the House of Commons) one is immediately struck by the integrity, sincerity, and honesty of the wildfowlers' case. They showed genuine support for much of the Bill but firm resistance to the tactics that were employed by the bird protectionist lobby who seemed intent on increasing the length of the closed season, invoking sweeping powers to create Bird Sanctuaries and give protection to brent geese. WAGBI was following the example set by Stanley Duncan. It was defending the right of the common man, but as always, prepared to adapt to change if, and only if, the case for change could be justified by proven facts.

By following this honest approach WAGBI gained the respect of Lady Tweedsmuir who was clearly impressed by the information passed to her by Eddie Parish, acting on behalf of the WAGBI Executive. Conversely the deluge of misinformation presented to the Wild Birds' Advisory Committee by the anti-shooting lobby was seen as unhelpful and in some respects even dishonest. The bird protectionist lobby showed their resentment by naming the new Act, 'A Wildfowlers' Charter.' Sometimes those against wildfowling 'whistle at the wrong time.' Wildfowlers are, and remain, a determined cohort.

The passage of the Protection of Birds Bill through both Houses of Parliament took many weeks and countless hours were devoted to steering the Bill to its eventual conclusion by late 1954.

Stanley Duncan's Legacy.

Stanley Duncan died on 30 August 1954. In December, that year, WAGBI honoured their founder by standing in silence at the Annual General Meeting hosted by the Hull and East Riding Wildfowlers' Association, his old punting partner Trevor Field, President, presiding over the solemn occasion.

In February WAGBI had a trade Stand at the Boat Show held at the Empire Hall Olympia. The exhibition included a fully equipped gunning punt and Colonel Hawker's gun was also on display. There is no record of how many new members were recruited but WAGBI was now clearly determined to move forward. In July 1958 the first Country Landowner's Association Game Fair was organised at Stetchworth. Thereafter, up until 2015, this annual event was to provide a showcase of the ongoing work of the Association, all of which has helped to promote membership growth.

In 'The Times' in October 1956, an unknown correspondent wrote, "there is no more quick and certain way to unite a group of enthusiasts in whatever activity, than to oppose them, or to hint that what they are doing is in some way socially undesirable." How right he was, WAGBI, an ailing Association in 1948 with annual income of less than £70, with only 300 members and a handful of affiliated clubs (which included Southport and District W.A, Morecambe Bay W.A , Blakeney & District W.A. and Frodsham & District W.A.) was, ten years later making arrangements to celebrate its Golden Jubilee. By 1958 the Association had the support of most wildfowlers. In fact many of today's wildfowling clubs were formed during the early 1950s as a response to the threats from proposed new legislation brought about by the 1954 Protection of Birds Act. By 1958 membership had grown and seventy seven clubs were listed as either affiliated or seeking affiliation. By March 1957 finance was on a much sounder footing and Lt. Commander John Anderton had been appointed to act as Honorary Secretary. The growth of the Association and

The WAGBI 1955 Boatshow exhibition

the work load created was such that John was soon to become the first paid staff member. He later became Director and led the association until his retirement in June 1988.

The vibrant British Association for Shooting and Conservation (BASC) that exists today owes its success to a dedicated group of wildfowlers who believed that shooting and conservation could go hand in hand. The transition period was overseen by two forceful Chairmen, namely John Ruxton and Bill Bailey, both of them were punt gunners. Not only did WAGBI defend the wildfowlers' rights but they showed their critics that they also had the conservation credentials to safeguard wildfowl and their habitat for future generations to enjoy. The wildfowler conservationist was born. Since that time the Association, with a change of name to BASC on 6 June 1984, has gone from strength to strength and now has around 150,000 members. Wildfowlers today have the assurance that the Association is better placed than ever before to ensure the future of traditional wildfowling.

John Anderton O.B.E.

The Peter Scott conundrum

Between the wars a new generation of fowlers began to emerge. Shore shooting for ducks and geese was the first attraction as there were relatively few restrictions to contend with on areas of coastal foreshore. In addition, the tradition of wildfowling attracted the adventurous, some of whom became fascinated by the age old sport of punt gunning. One such man was studying Natural Sciences at Cambridge in 1927 and found he could earn an income by selling paintings of wildfowl and waders that he observed out on the foreshore and marshland. That young man was Peter Scott. As a result of his wildfowling adventures he wrote two wonderfully illustrated books about his love of the sport of wildfowling. 'Morning Flight' 1935 was followed by 'Wild Chorus' in 1938. In each of these books Scott recounts factual stories, all written up from his wildfowling diaries. He shared with the reader red letter days and disappointments when shoulder gunning as well as exciting adventures experienced while punt gunning with his friends, Christopher Dalgety, Major Hulse, Michael Bratby, John Winter, Michael Dilke, and Johnny Rodick. Two of these friends were later to write classic wildfowling/punt gunning books of their own, Christopher Dalgety's book 'Wildfowling' in 1937 and Michael Bratby's 'Grey Goose' in 1939.

Peter Scott founded in 1947 the Severn Wildfowl Trust. Scott was Honorary Director and Michael Bratby was Honorary Secretary and James Robertson Justice, actor and punt gunner, was on the newly formed Council. All had their own punts and regularly went afloat. The development of the Trust and Peter Scott's career as a conservationist is legendary and for these he was later knighted.

Peter Scott and Christopher Dalgety (1907-1980) had met at Cambridge. They were closely involved with the work of the Wildfowl Inquiry Committee and saw any revision of the Protection of Birds' Act as an opportunity to scrutinise legislation affecting wildfowling and make what they regarded as sensible changes. Consulting the ordinary wildfowler was not high on their agenda. Scott wrote an article in "The Shooting Times" and voiced his opinion widely in other newspapers in what some saw as a rather tactless manner and by doing so upset many wildfowlers.

Scott's direct manner seemed to imply to many that he thought he knew best what was right for the sport and that he was becoming rather more critical of the behaviour of wildfowlers. This was of course to the delight of the bird protectionist lobby who now regarded Scott as their new ally.

It was Scott's overbearing influence on proceedings that upset wildfowlers; no one had shot more geese than him and he was fanatical about punt gunning, but here he was recommending a shorter shooting season, the protection of brent geese and non-shooting sanctuaries on their fowling grounds.

Scott maintained that brent geese numbers had declined dramatically. At a critical time during the Committee stage of the 'Protection of Birds' Bill in April 1954, Scott quoted figures given to him, in confidence, by Christopher Dalgety which shocked Lady Tweedsmuir, who was responsible for the Bill in the House of Commons. He alleged that 2000 brent geese were shot in six weeks in 1940 on the South coast by two punt gunners and two tons of brent were shot on the east coast. The evidence to support these figures was never forthcoming as Christopher Dalgety was sworn to secrecy and never divulged his source of information, despite being repeatedly challenged by the wildfowlers.

This letter appeared in 'The Shooting Times', July 16th 1954

> Sir, – We have followed with interest in The Shooting Times the story of killing 2,000 brent geese, and we have good reason to believe that we are the punt gunners involved in this mythical slaughter.
>
> We have been wildfowling on this coast for 40 years (and readers of The Shooting Times for over 30 years), and have never heard of such slaughter on the south coast.
>
> Now with 40 years' experience of punt-gunning, we do not believe anyone could kill 2,000 brent geese in six weeks. Our experience of numbers of wildfowl that can be killed agrees with the figures given in the letter you published from Mr. Parish.

Harold Pycroft

> During the hard winter of 1940, there were alot of brent in this district, the most we saw were about 2,000, and, having war-time permission to shoot on the harbour, and being asked to kill wildfowl for food., we, shooting together with our two punts, killed a quantity of geese. We have not killed so many before, nor have we done since, and no claim was ever made by us to have killed 2,000 geese. We did not keep any records and we are unable to give the exact number killed.
>
> A. V. G. Pycroft,
> H. Pycroft
> Chidham, Sussex

However, Scott's reputation as an expert on migratory wildfowl certainly influenced Members of the House during the debate. The damage was done and this was to lead to very bad relations between the Wildfowl Trust and WAGBI which took some years to heal.

Wildfowlers accepted the protection of brent geese on the basis that the ban would be reviewed after ten years. Mechanically propelled vehicles and boats were forbidden for the purpose of driving, taking and killing a wild bird. This was welcomed. The bore of a punt gun was restricted to 1¾ inches at the muzzle. The curlew was saved as a quarry species and agreement was reached to extend the close season to 1 September but the February wildfowling season on the foreshore, as we know it today, was saved. This is by no means a comprehensive summary of legislation introduced by the 1954 Act but it does serve to show the major restrictions that affected punt gunning.

Punt gunners learnt a salutary lesson that misinformation and emotional rhetoric was likely to be the greatest threat to their sport in the future. WAGBI was applauded for strenuously defending the foreshore wildfowlers' sport and this led to continued growth of membership and recognition that the Association deserved much more support for the work it was doing on behalf of all those who enjoyed shooting.

There followed a period of constructive dialogue and confidence-building meetings between WAGBI, The Nature Conservancy and The Wildfowl Trust. Each organisation grew to respect the others and new confidence led to greater cooperation. The common link was the recognition that the future conservation of wildfowl and waders in their habitat was the mutual interest of all three organisations.

When, in 1961, Scott wrote the Preface to the 'New Wildfowler' he showed real appreciation for the work that WAGBI was undertaking. Scott was no longer dictating to wildfowlers and although, by this time, he had given up shooting, he appreciated that the management of wildfowl shooting was in responsible hands. Under Doctor Jeffery Harrison's leadership, conservation had become a byword and some very good work was being done by wildfowling clubs, which of course continues to this day.

1963. Hunting methods under scrutiny from Europe

The International Wildfowl Research Bureau (IWRB) came into being following the demise of International Council for Bird Preservation in 1954. There was a general agrement that there was a need for future advice on the conservation and management of wildfowl in their habitat and this should be based on adequate and scientifically determined facts and not on hearsay.

At the first European meeting on wildfowl conservation, held at St Andrews in 1963, methods employed for hunting wildfowl were discussed at length. Punt gunning had been prohibited in Europe. (Germany prohibited punt gunning in 1884 and the Dutch followed in 1899) so it was not surprising that the policy of permitting punting in Britain and Ireland was questioned. It was Peter Scott who spoke with authority on the subject, highlighting the fact that few critics of punt gunning were honest enough to admit that they commented on and often condemned punt gunning without proper knowledge or experience. He no longer went punt gunning but certainly had experience of the sport. Whilst personally not now following this traditional aspect of wildfowling, he made it clear that he did not view punt gunning as a threat to the wildfowl population. He explained that punt gunning was a most adventurous and skilled form of wildfowling and, providing that it was pursued with moderation, there was no good reason why it should be discouraged and prohibited.* Support for this view was also given by Doctor Geoffrey Storey, a Council Member of the Wildfowl Trust and Vice-President of WAGBI. The Conference concluded that punt gunning was a dying sport and not responsible for any significant depletion of wildfowl stocks. It was wisely agreed that it would be allowed to die out naturally, as any attempt to curtail it might upset the harmonious relationship between all those interested in wildfowl conservation.

*Footnote: Writing in 1989 George Reiger, one of America's foremost wildfowlers wrote; "I met Peter Scott when he'd passed through Washington on a fund-raising tour on behalf of the World Wildlife Fund. I believe I annoyed him when, rather than show up with a copy of his autobiography 'The Eye of the Wind ', I brought Van Campen Heilners's 'A Book Of Duck Shooting' and asked Scott to autograph the page showing him about to go punt gunning. He knew the book well enough so that after regarding the page a moment and commenting that "those were good days," he turned back to the photograph of him touching up one of the profile decoys that Heilner had brought from America and remarked as he wrote his name and date," I'd rather be remembered this way."

1967. Protection of Birds Act

During the passage of the 1967 Bill wildfowling again came under very close scrutiny. Initially all went well and WAGBI did not oppose a proposal to ban the sale of geese or even new powers for the Secretary of State to curtail wildfowling during prolonged periods of severe weather. Punt gunning was discussed at the Committee stage but not in particularly controversial terms. Then, out of the blue it became apparent that Nicholas Ridley, Member of Parliament (MP) for Cirencester and Tewkesbury, was to put forward an eleventh hour Amendment to the Bill prohibiting the use of guns larger than 4 bore. Ridley focused his argument for this amendment on the belief that large bags of wigeon were being made on the Solway and at Holy Island by two punts and spoke of his shock when he heard of one shot of 360 wigeon. As discussions progressed it became apparent that his claim was without a shred of evidence and was totally wrong. Once again there was a confusion of thoughts that related to the true facts and it was only through the efforts of John Farr MP for Harborough (briefed by John Anderton at WAGBI) that resulted in the withdrawal of the amendment on 16 June 1967.

WAGBI's resolve was tested once more and John Anderton, assisted by Ted Conroy a Lancashire punt gunner, worked tirelessly for six weeks to establish the true facts. In recognition of the work John did to safeguard punting he was presented with a picture of grey geese painted by Noel Dudley.

This might have been the end of the Nicholas Ridley saga, but just before he retired as an MP, an interesting exchange of correspondence took place following a letter in the Daily Telegraph of 15 February 1992. At the time Nicholas Ridley was speaking out in the House during the debate related to fox hunting. He said, "I can think of a large number of entertainments which are not attractive to other people, but I defend to the utmost the right of those people to engage in those sports." The statement was spotted by Anthony McEntyre, a keen punt gunner, who wrote to Ridley questioning why he had effectively sought to ban punt gunning in 1967. He received the following reply:

Dear Mr McEntyre,

Thank you for your letter. I said in my speech anybody was entitled to pursue the sport of their choice provided it was not against the public interest.

In 1967 I tried to stop punt gunning because I thought two punts were taking too many ducks. The famous shot when 360 wigeon were killed in a gale by one punt shocked me deeply. What I sought to do was to restrict the calibre of the gun to restrict the number of ducks that could be killed at a shot.

However, I now think the punt gunners are not taking too many fowl. – leaving enough for other wildfowlers. It may thus now be in the public interest. But don't be too greedy in future.

Yours sincerely,

Nicholas Ridley

Anthony McEntyre

Peter Scott's influential intervention at the first IWRB Conference was fortuitous and John Anderton proved that WAGBI had the resolve to fight for punt gunners. However, a number of active punt gunners realised that there was now a pressing need to make sure they were well prepared for future questions about this traditional aspect of wildfowling. A fact sheet was compiled covering all aspects of punt gunning, together with a Code of Practice that set out a framework on which the sport was to be conducted.

Quite independently Keith 'Toby' Bromley made a documentary film in which James Robertson Justice and Laurence Thompson traced the history of punt gunning. They explained exactly what is involved when going afloat for a day on the Wash. 'The Puntgunners' is a brilliant film that has stood the test of time and stands as a tribute to three wildfowlers who are no longer with us.

A register of all active punt gunners is maintained to this day. The register serves as a record of the number of punts that go afloat each season, the estuaries punted and the annual bag returns of wildfowl shot together with the data related to the number of days afloat.

1981. Wildlife and Countryside Act

In April 1979 the EU Birds Directive effectively obligated the UK government to make amendments to existing UK bird protection, as it identified and sought to limit the number of species which could be shot or taken, as well as the means of taking them. It also restricted the trade in certain species and laid down general measures to improve the protection of habitats.

This new legislation brought about immediate pressure on EU member countries to amend their bird protection legislation. In 1979 the Conservative government issued a number of consultative papers in the run up to repeal and re-enact the proposed amendments the Protection of Birds Acts 1954 to 1967 and the Conservation of Creatures and Wild plants Act 1975. The proposed changes were the UK's direct response to the 1979 EU document, the Directive on "The Conservation of Wild Birds."

Inevitably changes in the law impacted on the sport of wildfowling. Revised legislation introduced a ban on the shooting of sea ducks, whimbrel, bar-tailed godwit, grey plover, jack snipe, garganey teal and bean geese. The sale of gadwall and goldeneye was banned. Semi-automatic shotguns were restricted to three shots. A bitter battle was fought by WAGBI over the curlew and the redshank but protection was granted. An acceptable and workable criteria to restrict some forms of shooting during prolonged periods of severe weather was also to eventually evolve.

But there were successes too. Through sensible well-reasoned discussion the February foreshore wildfowling season was preserved, Sunday shooting would be allowed to continue where permitted and despite strongly voiced opinions about moonlight shooting and punt gunning, they remain permissible to this day.

The passing of the Wildlife and Countryside Act in 1981 fulfilled the UK's obligation to respect the demands of the EU's Birds and Habitats Directives. To date, and even after a number of EU countries have been taken to the European Court of Justice, there are still countries that have not fulfilled their obligations under these Directives.

Wildfowlers have always recognised that their quarry species are largely migratory. Managing and understanding the movement of wildfowl has been helped by ringing records, ably assisted by wildfowlers who ringed and released many mallard and then fed back information when birds were recovered. But essentially it was now recognised that more attention had to be devoted to the preservation of wetland habitat which increasingly was seen to be the long term focus of any new conservation initiatives. This objective was a shared international responsibility and thankfully there is, today, greater unity than ever before, brought about by sensible discussions between all interested parties.

Back in the 1960s the much respected voice of Dr. Jeffrey Harrison OBE WAGBI's Honorary Director of Conservation and Research made a remarkable contribution to the early formative discussions. Jeffrey, a keen wildfowler, showed that wildfowlers and naturalists could and should work together: in fact, he showed it was essential that they did so. We cannot put a precise date on the emergence of the wildfowler/conservationist; the seeds were certainly sown by Stanley Duncan but since then they have flourished and strengthened right up to the present day.

The Ramsar Convention (1975) is the international treaty that provides the framework for national action and international cooperation for the conservation and wise use of wetlands and their resources. At the time of writing there are 160 Ramsar sites in the UK mainland and many allow responsible wildfowling to be enjoyed by members of the current 146 BASC affiliated wildfowling clubs and associations that exist today. Club members assist with the management of the inner saltmarsh over an estimated 760 linear kilometres of coastline which equates to 120,000 hectares of land under the management influence of wildfowling club members. Almost without exception, the coastal sites are designated as Sites of Special Scientific Interest (SSSIs) as they originally formed the building blocks for site based nature conservation. Wildfowlers now have responsibility for the wellbeing of the resource they have the privilege to exploit. Surely there is no better way of ensuring that habitat and all bird species safeguarded for the future. Many sites are now also covered by a higher level conservation status known as Special Protection Areas (SPAs), classified very often for rare plants as well as vulnerable birds.

The ever growing complexity of the conservation of wetlands has brought about new responsibilities for the wildfowler. BASC clubs and associations now seek formal consent for their sport which is classified as a "potentially damaging operation". With the help of BASC, all across the country Site Management Plans are drawn up and submitted to the controlling authority. In most instances the management plans are comprehensive and are endorsed by all consulted interested parties. The positive outcome is that at last there is endorsement that wildfowling, carried out responsibly, is compatible with wider nature conservation interests.

The historical importance of WAGBI

16

THE 1990 LINDISFARNE NATIONAL NATURE RESERVE INQUIRY

"Observation is the hard path:

Speculation the easy one"

Anon

With the growth of Special Protection Areas (often exceptional wildfowl and wader habitat) came a corresponding number of local regulating authorities. In the case of Lindisfarne National Nature Reserve (formative discussions in 1953 resulted in the reserve designation on 15 September 1964) the Nature Conservancy Council (NCC) were to have the overall responsibility for managing the reserve and employing wardens who would be actively engaged in supervising and managing the shooting area during the wildfowling season. The Northumberland and Durham Wildfowlers' Association was formed on 18 September 1953 under the chairmanship of Dr Frank Stabler, a Surgeon Commander R.N.V.R., noted gynaecologist and a respected punt gunner who later became Chairman of the Lindisfarne Wildfowl panel. It is interesting that the inaugural meeting of the Club was attended by eighty sportsmen who recognised that their collective voice would be more likely to preserve wildfowling for local fowlers with the coming of the Reserve (reported in Morpeth Herald and Reporter September 1953).

By 1990 statistical analysis of data related to over wintering numbers of wigeon was causing alarm. In 1983 the maximum wigeon count was 30,000 and looking back, Captain L. Scott Briggs is recorded in the Berwick Advertiser 26 December 1935 counting up to 30,000 wigeon. This was at the time when punt gunning was at its height on the Fenham Flats. By 1989 the maximum count was 17,000 and the strength of what English Nature (formerly NCC) called the 'wigeon visit' was declining whilst there was no obvious increase in the strength of the 'brent visit', which otherwise might have accounted for the falling wigeon numbers. The report concluded, "we suspect that additional factors are influencing the decline in wigeon and this merits further investigation."

There had always been a suspicion that punt gunning was a major disturbance factor resulting in the movement of fowl on an estuary and this opinion had even been expressed by foreshore shoulder gunners. At Lindisfarne punt gunning was now managed by the issue of permits

Frank Stabler (left.) and Dr. Peter Basham had a punt shed on the mainland side of the Holy Island Slakes. Here they launched their punt using rollers to reach a series of shuttered sluices in a narrow channel the width of a gunning punt. This ingenious engineering feat enabled them to reach the punting grounds where the wigeon and brent geese gathered in great numbers around the Foulwork Burn.

with only eight named punt gun permits being issued, four to Holy Island punt gunners and four to visiting punt gunners. All punt visits had always been closely monitored by the wildfowling wardens. It came as a surprise that two Nature Conservancy Officers, D.J. Townshend and D.A. O'Conner, wrote a report predicting that restrictions on punt gunning would lead to an increase in peak wigeon numbers and result in an increase in the length of time that they remained on the Reserve. Shore shooters pricked up their ears and one wonders if the 'divide and rule' Trick' was being played.

In 1990 English Nature approved a five year scientific study of punt gunning at Holy Island. From the 1990/91 season new regulations were placed on all punts with punting allowed only on three days a week and on no consecutive days. These were draconian measures when one considers the level of punt gunning at the turn of the century when Abel Chapman and Payne-Gallwey were punting. At that time punts would have been afloat daily, weather and tides permitting. The islanders would have valued greatly the food source and meagre funds they would have secured from the sale of fowl. The new controls were put in place for five years after which two scientists, Steve and Tracey Percival from the Ecology Centre at the University on Sunderland, would report on their findings.

Punt gunning was being called into question and this time it was on a National Nature Reserve. There was no doubt that the results would be watched most closely by other reserve managers.

The report, "Analysis of Punt gunning Data: Possible Effects of Disturbance on Wintering Waterfowl at Lindisfarne NNR" was published in April 1995. The report concluded that there was no evidence from bird counts that punt gunning was having a major deleterious effect on numbers of any of the species investigated and secondly there was no increase in wigeon or brent numbers following restrictions on punting activity. Numbers remained fairly stable at pre 1990/91 levels.

Once again confusion of thought and personal opinion had threatened punt gunning. Fortunately the scientists who undertook the analysis were professional, but those that were to read and interpret the report were less so. Mr. Martyn Howat (later to become Chairman of BASC, 2012-2014) the North East Regional Officer for English Nature, had the authority to halve the punting area and much reduce the shoulder gunning area despite an earlier agreement that the wildfowlers had negotiated with Colonel Crossman (Holy Island Slakes landowner) that Budle Bay would be the agreed non-shooting sanctuary area. Howat justified his action on the basis that to resist the increase in reserve area might have resulted in a total ban on all wildfowling and the EU Habitats Directive legislated that a larger reserve area was needed by law. Today, weekend punting is not allowed and a booking system is in operation to avoid more than one punt going afloat in the much reduced shooting area. However, the long tradition of punt gunning, first introduced on the Slakes, by a Norfolk gunner in 1829, still continues, albeit on a much reduced scale.

Ralph Wilson

Writing in 1891 Abel Chapman, naturalist and regular visitor to the island, noted that when shooting disturbed wigeon and brent on the Holy Island slakes they sought the sanctuary of open sea beyond Guile Point, in Burrows Hollow and the Skate Roads. It was here that they fed unmolested on the vast amounts of Zostera that had been torn from the Slakes by wind and tide only to float out on the twice daily ebbing tide. This floating Zostera provided rich pickings for the wigeon and brent geese.

Today the large non-shooting area encompasses not only Budle Bay but has been extended to include the Zostera beds in the Foulwork Burn and the Stinking Goat enabling the wigeon and brent to stay on the feeding grounds throughout the day and night. The natural flight of wigeon, on a rising tide, moving in from the open sea where they have been feeding and roosting is virtually lost, so too is all the floating Zostera as the wigeon no longer take advantage of this valuable food supply.

Chapman also noted that brent geese seldom arrived before January (an article about Selby Allison's daughter's wedding to Mr Tom Yetts in the Berwick Advertiser 17 January 1908 confirmed that brent geese had just arrived) whereas today they arrive in September together with an increasing number of dark-bellied brent geese and they peak in October. This coincides with the maximum wigeon numbers resulting in battalions of fowl all competing for the same feed. Increasingly it is observed that wigeon at Holy Island are foraging inland, which suggests pressure on their traditional feeding grounds.

The late Ralph Wilson M.B.E., a Holy Islander and former Harbour Master had been a punt gunner/wildfowler all his life and he had always closely observed wildfowl at Holy Island. His opinion was that with the introduction of a non-shooting zone on the southern Slakes, wigeon would move away sooner rather than later due to feeding pressure. He reasoned that the non-shooting area would initially prove attractive as an undisturbed feeding area but, as the bird numbers increased, wigeon would move on and there would be an increase and faster turnover of birds using the site. This seems to be the case and to this day there remains little information about the turnover of wigeon numbers and their eventual pattern of distribution. It appears high time that a better understanding is gained on how long wigeon remain on the Slakes. Satellite tagging and tracking of birds opens up new opportunities to really understand the movement of wildfowl. Counting ducks can be very misleading as it is impossible to tell if you are counting the same fowl every day, especially when the count is carried out on a site which is a known major staging point before further dispersal (confirmed by declining wigeon numbers which often follow the November full moon). The policy introduced by English Nature does not appear to have achieved their objective but it has much reduced the opportunity for wildfowling. It also leaves many questions either unanswered or ignored. When and where, for instance, do the light bellied brent geese disperse and why are the increasing number of dark bellied brent geese seldom referred to in the wildfowl counts? So many questions and few clear answers.

It begs the question, whether the southern Slakes will ever be re-opened for fowling or is Natural England (as English Nature is now known), really only wanting to restrict still further the long tradition of wildfowling at Holy Island?

The observations of 'the common man' are too often dismissed as unscientific anecdotal evidence. 'Common man' offers only what he regards as common sense and seeks no reward. If he is wrong, he will stand corrected and becomes a little wiser. He asks only that he should not be ignored. There is a strong case for much wider recognition that practical experience, in conjunction with scientific evidence, is valuable. The ultimate aim must be to distinguish between evidence and belief.

To achieve this may mean commissioning more independent research so we must all support BASC as it continues to represent our sport. With sound funding, independent research can go a long way in eliminating all forms of bias that has always been a threat to our sport.

Punt shed, Holy Island

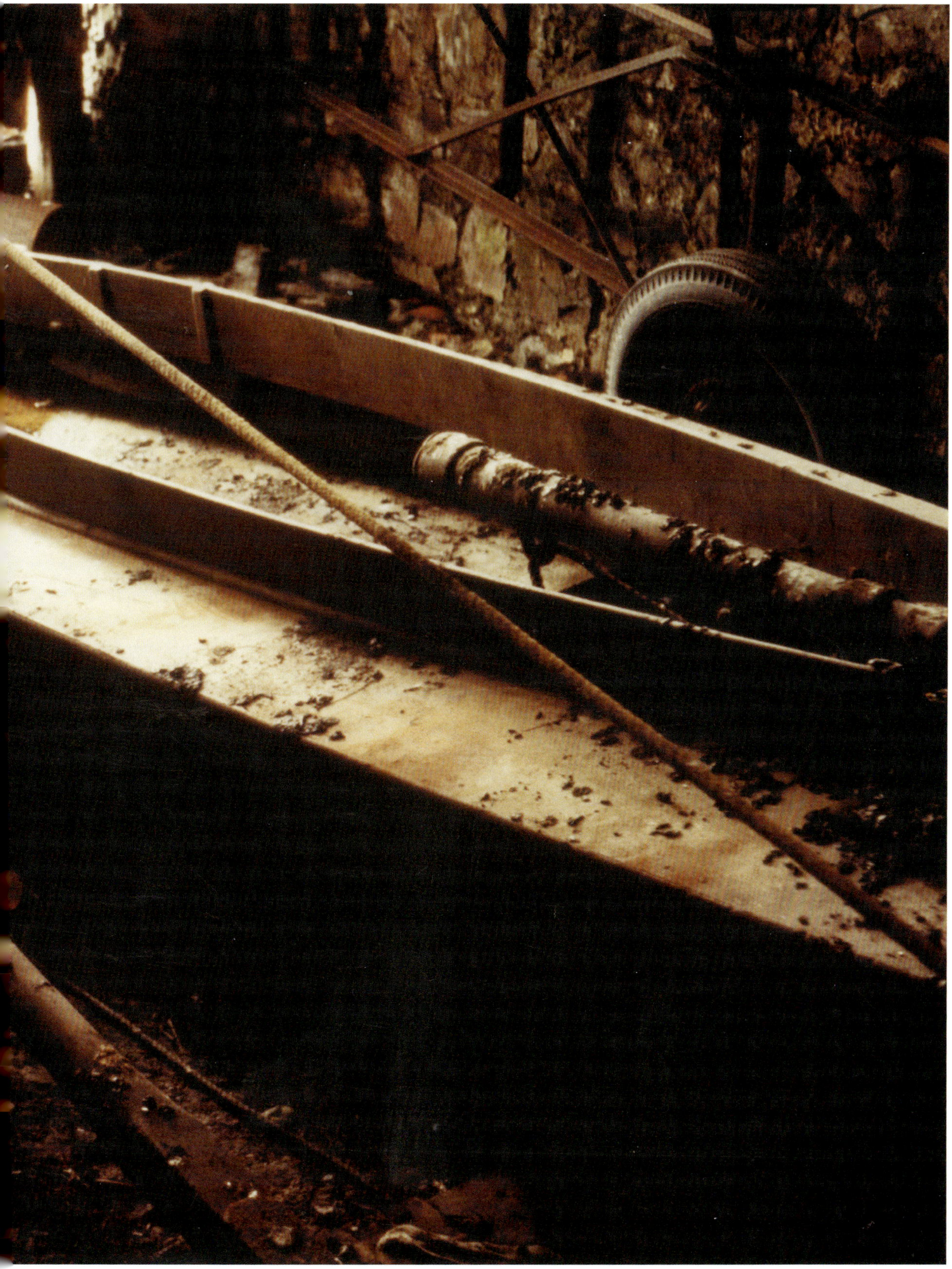

Christopher Dalgety's account of an early wildfowling adventure with Peter Scott in December 1929

"The watching so often stayed the shot:

That at last it grew to be a habit."

Richard Jefferies

Whilst at Cambridge University Peter Scott became friends with Christopher Dalgety, (Scott graduated in History of Art in 1931). Dalgety was studying Forestry but it was his expertise and knowledge of birds that led him to be appointed in 1927 as the expedition ornithologist to Edgeoya (Edge Island), located south east of the Svalbard archipelago in the Arctic Ocean, midway between continental Norway and the North Pole. This was the first of five Arctic expeditions which he embarked upon between 1927 and 1934.

Major C.W.W. Hulse 'The Expert'

Both Scott and Dalgety shared a passion for wildfowling but in 1929 their knowledge of punt gunning was in its formative years. It so happened that they met Major C.W.W. Hulse at Creetown whilst on a wildfowling holiday in Scotland. Scott was invited to go afloat with Hulse and thenceforth Scott and Dalgety always referred to Hulse as 'The Expert' in their wildfowling books.

Following discussion with Hulse, Scott and Dalgety commissioned Mr Mathie, a boat builder from Cambridge to build for them a sea-going punt. She was built to Hulse's design incorporating all the modifications that he had considered since his own punt was built. They named their new punt '*Kazarka*'* and she was launched on 11 December 1929. Scott later wrote that she was probably the best double punt in the country at the time.

*Kazarka is the Russian name for small black geese

The following adventure took place on the Wash shortly after the punt was launched. The account is quoted directly from Christopher Dalgety's wildfowling diary and the accompanying sketches were given to Christopher by Peter Scott.

Monday 23 December 1929

"Peter and I had breakfast and left Lynn at about 6 o'clock. There was a fairly thick fog and sou 'easterly wind. We took the car right down to the sea wall at Horseshoe Hole Farm. As I turned the car at the end of the inner bank the headlights came onto a short eared owl which got up from the fence post and flew over the bank to the saltings. It was getting late before we left the car so we hurried along the drove and out towards the 2 poles at the saltings edge. All the geese were already on the saltings and could be heard further to the east of us. We were apparently too late. After waiting a very short while we decided we were in a useless position and had better move. As Peter wanted to stalk the geese up the creeks, I left him and went back via the drove to the North Pole. As I walked around the corner I put up about nine geese which I might have stalked behind the bank if I had seen them earlier.

From here I could hear the geese on both sides of me and apparently in scattered parties, so I went straight out on the saltings and waited. After a short wait a muffled shot sounded from Peter's direction and all the geese to the west of me went out onto the mud. After waiting a bit longer, I fired a shot in the bottom of my creek, hoping that it would put up the geese to the east of me and that they might come over me. The only response was from two Redshanks. Not a sound from the geese. I now decided to shoot over the top and see what that would do. An unfortunate dunlin then came by and I shot it. Still no response from the geese, so I concluded they had made a move in silence. As there were now no geese close to me it was all right to shoot at anything, so I had three or four shots at redshank without hitting any. I was returning to the pole when I saw two Curlew and ran and jumped into a creek. The leading Curlew had half seen me in the fog and came to satisfy his curiosity. I let him come right over, so as to get his companion in range too, and then shot him. But the other was too quick for me. As I reloaded and shut the gun a Mallard jumped from the creek into which the Curlew had fallen and I got that. Peter now appeared on the scene to see what all the shooting was about. We were returning together when some geese came in and settled about two hundred yards away. I started down the creek to stalk them as Peter said it was my turn, and he had already stalked to within shot of one lot and only got a bag full of feathers. As I went down the creek more and more geese came in, so Peter ran up behind me and we tried to do a racing stalk so as to get under the flight line. Then, most of the geese got nervous and made off eastwards. There was still a small lot on the ground and others could be heard coming up through the fog. One lot circled and was coming straight for me when they swerved off with sudden loud frmph-frmphs of their wings and squeaks of consternation. I was certain they had not seen me and was puzzling over their action when a Peregrine came into my range of vision. She must have passed right underneath the geese. We seemed to have already wasted enough time by messing about in the creeks, so jumped out and ran to intercept the rest of the flight. This of course put up the few geese that were left.

Peter and I were running together again. Some geese could be heard coming and quite close. We dropped into the nearest creek. It was a bad one for cover. The geese turned off at the last moment and we both got the same bird which was the only one within shot.

I could hear the geese on the saltings down by the Windmill, so I started off to put them up so as to make them go out hungry and thus come in again before long. A Curlew got out of a creek close to me and I got him. The sound of the shot put the geese out. I sat down to wait and listen. The old rusty Windmill was screeching away at regular intervals. Carts were rumbling, and men calling to horses in the fields. Hoodie Crows and gulls calling all round.

A Harrier flapped along by the sea wall, but too far away to make sure of the species. Some goose noise came up from the West, and soon the geese appeared through the fast thinning fog. They came straight over, but too high, and I did not get one. The fog was clearing so fast that it appeared possible for us to take the punt out, and so I started back to Peter. He had got another goose and two mallard. Quickly returning to the car. We exchanged our shore shooting outfits for the punting gear and made for the creek, where the punt was. We were late for the tide, probably too late, and had to hustle along.

We found that the punt had drifted broadside at high water and was supported at bow and stern across the creek! However, no damage was done and we soon had her in the water and started down the creek. Three minutes later we could not have got out at all, and as it was we had to get out and push her over some shallows. As soon as we were in deep water we stopped to bail out, load the gun and clean up and stow everything properly. Large flocks of knots were following the ebb tide and congregating in the mouth of our creek. There were also a few ducks about, but no big lots.

At last we were all ready and everything in its proper place. There were so many knots near the mouth of our creek that we decided to go to them. We got much too close and Peter could not bring the punt to bear on them at their thickest, then they began moving and eventually I had to

Scotsmans Sled 23rd Dec 1929 about 4.45pm. Original sketch by Peter Scott.

take a shot where they were not very thick. Peter had told me about having to aim high and I shot right over them. We picked up 39 knots and 2 dunlins and only lost about 2 birds wounded. We now went on down a shallow lead to the west of Scotsman's Sled and anchored to wait for the tide to drop. While waiting there were a number of geese flying about. One came over and I gave him both barrels of the cripple stopper but hit him too far back. Finding it was 3 o'clock we began pulling down and sighted a nice bunch of wigeon. We set to them and Peter made me take a very long shot which I would not have pulled at. We got 6 birds and lost one which got up and flew away. We now went on down to try and go round and up the Nene. This was a ridiculous and suicidal thing to attempt with a rising wind and falling night and ground that neither of us knew. When we sighted the light at the northern end of the Inner Westmark Knock, we put up the sail and went along the edge of the mud. The sea was breaking on our stern and sides, and every now and then coming in.

We were running fast before the wind and every now and then she buried her nose and was in imminent danger of burrowing. The Wreck and the Westmark Knock were lost in the dusk behind us and still no land in front. Then came a sandbar which we had to pull over. Then we thought it was safe to make across the wind, and put down our lee-boards. Now it was very slow work and Peter's time was taken up with the steering oar and sheet while I had to sit on the patent lee-boards to keep them in place so that neither of us could bail. Conversation was flagging a bit and our jokes fell rather flat. At last, the mud showed in front of us and a bit later, the leeboards struck bottom and then we went on to the lee shore with the waves breaking into us. We got the sail down and stowed alongside the gun which we had to take in long before in order to lighten the bow and turn up the bow wash streaks (sic). Then I held her head to wind while Peter bailed out. When she was fairly empty again, we began pushing her along the mud edge towards the South and East again. We soon gave it up and got out and waded and man-handled her along. Practically every wave broke into her and an occasional one came in green whenever we had to round a point. We soon found that the best way was for me to tow her

Nene channel 23rd Dec 1929 about 5.10pm. Original sketch by Peter Scott.

Nene channel 23rd Dec 1929. About 6.p.m.

while Peter sat in the stern and bailed. Thus we went on for what seemed an age, but it was vastly better than the passive inactivity of sailing and we at least had the mud close to us and were in shallow water. If the worst came to the worst we could now make everything as fast as possible, anchor her to the big gun and make our way across the mud, though we did not know if there was a channel the other side though we thought we were across the channel of the Nene and that the Holbeach Marsh saltings were about 1½ miles across the mud and that any channel we met would be wadeable. The apparent proximity of motor headlights also made us think we were near the Holbeach side. At last we saw mud on the other side of us and thought we were in a channel. But no luck, it was a shallow bay and we could hear the sea breaking upwind of the newly found mud. I left Peter in the punt to signal me with the torch while I went over the mud to the West to find out what I could of what lay beyond. After about half a mile of soft going I did not want to go further in case the rain got any thicker and I lost Peter, so I returned with no news. Peter now went out to the East and reported a good channel and a sea which was not so bad as what we had come through. He thought we could reach it by going a short way back and following round the edge of a point. After walking across, to have a look for myself, we towed her round and began going up the channel which appeared to be fairly deep. After a short way the bank shelved down so abruptly that the water was too deep to tow from the upwind side of the boat and handling her from the downwind side was impossible as the continual lurching nearly knocked one off one's feet. The only thing was to get in again and row. The tide had turned now and our greatest danger lay in the possibility of it rising quick enough to make a large expanse of open water upwind of us.

Now we were rowing along under a 4 foot mud bank with the wind on our port bow. The wind prevented fast rowing and the necessity of continuous bailing made it worse. Once we got too far around and a large green wave caught me on the shoulder and came in the whole length of the starboard side. Two or three of them would have sunk us, but luckily we caught no more big ones. At last out of the darkness loomed a pole with a bush on top and we were almost certain we were in the Nene. I began wondering how cold it would be if we had to climb a pole and lash ourselves on! Now there were poles every 200 yards or so and the sea was improving the

Nene channel 23rd Dec 1929 about 6pm. Original sketch by Peter Scott.

whole time. The far bank came in view, and we were too thankful to say much about it. After another long stretch we came to rocks and knew we were in the last straight and were safe and "mirabile dictu" exactly where we wanted to be. At last the West Lighthouse showed against the sky in front of us. Then we found a big creek and anchored and made all fast, took the birds and left the rest of the gear and clambered ashore. The Tinbys had gone to bed at the lighthouse, but Mr Tinby stuck his head out of the window and said there was no telephone nearer than Sutton Bridge, so the only thing for it was to walk the 3½ miles there. It had been 9.15, when we got ashore and as I had forgotten the sandwiches we had not eaten since 6 am breakfast except for 2 or 3 aged and mature sandwiches which had been left in the punt. We tried the first lighted farm we came to for either telephone or nourishment. They gave us some separated milk which was one of the best drinks I have ever had. They said there was no telephone near and no chance of a lift on the road. After walking about half a mile a car came up behind us. When we stopped it and asked for a lift we were surprised to find it was the same farmer who had said there was no chance of getting a lift. There was only him, his wife and small child in a large 4 seater, so I think they might have offered us a lift first instead of rather hesitating before giving us one when they knew exactly our plight. However, we were saved about three miles walk and hired a car and got a welcome meal at the Globe on our return."

We know that Scott continued wildfowling into the 1950s regularly visiting Wexford Slobs in Southern Ireland as a guest of his good friend Lt.-Colonel Bill Bradish whilst Christopher Dalgety records in his diary punting adventures up until 1949.

Footnote 1: Over the next decade Christopher Dalgety had a further six punts built along the same design. Peter Scott and Michael Bratby commissioned Banhams of Cambridge to build their punt which was called 'Grey Goose' (1937) (note there is mention of another punt called 'Grey Goose' but this was an old punt left on the inland Washes). To read of the adventures they had together in 'Grey Goose' you must turn to the pages of Michael Bratby's book of the same name published in 1939. Today 'Grey Goose' and two of Dalgety's punts still survive, one of which is still occasionally afloat each winter, surely a fitting tribute to her construction and the men that built her

Footnote 2: Peter Scott, writing his account of this day afloat in his book, 'Morning Flight' wrote, "I never remember to have been so frightened for so prolonged a period."

Christopher Dalgety(left) and Peter Scott afloat together in 'Kazarka' with the 2 inch Patstone puntgun

18

THE STORY OF IRISH TOM AND ADVENTURES WITH JAMES ROBERTSON JUSTICE

"Part ranging in figure wedge their way,

Intelligent of season, and set forth

Their airy caravan: high over seas

Flying, and overland, with mutual wing

Easing their flight."

Anon

Payne-Gallwey writing in 1882 in his book 'Fowler in Ireland' tells us about a large muzzle-loading punt gun. He wrote that the barrel measured 12 ft. 11 inches, weighing 375 lbs, and made from Siemen's steel (normalised) with an overall length of 13ft. 8¾ inches. The bore was a little over 2 inches; handling a charge of ¾ lbs of powder and 3¾ lbs shot. The gun was credited as being made by Messrs. Allport of Cork, for Mr Graves of Limerick, who punted Tralee Bay. Thereafter, from 1877 to 1892, we speculate that the gun may have passed to Captain Vincent who punted the Fergus Estuary with his puntsman 'Sambo' (Peter Considine) using the yacht *'Scoter'* as their wildfowling headquarters. Little is known about the punt gun's history until it re-emerged in 1933.

Captain Gilbert S. Bradish of Strandfield, Wexford was a colourful Irish character and avid punt gunner, an ex-champion weightlifter and Indian tea planter. He was well known for his skill with punt and gun and regularly corresponded with Stanley Duncan. In July 1933 Bradish advertised several muzzle-loading punt guns on behalf of the widow of a deceased wildfowler. One gun, known as, 'Irish Tom' appealed to Duncan. He saw the opportunity to convert this gun into a breech-loader and, in so doing, to create the largest breech-loading punt gun ever made. So he decided to purchase the gun.

In an article in the 'Shooting Times and British Sportsman' written by Duncan in December 1934 he describes the process. W.W. Greener is credited with making the gun barrel from Whitworth steel. At this time large bore barrels could only be made by the Birmingham trade but often ended up credited to a different maker, in this case being Messrs. Allport.

Trevor Field loading Irish Tom

With the assistance of Mr H. G. Goade, whom Duncan describes as a north country wildfowler and Ordinance Engineer, the following work was undertaken; "Separating the stock from the barrel we proceeded to cut two inches off the breech end. The breech end was then 'capped'. The cap extension not only shrouded the original breech end of the barrel by a screw length of 5 inches but also facilitated the provision to carry a screw breech plug (Whitworth pitch thread 3 inches long) and swivel head being immediately behind the inserted cartridge."

Once the conversion was completed the gun was sent to the Birmingham Proof House and on Duncan's instruction proofed for 50oz of shot. Amusingly Colonel Charles Playfair, the Proof Master, contacted Duncan suggesting that there was, he suspected, a mistake in Duncan's request as he had never proofed a gun for such a huge load. Duncan assured him that there was no mistake and the gun passed proof with flying colours. Henceforth the gun was referred to as Irish Tom and was put into service on the Humber estuary. Duncan had to build a specially designed punt, 24ft 6 inches long with a 4ft 6 inches beam to withstand the recoil. Writing in 1933, he goes into great detail about how this was achieved. .

Duncan took great pride in the conversion of Irish Tom to a breech-loader but sometime after the work was completed, he decided to sell this massive gun. The reason for this may be that the conversion work had cost him in excess of £200, a sum which he freely admits he could ill afford on top of the price he had paid for the gun. The gun first went on display at Cyril Duncan's Hull gun shop. Cyril then instructed his manager Mr A. Karsh to pack and dispatch the gun to London where it went on display at Thomas Bland's gun shop 4/5, King Street, Strand. Bill Caseley, who worked in the gunroom at Bland's recalled dropping it on his foot! The next person to use the

'Irish Tom' outside Cyril Duncan's Hull gun shop (bottom gun in rack)

gun was Major Ronald Armstrong-Jones K.R.R.C. who wrote an article headed, 'A Wildfowler on Leave' in the 'Shooting Times and British Sportsman' in March 1943. In his article he recounts how he and his puntsman Evan Lloyd almost made a magnificent shot but at the crucial moment 'Big Bertha,' as he nicknamed it, suffered a misfire and they did not get a feather. In disgust he must have returned the gun to Blands and never completed the purchase of the gun from Stanley Duncan. We suspect he only had the punt gun on loan for a short time in order to assess its worth.

Bill Caseley later told another story, "some actor feller came into the shop and negotiated for its purchase." This turned out to be James Robertson Justice.

In 1954 Robertson Justice bought a house called 'Spinningdale' situated just outside the village of Spinningdale overlooking the Dornoch Firth in the north east of Scotland. The house, built in 1920, was formerly owned by Mr A. M. Chance (1870 – 1954) a wealthy gentleman with a lifelong interest in punt gunning. Records show that during 33 years of punting on the Dornoch Firth Chance recorded a total of 409 shots averaging 12.4 birds per shot, most of which were wigeon, teal and mallard. Punt sheds had been built below the house and James kept a number of outfits, both singles and doubles for use whenever he stayed at Spinningdale. At some time 'Irish Tom' must have been brought to the northern firths.

'Spinningdale' was James' much loved home up until 1970 when he was forced to sell it. He departed leaving his punts in the punt shed and presumably the gun was left at the boatyard for safe keeping. In the same year that James died, (1975) John Richards, then working for WAGBI, received a telephone call from Mr and Mrs Grant owners of the famous Grants of Dornoch butcher business. They had recently bought 'Spinningdale' and were anxious that the wildfowling equipment should find a suitable home at WAGBI Headquarters. As a result

James's widow (his 2nd wife), Irina von Meyendorff (known as The Baroness) gifted three punts and one muzzle-loading punt gun to the Association. Irish Tom was not found at this time. John Richards and Anthony McEntyre then travelled to Spinningdale and returned with the punts and gun in March 1977 and placed them in WAGBI's care.

Major John Rippingall was responsible for ensuring that Irish Tom was eventually restored to its former glory having found the derelict, neglected barrel of the gun in the Inverness boatyard. With the approval of 'The Baroness', the gun was delivered to Allan Owens, a skilled engineer living in Essex. He replaced a large section of the barrel which had been removed by the Inverness boatyard. Allen, to his great credit then built a complete action, breech plug and cartridge case, and Jim Spalding stocked the action. The work was completed early in 1983. Today the gun can be seen on display at BASC's headquarters in the Duke of Westminster Hall, below Julian Novorol's painting 'Wigeon over the Black Hut' the birth place of WAGBI and a place where Duncan went afloat with the gun.

James Robertson Justice's story

To gain a real understanding of the life of James Robertson Justice we must refer the reader to the book 'What's the Bleeding Time?' written by James Hogg. It is a highly amusing biography of the renowned actor who found true happiness in his pursuits of falconry, fishing, wildfowling and in particular his love of punt gunning. We have already mentioned the part he played in the making of the film 'The Puntgunner' with his lifelong friend Toby Bromley. It is noteworthy that this larger than life figure was invited by Peter Scott to become a founder Council member of the Severn Wildfowl Trust in 1946. His formative wildfowling years were spent chasing geese and ducks around Wigtown Bay and there are many legendary tales told of his exploits in the immediate post-war period, often using his single Holland and Holland sidelock, hammerless 4 bore (made in 1897) which he called 'Whispering Jack Baritone'. James handled this monster apparently with the ease of a four-ten and regularly dispatched grey geese at great range. In later years the gun passed to Laurence Thompson along with other wildfowling equipment including Toby's punt and Holland and Holland punt gun, formerly owned by Christopher Dalgety. Laurence acted as puntsman and friend to Toby Bromley who had inherited the punts and guns when he married Irina von Meyendorff shortly after James died.

James also claimed that it was he who first suggested to Peter Scott that they could use the Schermuly Pistol Rocket Apparatus for rocket netting geese.

James Robertson Justice

At the time the apparatus was used for life saving exercises at sea. He was always full of innovative ideas and it was in 1947 that he and Peter Scott tried out the apparatus on the grassy field in Sussex which was the proofing ground of Messrs Schermuly Brothers Pistol Rocket Works based at Newdigate. Subsequently they went on together to catch and ring many Icelandic pinkfooted geese which ultimately led to a better understanding of the migration and breeding habits of this and many other species of geese.

James' fowling HQ at the Bull hotel

In January 1953, James was 45 years old. He had long since established his wildfowling headquarters at The Bull Hotel, Long Sutton where the landlady, known to all wildfowlers as Mrs Mitchell (daughter of Mrs. Stuart former proprietress of 'The Bull' for 32 years), administered an informal welcome to fowlers who regularly visited her hotel. By "informal" we mean 'a help yourself bar' based entirely on honesty ("write it in the book") and a kitchen that worked on a self-help basis but always a wonderful, 'full house' cooked breakfast on return from flight. Hotel heating largely depended on open coal fires which you were expected to keep well stoked. Bedrooms were always cold and bathrooms freezing. On one occasion a visiting wildfowler struggled down stairs for morning flight with evidence of a severe head wound. His pals thought he had fallen on the stairs on the way to bed (not unusual) but he announced that he had just slipped on the ice in the bathroom! Despite somewhat Bohemian conditions, it was a great hotel and the whole regime was based entirely on respect for the grand lady of the house and many happy times were spent in this charming old coaching inn. All guests were expected to behave like gentlemen. (At least until Mrs Glenndenning Mitchell, to give her full title, had retired to her bedchamber). This was the hotel where James loved to stay and where he was held in great affection.

1953, James' account of his holiday on the Wash, afloat with Irish Tom

"On the 30 January 1947 Johnny Drysdale and I picked up 70 wigeon to a shot with my small pound and a quarter Greener punt gun, and I very much doubt if, considering the size of the gun, I shall ever have a better shot. About the same time, however I managed to acquire, from Stanley Duncan, his immense Whitworth, screw breech 3lb gun, with a barrel 13ft long and weighing upwards of 330lbs. It was quite obvious that the 19ft 6 inch punt was not man enough to carry this enormous piece of artillery about, and I had resigned myself to having a new punt built when Peter (Scott) told me I might collect his old 24 footer '*Kazarka*' which had been lying on the Nene bank since 1939 and was, not to put too fine a point on it, in a pretty poor condition. It was towed to Cambridge where Messrs. Banham faithfully carried out all the repairs necessary, to my own set of drawings, and there perforce until 1952, she remained.

For four years, owing to a variety of reasons, I was unable to go afloat in a punt. During two winters I was festering under a dreary Californian sun, while dreaming of the mudflats and tideways of the great estuaries at home, so that it was not until January this year (1953) that I found myself able once more to arrange a punting expedition.

The punt, in the meantime, had been brought down to Hampshire, from Cambridge, only for us to discover, on arrival, that she had split in half a dozen places just above the chine. The copper sheeting was removed, we wopped on a liberal application of plastic caulking, and resheathed with new 8 inch wide copper. She was then put in the Test for the summer to take up, and appeared to make but very little water, not enough to matter anyway. Luckily, a gang of Hampshire County Council people were building a new bridge just up the road when the time came to load the punt on to the trailer, and wet as she was, it took the combined efforts of six middling powerful men to lift her.

I arrived at our Headquarters without any untoward incidents to find that a spring shackle on the trailer had broken and that the spring had bored a hole in the side of the punt. This was repaired by cutting out the hole, fitting a new bit of wood, covering and caulking with a thick dose of Bostick, and resheathing with a wider piece of copper, which thank Heavens I had had the sense to bring with me.

All this took a day or two, and the first week we spent doing a little desultory flighting at the geese, duck and indeed pigeons, which a friendly farmer wished destroyed. We needed some food for the hawks anyway and the tides were wrong for punting, so that no time was wasted. During the day we flew the hawks two or three times, Geoffrey's goshawk killing three rabbits and a pheasant on the new enclosure and his Cooper's hawk a couple of moorhens in excellent style. Unfortunately, my peregrine seemed disinclined to do any work, though she did have a smack at a carrion crow on one occasion.

In the meantime, we had acquired the services of Jim Rowson and his motor boat, so that for the first time for years we could look forward to punting in reasonable comfort and indeed a hot meal in the middle of the estuary. On Saturday, just a week after we arrived, the tides served and we were all ready to go afloat when Jim rang up to say that he had magneto trouble, and that he would be unable to start until Sunday. This was a blow, but Geoffrey improved the not so shining hour of the morning flight by getting himself a pink-footed goose. Three of us went to the evening flight where we were edified by some, 'Milford snobs and tit-poppers' shooting at geese at least three hundred yards up. This is what comes of so called 'sporting journalists' writing about 'the high goose of my life.' Anyhow, the resulting communication would have scorched a donkey's rudder. And I hope they blushed a little on their return. The fog was very thick, and though we heard numberless mallard, wigeon and geese none of us had a shot.

On Sunday morning we launched the punt with difficulty and put to sea, having stowed the gear and got the big gun aboard some days previously . I should point out that, in accordance with Mr Duncan's advice, I had sawn 2ft 6 inches off the barrel of the big gun which made the whole thing much handier.

Half past four is a horrible time to set out on a January morning. But five o'clock found us snug in the cabin of the motor boat leaving Jim to do the driving. Dilly (James' first wife) who was aboard as cook and motorised cripple stopper produced a cup of coffee, and we settled down to a rather cramped cat-nap for about an hour until it should be light enough to shoot and we should reach our fowling ground. The fog was pretty thick and we did in fact miss the end of the channel in the gloom. As soon as it was light we found ourselves in 'The Eye', but visibility was so bad that it was almost impossible to see fowl before they saw us.

Eventually, though a small shot presented itself, and as we had never tried the new gun, I decided to take a chance. Geoffrey Ivor-Jones had been warned not to get his snout too near the stock of the gun, but in his excitement forgot the instruction and gave himself a bloody nose when she went off. It was an easy stalk to about a score of birds, of which we picked up fifteen, all stone dead. The gun appeared to be satisfactory, at least with a light load of 2 lbs we had fired, and we returned to the motor boat for breakfast. The fog clamped down again and the tide was flowing fairly fast by the time we were ready, cleaned up and stowed. Most of the mud banks were now covered so we set off homewards. By this time the embankment of the home river had enough water over it to float the punt across and there was a good shot on the shore of 'The Lagoon' only a short distance above us. The motor boat was put about, and we steamed about a quarter of a mile against the tide before casting off. I knelt down to paddle across the channel of the lagoon, and arrived on the shore about 500 yards below the fowl, still unsuspecting. We then set to them in the approved style, and reaching long range, before I realised that they were mostly geese. At this moment, they began to walk somewhat rapidly away from us but along the shore. At about 70 yards for the punt was travelling quite fast by now, with the tide and my effort combined I told G to pull if a feather showed. He did, but shot underneath the birds, and we picked up a mere four. Probably a good thing, for I have no ambition to shoot many more geese. Curiously enough on an estuary reserved almost entirely to pinkfeet, the four were all whitefronts. And so home along with fifteen wigeon and four geese aboard. As we shot the bridge below our mooring we all spat for luck, a ritual which was religiously carried out, morning and evening for the rest of the trip.

Next morning we were well down the channel before a shot presented itself; but what a shot. There were three lots of wigeon, the first about a quarter of a mile long by twenty yards thick, solid jam packed wigeon, about half a mile below them about 300 birds, between which it would not have been possible to insert a feather, and then another huge bunch of several thousand birds. The tide was still ebbing when we cast off, with the intention of going upwind and tide to the really big bunch. As we approached the shore though, a shrimper came past astern and waved us down. I thought he might have seen the upper bunch shift, so turned downwind, (always a mistake) and set up to the 300 birds. G by this time, had butterflies in his stomach, and was also a little apprehensive of being hit in the face once more by the stock of the big gun. He had acquired a split lip from his second shot, at the geese and we had shortened the breeching rope by the 18 inches it had stretched with the first two bangs. The 300 lifted at long range, but settled with a lower bunch and at 40 yards G pulled the lanyard. When the pillar of cloud cleared G was already ashore with the shoulder gun while I took the punt straight down below the swimmers and rounded them up. I knew we had a goodish shot but was delighted when we counted up to find that we had 53 wigeon aboard - my third best shot. This seemed enough to shoot for a day and we did not wish to ruin this very promising ground by overshooting. So as the tide had now turned we decided to call it a day. There was a German freighter lying off, waiting for water to take her cargo of timber up river and we went alongside to attempt a little barter. I hailed her in my best Hamburger Platt, "Wollen's mal einije wilds enten gegwn 'ns Flshchs Schapps tauschen?" Sure enough, down came a boarding ladder, and Dilly and I clambered aboard to be most hospitably entertained in the wardroom. They had a crew of 18 so we left them a dozen and a half of wigeon in exchange for a litre bottle of Swedish Aquavit, which I dislike, but which was much appreciated by the others!

On Tuesday morning H.R.H.* arrived from Sandringham at 0600 and we put to sea at 0645. There was a good shot where the big bunch had been the day before but the wind was stronger and against my better judgement I decided to have a try for them downwind. Toby had arrived with his punt the previous evening and it seemed a reasonable opportunity to try a double punting act. Toby had the inshore position with Geoffrey as his gunner, whilst H.R.H. and I took the deeper water offshore. As it happened the scheme was a failure, for at long range Toby went aground and we were left to proceed alone. H.R.H. was quite dry in the gunner's position forrard but there was a bit of a lop on and the water was coming in astern over the wash strakes soaking me fore and aft. As so often happens in punting downwind the birds smelt us and started to roll, the near ones rising and settling two hundred yards further on. This went on for about a mile and a half until we really got into range but by this time the birds were not sitting nearly so tight and I would not in normal circumstances have taken a shot. However, I was very keen for the gunner to get at least one shot on his first attempt and at about forty yards I told him to pull when a feather showed. We picked up 14, all dead but must have disturbed ten thousand wigeon in doing so. Not a very good thing to do. Then back to the motor boat for breakfast, after which there was quite a good shot on the shore where we had had the 53 the day before. This time we went upwind to them and had no trouble at all in getting within easy range. It would not have been a very big shot in any circumstances but the birds were so late in jumping that most of the shot went above their heads and we picked up a mere 21. In a way a good thing because it

* His Royal Highness The Duke of Edinburgh

Toby Bromley and James Robertson Justice in one punt, H.R.H. Duke of Edinburgh and Geoffrey Ivor-Jones in Peter Scott's punt '*Kazarka*'

doesn't do to get a really big shot on one's first day out with the big gun. It all appears too easy and it is difficult for the gunner to appreciate the years of practice, sweat and discomfort which go to handling a punt with adequate skill in a tideway.

Another shot showed in the Eye and Toby again with G. as his gunner set up to them whilst we sat aboard the motor boat eating cold pheasant and having a grandstand view. The birds looked big and from their charming there were certainly some mallard amongst them but Geoffrey was too late with the shot and the total score was only 2 mallard. It should have been at least 20. This finished the day.

Wednesday the fog was thicker than ever but we tried the two punts once more. As it happened I never set foot in mine for there was only about half an hour in which it was possible to see more than one hundred yards and the birds always saw us first. Toby and Geoffrey had one stalk but it was ruined at the last minute by a shrimp boat which put up their quarry when they were about seventy yards off. Geoffrey fired, but again the shot was too late and the score only 1 brent. After this we cruised around for some time exploring another channel but for some unknown reason, possibly not unconnected with the fog, the birds were nearly all on the water. There was one line of mixed wigeon and brent which extended for fully two miles and packed really tight and including some dozen or so Berwick swans but they were unapproachable and we went home.

Thursday, our last day saw only the four of us afloat, Jim, Dilly, Geoffrey and myself and as soon as we reached the channel mouth we saw a good shot. As usual though by the time we had lashed up and stowed and loaded the big gun they had started to shift. There was a big ebb and the stalk was a difficult one across about a quarter of a mile of mussel scaups, interspersed with old stakes and whatnot. Again we were going to the birds downwind and this time they sat perfectly and I was most disappointed when the gun went off to see that we had made a very poor shot. Geoffrey had shot over them shooting from the rest which is a very bad thing and we picked up a measly 7 when it should have been 47. The motor boat was in the channel on the other side of the middle ground which was dry at each end. I thought we could get across below in the middle, but we failed by thirty yards and there we were high and dry until the flood should float us, in about an hour and a half. I had no rollers aboard and it was quite impossible to shift the punt on the sand, so we had to sit it out. A dozen or so of large mussels did well as an appetiser for breakfast after which we settled down to a game of cricket with a paddle for a bat, the rubber sponge used for mopping out the punt for a ball and setting poles for wickets.

Score, when tide stopped play.

	R.	W.
Mr G. Ivan Jones' XI	3	3
Mr J.R. Justice's XI	2	3 (in play)

No bowling analysis was kept.

As soon as we got aboard the motor boat, we saw a really good shot up 'The Eye'. The bacon and eggs disappeared with the speed of nuclear fission and we were ashore and setting to fowl within fifteen minutes. Upwind, and a good flood to push us along made the stalk fairly easy and we were within long range and alongside the outliers before a bird shifted. Then the outliers joined the main body and I told G to shoot at will. We were not more than forty yards from the nearest birds when they started to rise. Geoffrey still didn't pull until I exhorted him at the top of my voice; "Pull, pull for the **** love of Christ." This time he took them just right. Dilly with the landing net picked up 21 while we had 55 wigeon and a couple of teal, total 78, my best shot to date. A very satisfying trip back to our home creek then the labour of loading the punt on to the trailer again but thanks to some kind friends there was enough manpower to make the chore not too strenuous.

Over the journey home some 200 miles with a twenty four foot punt towing, a dense fog for about 80 miles and in the dark, I would prefer to draw a veil. Dilly isn't speaking to me yet!"

James' drama on the Wash a year later. January 1954

Almost to the day a year later James, accompanied by Geoffrey, was once again punting the Welland Channel in the company of Jim Rowson's motorboat. They were out in the Wash down at Cut End and having left the motor boat around midday they were stalking some wigeon when a gale of wind with gusts of wind between 80 and 90mph caught them unaware. The motor boat would have been a safe haven but it was too far away and they quickly found themselves in difficulty taking on water and being swamped by the heavy sea. As fortune had it there was a Shrimper, manned by 'China' Ingham of Fosdyke close at hand. He was able to get James and Geoffrey on board and lashed the punt and gun to his stern block. The gale was so severe that the heavy punt, carrying James's gun plus £450 of on board equipment, shipped too much water and sank in 30 feet of water. Meanwhile, Jim Rowson and Geoffrey's wife were also in trouble as the motor boat was holed and they abandoned ship, walking 5 miles across the marshes in extremely difficult conditions, falling into many creeks on the way. It was Mrs Ivan Jones' first time accompanying her husband on a punting trip: history does not reveal if she ever went again! The punt and gun were recovered the next day but James took to his bed at The Bull with a severe attack of influenza. Mrs Mitchell, proprietor of 'The Bull' always maintained that James never had any money to pay his bill, but to secure his debt he left his guns with Mrs Mitchell until he claimed them again when, as he put it "his ship came in."

James was to die penniless on 2 July 1975, but what a wonderful life he led. All puntgunners must be thankful for his contribution to 'The Puntgunners' film. It is a lasting legacy to his love of the sport and was one of the very last films he was involved in making with his friend Toby Bromley, along with two other outstanding films, The Falcon Gentle and The Chalk-Stream Trout. The standard of filming and the content achieved in the punt gunning film and the hawking documentary were adjudged by the British Film Institute to be of sufficiently high quality to warrant permanent preservation, with the master films consequently stored in the National Film Archive. James would have been immensely proud of that achievement.

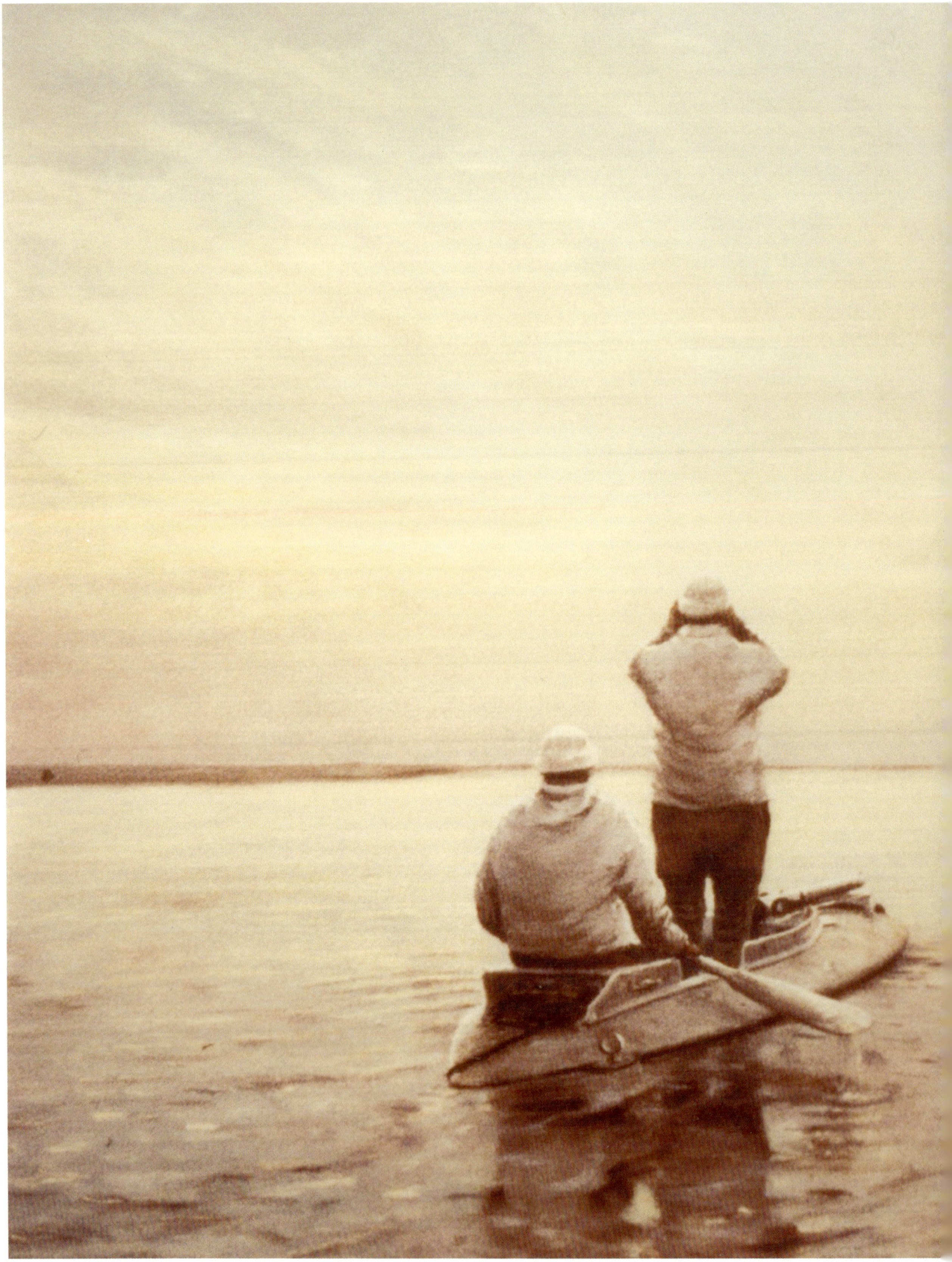

THE STORY OF IRISH TOM AND ADVENTURES WITH JAMES ROBERTSON JUSTICE

19

Julian Novorol recounts the story of a day afloat on the East Coast that brings 'double trouble'

When the long Tale, renewed when last they met,

Is splic'd anew, and is unfinished yet.

George Crabbe 1754-1832

Whenever Julian and I meet we inevitably reflect on the adventures we have had together. Those adventures span a period of more than thirty years so we thought we would add just one of our own stories to our book.

We greet each new wildfowling season with great anticipation, discussion and excitement. No two days afloat are ever the same and because we live in different parts of the country getting together has becomes a special occasion which we both look forward to each year. Here is one story told by Julian; it takes place on his home punting grounds

John Richards.

Leaving the 4x4 we set out from the seawall an hour before dawn, following a route along the narrow boardwalk across the saltings, to the jetty, where we pull the dinghy to the steps using the endless line. She is our ferry to the gunning punt moored close by in the deep water channel. We load the dinghy with all the items essential for a day afloat including binoculars, food, shoulder guns, the breech of the double Holland and Holland, 'Gallwey' punt gun plus plugs and cartridges. A few strokes on the oars and we reach the punt, climbing aboard the cover is rolled up. The plastic cover is thickly encrusted with frost and fingers tingle and ache as the cover is stowed and put into the dinghy. Everything has its allotted place in a gunning punt and once sorted we leave the dinghy astern attached to the punt's mooring and we set off down the creek taking advantage of a strong ebb tide.

Spirits are high, there is a stiff breeze from the southeast and a prolonged hard frost has resulted in much of the inland fresh water remaining frozen. Displaced wildfowl and waders would now be frequenting the intertidal marsh increasing our chance of a shot.

It is still dark as I pull hard on the oars and John paddles astern guiding the punt down the winding creek. A pale blue glow along the eastern horizon heralds the first signs of dawn. Conversation is minimal; we absorb the atmosphere of our surroundings, breathing in the crisp fresh air which holds a definite tang of the sea. The only sounds are the rhythmic knock as the oars are worked in their rowlocks and the swish of water caused by the blades of the oars and the paddle as we make our passage. The wind carries the occasional sound of alarmed waders but the marsh has yet to come alive with the coming dawn. We round a sweeping bend and hear a new sound; seals are slipping down the steep mud banks and splashing into the tide. It is still too dark to see them but soon some start to surface astern of the punt. They are inquisitive by nature and more and more appear in the reflection of the eastern light. Suddenly one surfaces within a yard of us and immediately flings itself sideways vanishing in the wake left by the punt.

We have now travelled a mile or more from the mooring and are fast approaching the mouth of our home creek where the confluence occurs with the main channel. It is here that we hold up to assess the prevailing conditions; should we go east or west? It is essential to sense the wind now that we have left the shelter of the home creek. This morning the wind is coming from the direction of the dawn and instinctively we know that this will be the best direction for us to head.

Looking to the west it is still too dark to see clearly; we know that there will be ducks along the channel sides but experience suggests that downwind stalks are seldom successful and with the lightening sky behind us a successful stalk almost impossible. As we glass westward we hear the soft rolling call of brent geese travelling over the tide. Now their calls are answered by more brents opposite, on the south side of the channel. There is just sufficient light to make them out scattered along the tide edge. The light is now improving and glassing east we make out a darker line of birds. The tide edge where they are sat and their appearance suggest that they are probably ducks. It is a place on the estuary that we know ducks favour and everything now suggests that they may offer the chance of an upwind stalk.

The time has come to discuss tactics; a welcome coffee and an excited conversation follows. We conclude that we must cross the open water channel but, in so doing, position the punt so as not to disturb the brents that are clearly not far from the ducks. In no time we are across the broad expanse of water and pull in west of the geese. With the coming of daylight and the sunrise it is time to pause again, listen to the brents that are now calling more loudly and watch the movement of waders that fill the air.

While we wait we see several packs of wigeon and teal pass high overhead heading seawards but our birds to the east hold their position. The prospects of obtaining a shot are improving so we decide to load the double gun. After attaching the breech I manoeuvre on my knees over the punt foredeck to cover the puntgun muzzle with a thin piece of grey plastic to ensure that no water enters the muzzles. One wave might otherwise wash water into the bores and if this reached the cartridges this could lead to a misfire.

The sun is slowly rising and sits like a blood red disc on the horizon. It gives light to our day but as every wildfowler will know this is the time when it feels as if the temperature has dropped and it is bitterly cold. A time now for more coffee before pushing along to a point where we can view the tide edge more clearly. The brent, numbering perhaps two hundred, are well beyond the point and undisturbed by us but they have begun to walk up the mud towards the saltings. One small lot now lifts from the tide edge and flies low over the saltings, they then circle, setting their wings and landing in dead ground. After a bitterly cold night the geese are keen to feed on the saltings that appear to be relatively frost free. The movement of geese now triggers off a response from the remaining geese ahead of us. Up they get and follow the flight line to where the first geese alighted. But not all are gone. Between the punt and the ducks we can now clearly see three asleep at the edge of the tideline.

The air is cold and the atmosphere hazy due to the stiff easterly wind. The duck appear well placed and through the glasses we can now see that they are mainly teal with wigeon intermixed among their ranks. They are no more than half a mile from us and appear to have no outliers which so often spoil a stalk. We have only the three brent to pass so decide it is time to attempt a stalk. Hopefully they will move without alarming the duck.

Before we set off John takes the bailer and washes water over the decks to melt any remaining frost. The wet deck will reflect the colour of the sky and help to hide the low profile of the punt. All is ready and we lay flat, John behind the gun and I am in the stern ready to commence the stalk. It is then that we hear a distant boat engine coming faintly on the wind. Our hearts sink as a boat slowly emerges from the haze. A grey shape coming from the Walton Channel but unmistakably making its way towards us. I recognise it as the oyster boat and his destination we know to be astern of us in Kirby Creek. He must pass the duck but he has given them a wide berth and they appear undisturbed. We hold our breath, he is past them. Then suddenly they lift as one, circle and alight back on the mud. To our dismay they are well away from the tide edge and are now well out of range.

As the working boat passes the oysterman steps from his wheelhouse and gives us a cheery wave. We respond likewise, he is a friend and a fellow wildfowler, as were his father and his grandfather. Generations of punt gunners were brought up in his family and he will be well aware that he may have spoilt our chance of a good shot but in the same way we understand he has to tend the oyster beds to make a living.

The noise of the boat engine fades into the distance and we can now do nothing but wait in the hope that the ducks will return to the tide edge. Searching with our glasses we see a small group of mallard on the edge of a channel where it is unusual to see ducks and not far from them a pair of gadwall. We assume these ducks have been frozen out from their regular inland haunts. They are strangers on our shore unaccustomed to estuary life. They walk about uneasily and protest noisily about their new surroundings. Further inland a few golden plover are on the move, their plaintive cry filling the air as they swoop down and rise again before finding a place to alight.

The sun is now well up and feels warm on our faces. However, the chill air from the easterly wind penetrates even the thickest of coats. We must be patient, the continual movement of birds, mainly waders keep us alert, but small packs of brent are hunting the inner marsh probably brought about by the turning of the tide. Over the saltings we spot a large pack of birds flying low and fast twisting and turning as they follow the line of the main creek that runs through that part of the marsh. We recognise them instantly as teal. Our spirits are lifted as the pack heads our way turning into the wind and alighting on the water a quarter of a mile to the east. We watch them not knowing if they will stay or rise and pitch again. These birds seem settled and quickly make their way, one after another, to the shore line. Soon they appear to us as a thick black line, perfect for an upwind stalk from the position we now hold.

All feelings of cold and discomfort are forgotten. Our patience has been rewarded and before us there appears to be a grand chance. John checks every inch of the shoreline between us and the ducks. In the excitement we had not noticed that the three brent had departed; even the wind appeared to be on our side, increasing just enough to provide a little chop on the water to help give cover to the 24 foot gunning punt as we make our approach to the teal. The once blood red sunrise is now subdued and increased cloud cover obscures what little sun there is. We lay flat in the punt and now merge into the grey surroundings. Our excitement mounts and at two hundred yards the gun is cocked as the slightest sound or movement may alert the fowl; I am using the three foot setting pole concentrating on as little perceivable movement as possible, much of the time my hand and the pole are completely submerged but always in contact with the soft mud beneath the punt to hold her line.

At one hundred and fifty yards not a bird has moved but we know that from now on these wild birds will be a challenging stalk. Their survival is dependent on awareness to the slightest danger. Our hearts sink as we hear the alarm calls of redshank flying low and fast towards our position. This immediately triggers alarm amongst some wigeon in the saltings that we were unaware of. A small group head for the open water where they find safety. Our teal now have their heads up and characteristically some walk up the mud slope to see what caused the wigeon to flush.

While all this is happening we 'hold up' waiting for the danger to pass. Our teal settle down but are no longer in a dense group. But all is not lost and we prepare to push a little closer. The reason for the unease amongst the birds now becomes apparent. A marsh harrier is working the edge of the salting causing continued unrest and alarm. We can do nothing but watch as the harrier changes course and heads across the channel but now well to the east of our chance of a shot. In so doing more wigeon are flushed together with a good number of waders. Bird movement everywhere now. Once again, to our dismay, many fly towards our position dropping in on either end of the teal. We now have a glorious close up of thirty godwits between us and the teal and a dozen avocets beyond. All we can do is hope the waders will go. Twenty long cold minutes later nothing has changed except the flowing tide has now herded the teal up into an even tighter group. We watch as gradually the water reaches the top of the sloping mud bank and now the teal are being washed off their feet and spreading out on the broad front of the tide as it flows forward over the flat mud. The tide travelling fast now triggers the waders to commence feeding, running and walking over the mud chased by the oncoming tide.

We know we have lost any chance of a shot. Without disturbing the birds I gradually turn the punt and pole quietly away, the gun is uncocked and once we are a safe distance from the feeding birds we sit up in the punt. The adventure this morning had brought us very close to success but we have been there many times before and the excitement had been intense. If a shot was the only reason that we go punt gunning we would have given it up many years ago. We agree it is probably the least important part of punt gunning and it is the memories forged on the many blank days that are often the focus of later discussion.

Julian and John with punt and double gun

With the wind at our back we set the sail to ease our passage back to our mooring. We speed along, water curling away from the prow of the punt. An occasional wave rolls up the foredeck and I ease the sail sheet to prevent the punt from plunging. The sail is exhilarating , our spirits are high and we have had a great morning. With luck there will be another chance to get on terms with the teal if the weather holds for the next day or so. As we cross the channel three long tailed duck come flying by low over the water. They turn and do a complete circuit round the punt, we imagine this is out of curiosity. It is an enchanting encounter with these beautiful seaducks as they are a rare visitor along this coast.

We now enter our home creek and soon we are amongst the seals again. Fifty or sixty are hauled up on the mud. They are undisturbed by our presence only bothering to lift their heads and look inquisitively at us. We soon leave them behind and with the running tide our mooring is quickly in sight again. Our day is done, the covered punt is back on her mooring and we ferry the equipment back to the jetty and onwards via the boardwalk to the vehicle. At last we are out of the cold wind; we sit for a moment reflecting on a great day afloat. We drain the last of the coffee from the thermos flask but the prospect of a stronger drink has greater appeal. We head for home.

There are always a surprising number of tasks to be undertaken after a day afloat, dealing with wet clothing, cleaning guns and binoculars, oiling the breech which inevitably will have been covered by salt spray. That done, we sit, with the dogs round us, in front of a log fire discussing the many compelling elements of punt gunning. Little has changed since Hawker's time; wildlife legislation has ensured that technical innovation will never interfere with tradition. No quarry pursued by puntgunners is threatened. Our wildfowling club is well run. Much of the ground where we have been on this day is owned by the club and is included in the boundaries of the Hamford Water National Nature Reserve. Natural England are our partners in management and recognise that a sustainable level of wildfowling can be maintained.

The log fire crackles and we reflect what might have been . There will be other opportunities. The amber nectar looks inviting and we raise our glasses toasting ' Saltwater, Webbed Feet and Blackpowder'. Memories last forever.

❦ 20 ❧

Conclusion

"With fiery burst,

The unexpected death invades the flock;

Tumbling they lie, and beat the flashing waves,

Whilst those remoter from the fatal range.

Of the swift shot, mount up on vigorous wing,

And wake the sleeping echoes as they fly."

Anon

Few punts now go afloat each winter. For the gunners who man them, their motivation is likely to be a determination to experience the excitement of punt gunning written about by famous authors of classic wildfowling books. Perhaps, it is the spirit of adventure which still attracts this small number of devotees? Stripped of literary glamour, punt gunning is arduous; it is often uncomfortable and can be physically demanding. Its reward in terms of the bag is surprisingly small; a red letter day might happen once in a lifetime and only if you stick at it.

Punts that are used today follow the traditional design that Colonel Hawker wrote about over 150 years ago and punt gunners must learn to handle these frail craft sometimes miles out on a remote estuary. This inevitably means participants must have an intuitive understanding of the sea and the influence of the tides in the harshest of winter weather conditions. Historically the professional wildfowler found a single handed punt more useful, but nowadays most amateurs use double punts. In a double handed punt the day becomes a shared experience, each relies on the other and inevitably you learn a great deal about your companion. If an enduring relationship develops, although at times it will be severely tested, a strong friendship is likely to grow, which will last a lifetime.

Conclusion

The truly compelling element of punt gunning is to be found far out on remote estuaries where the gunning punt takes its occupants. It allows the fowlers to merge with the magical landscape of marshland, mudflats and creeks where wildfowl, waders and seabirds feed and roost far from some distant shoreline. It is here, with the scent of the tideway, that you are able to observe and listen at close quarters to birds of the estuaries in their natural surroundings.

Wildfowlers have for centuries hunted truly wild birds and long may this tradition continue. Today a network of countrywide wildfowling clubs and associations, with membership drawn from a broad section of the community, help to ensure that the habitat, which is essential for wildfowl and wader survival, continues to be managed in a responsible and sustainable way.

The End

Bibliography

Batley, Desmond. *A Goose in Galloway.* GC Books, Wigtown, 2011.

Begbie, Eric. (Editor). *New Wildfowler: Third Edition.* Stanley Paul, London, 1989.

Benham, Harvey. *Down Tops'l: The Story of the East Coast sailing barges.* Harrap, London, 1951.

Benham, Harvey. *Last Stronghold of Sail: The story of Essex sailing smacks, coasters and barges.* Harrap, London, 1948.

Bishop, Billy. *Cley Marsh and its birds.* Boydell Press, Woodbridge, 1983.

Bratby, Michael. *Grey Goose.* Geoffrey Bles, London, 1939.

Booth, E.T. *Rough Notes on Birds Observed During 25 years Shooting and Collecting in the British Islands.* R.H. Porter, London, 1881.

Chapman, Abel. *Bird-Life of the Borders.* Gurney & Jackson, London. 1889.

Chapman, Abel. *First Lessons in the Art of Wildfowling.* Horace Cox, London, 1896.

Christy, Robert Miller. *The Birds of Essex.* Edmund Durrant, London, 1890.

Clement, Lewis. *Shooting, Yachting, and Sea-Fishing Trips: At home and on the Continent, by "Wildfowler," "Snapshot."* Chapman & Hall, London, 1877.

Clement, Lewis. *Shooting Adventures, Canine Lore and Sea-Fishing Trips, by "Wildfowler," "Snapshot."* Chapman & Hall, London, 1879.

Clement, Lewis. *Modern Wildfowling, by "Wildfowler" of "The Field."* Horace Cox, London, 1880.

Clement, Lewis. *Public Shooting Quarters: being a descriptive list of localities where wildfowl & other shooting can be obtained, by "Wildfowler" of "The Field."* Horace Cox, London, 1881.

Collins, John and Dodds, James. *River Colne Shipbuilders: A portrait of shipbuilding 1786-1988.* Jardine Press, Wivenhoe. 2009.

Dallas, Donald. *Holland and Holland - The 'Royal Gunmaker': The complete history.* Quiller, Shrewsbury, (2003) 2014 2nd edition.

Dalgety, Christopher T. *Wildfowling.* The Sportsman's Library series, Philip Allan, London, 1937.

De Visme Shaw, L.H. *Wild-Fowl.* Fur, Feather & Fin series, Longmans, Green & Co., London, 1905.

Downing, Graham. *A Sporting Century: The history of the British Association for Shooting and Conservation.* Quiller, Shrewsbury, 2007.

Duncan, Stanley; and Thorne, Guy. *The Complete Wildfowler (Ashore and Afloat).* Grant Richards Ltd, London, 1911, and Herbert Jenkins, London, 1950 revised edition.

Folkard, Henry Coleman. *The Wild-Fowler: A treatise on ancient and modern wild-fowling, Historical and Practical.* Piper, Stephenson & Spence, London, 1859.

Folkard, Henry Coleman. *The Sailing Boat: A treatise on English and foreign boats and yachts, etc.* Longmans, Green & Co. London, (1853) 1870 4th edition.

Greener, W.W. *The Gun and its Development.* Cassell, Petter, Galpin & Co., London, 1881.

Halliday, W. *The Book of Migratory Birds: met with on Holy Island and the Northumbrian coast, to which is added descriptive accounts of wildfowling on the mud flats, with notes on the general history of this district.* John Ouseley Ltd., London, 1909.

Harrison, Jeffrey G. *A Wealth of Wildfowl.* Andre Deutsch, London, 1967.

Harrison, Jeffrey G. *The Wildfowl of the Elbe Estuary.* The Hamburg Shooting Association, Hamburg, Germany, 1950.

Harrison, Jeffrey G. *Pastures New: A wildfowler naturalist explores north-west Germany.* Witherby, London, 1954.

Hawker, Peter. *Instructions to Young Sportsmen: in all that relates to guns and shooting.* Longmans, Brown, Green & Longman, London. (1814) 1844 9th edition.

Hawker, Peter. *The Diary of Colonel Peter Hawker: 1802-1853.* Longmans, Green & Co., London, 1893.

Higson, Daniel. *Seafowl Shooting Sketches: Being chiefly a series of adventures on the River Ribble in pursuit of wild fowl, etc.* Alfred Halewood, Preston, (1887) 1909 revised edition.

Hogg, James. *James Robertson Justice: 'What's the Bleeding Time?' A biography.* Tomahawk Press, Sheffield 2008.

Humphreys, John. *Stanley Duncan, Wildfowler: Founder of the Wildfowler's Association of Great Britain and Ireland in 1908.* B.A.S.C., Rossett, 1993.

Hutchinson, Horace G. (Editor). *The "Country Life" Library of Sport: Shooting.* Country Life, London, 1903.

Huxley, Elspeth. *Peter Scott: Painter and naturalist.* Faber & Faber, London, 1993.

Kavanagh, Arthur MacMurrough. *The Cruise of the R.Y.A. Eva.* Hodges, Smith & Co., Dublin, 1865.

Lacy, Richard. *The Modern Shooter: Containing practical instructions and directions for every description of inland and coast shooting.* Whittaker & Co., London, 1842.

Lowe, Percy R. *International Wildfowl Inquiry, Volume 1. Factors affecting the general status of wild geese and wild duck.* Cambridge University Press, Cambridge, 1941.

Macpherson, H.A. *A History of Fowling: Being an account of the many curious devices by which wild birds are or have been captured in different parts of the world.* David Douglas, Edinburgh, 1897.

Marchington, John E. *The History of Wildfowling.* A & C Black, London, 1980.

Morgan W. A. *The House on Sport.* Gale & Polden, London, 1898.

Norman, Bernard J. *Walton-on-the-Naze in Old Picture Postcards.* European Library, Zaltbommel, Netherlands, 1991.

Payne-Gallwey, Ralph. *The Fowler in Ireland: Or notes on the haunts and habits of wildfowl and seafowl including instructions in the art of shooting and capturing them.* Van Voorst, London, 1882.

Payne-Gallwey, Ralph. *The Book of Duck Decoys: Their construction, management and history.* Van Voorst, London, 1886.

Payne-Gallwey, Ralph. *Letters to Young Shooters (Third Series): Comprising a short natural history of British wildfowl, and complete directions in shooting wildfowl on the coast and inland.* Longmans, Green & Co., London, 1896.

Perry, Richard. *At the Turn of the Tide: A book of wild birds.* Lindsay Drummond, London, 1938.

Perry, Richard. *A Naturalist on Lindisfarne.* Lindsey Drummond, London, 1946.

Sedgwick, Noel M.; Whitaker, Peter; and Harrison, Jeffrey G. (Editors). *The New Wildfowler.* Herbert Jenkins, London, 1961.

Sedgwick, Noel M.; Whitaker, Peter; and Harrison, Jeffrey G. (Editors). *The New Wildfowler in the 1970's.* Barrie & Jenkins, London, 1970.

Scott, Peter. *Morning Flight: A book of wildfowl.* Country Life, London, 1935.

Scott, Peter. *Wild Chorus.* Country Life, London. 1938.

Scott, Peter. *The Eye of the Wind: An autobiography.* Hodder & Stoughton, London, 1961.

Sharp, Henry. *Practical Wildfowling.* Upcott Gill, London, 1895.

Sharp, Henry. *The Gun: Afield and afloat.* Chapman & Hall, London, 1904.

Skinner, Jean. (Compiler). *Through the Lens with Stanley Duncan.* B.A.S.C., Rossett, 1988.

Stammers, Michael. *A Maritime Fortress: The Collections of the Wynn Family at Belan Fort, c. 1750-1950.* University of Wales Press, Cardiff. 2001.

Walsh, John Henry. *Manual of British Rural Sports, by "Stonehenge."* Routledge, London, (1855) 1856 2nd edition.

Walsh, John Henry. *The Shot-Gun and Sporting Rifle, by "Stonehenge."* Routledge, Warne & Routledge, London. 1859.

Walsingham, Lord; and Payne-Gallwey, Sir Ralph. *Shooting: Moor and Marsh.* (The Badminton library series). Longmans, Green & Co., London, 1887.

Warren, Henry C. *Essex.* (The County Books series). Robert Hale, London, 1950.

Wentworth Day, James. *Coastal Adventure: A book about marshes and the sea; shooting and fishing; wildfowl and waders and men who sail in small boats.* Harrap, London. 1954.

Wentworth Day James. *The Modern Fowler: with a guide to some of the principal coastal wildfowling resorts of to-day.* Longmans, Green & Co., London, 1934 and 2nd edition, Batchworth, London, 1949.

Whitaker J. *British Duck Decoys of Today 1918.* Burlington, London, 1918.

White, Archie. *Tideways and Byways in Essex & Suffolk.* Edward Arnold, London, 1948.

Wrigley, John. *Notes on the Bird Life of Formby.* Printed for private circulation, Liverpool, 1892.

Young, Jonathan. *A Pattern of Wings: and other wildfowling tales.* Unwin Hyman, London, 1989.

ESTABLISHED 1835.

Winners of all "The Field" Rifle Trials, 1883.

GOLD MEDAL, INVENTIONS EXHIBITION, 1885.

HOLLAND & HOLLAND

Gun and Rifle Manufacturers

98, New Bond Street, LONDON, W.

Gun and Rifle Makers by Special Appointment to . . .
His Majesty The King of Italy.
His Imperial and Royal Highness The Crown Prince of Austria.
Their Royal Highnesses The Comte and Comtesse de Paris.

Factory: 527 to 533, HARROW ROAD, W.

Shooting Grounds: KENSAL RISE, W.

Telephone Nos.: 98, New Bond St., 7475; Shooting Grounds, 7474, Factory, 7472.
Telegraphic Address: "Armourer, London."

AGENTS IN INDIA FOR THE SALE OF OUR ARMS AND AMMUNITION:
MESSRS. KING, KING & CO., BOMBAY.

[Index, see page 112.]

SINGLE STEEL-BARRELLED PUNT GUNS.

THE "LONDON" IMPROVED MODEL.

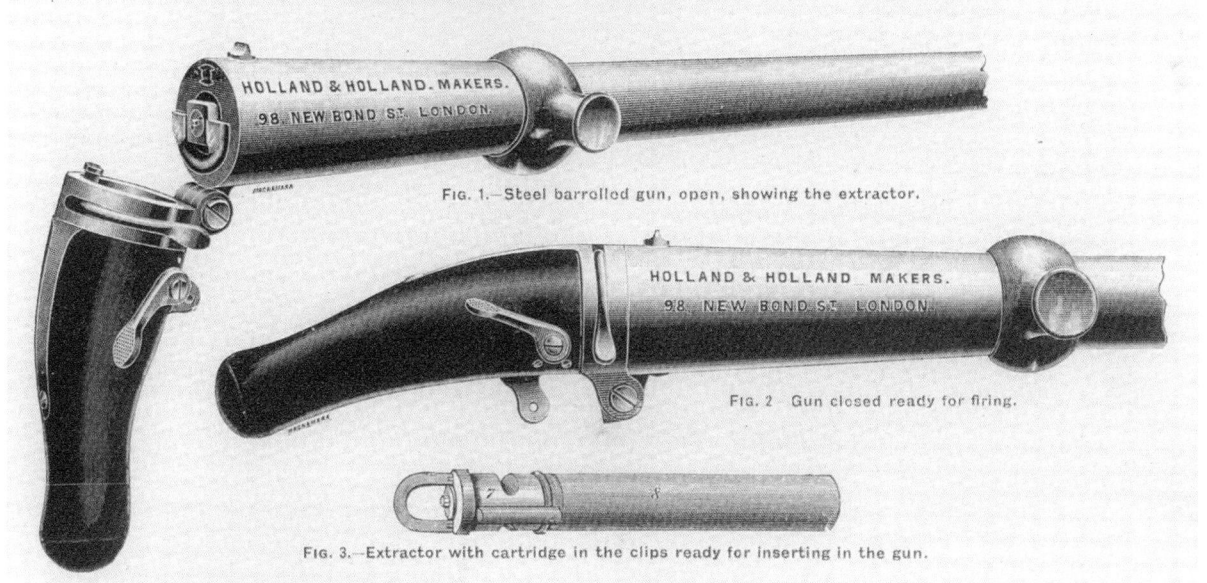

Fig. 1.—Steel barrelled gun, open, showing the extractor.

Fig. 2 Gun closed ready for firing.

Fig. 3.—Extractor with cartridge in the clips ready for inserting in the gun.

HOLLAND'S steel-barrelled central-fire hammerless guns are acknowledged to be the strongest, simplest, and best shooting Punt Guns made. They are constructed upon two principles—the patent screw-breech, with extractor head attached, as invented for Sir R. PAYNE GALLWEY's big gun; and the falling breech action, named the "London."

The above guns are arranged and chambered either for solid brass or paper cases. We have found the latter to answer the best generally, and they are made to any bore up to two inches.

We have received most satisfactory reports respecting these guns from time to time, and beg to call attention to the following favourable notices respecting them.

Press Notices and Testimonials.

Extract from "THE FIELD."

"It is well known that a great difficulty is usually experienced with ordinary breech-loading guns, on account of the heavy charges which are fired jamming up the action, and making it sometimes all but impossible to open the gun and extract the exploded case. Now in Messrs. HOLLAND's gun it will be noticed:—Firstly, that the whole of the recoil is taken, not by any hinge or breech-piece, but by the solid breech-end itself; secondly, that the extractor is so arranged that there is no chance of any of the exploded cases sticking; thirdly, the whole is perfectly gas-tight, there being no chance of the gas escaping into the lock, the limbs are nickel plated to save them from rust; fourthly, the quickness and facility with which the action can be opened, and the gun charged or cartridge exchanged, are undeniable."

Appendix 1

From research undertaken by Mr John Bishop in 2014

Holland and Holland Punt Guns

Year	Holland and Holland Punt Gun Serial Numbers										
1872	2321										
No guns recorded 1873 until 1880												
1880	6265	6317	6373								
1881	6422	6865	6901	6903	6916	6917	6981	6987	6994	6998	6999	7003
1882	7048	7049	7142	7170	7304	7305	7397	7470	7471	7633	7634	
1883	7526	7849	7050	7867								
1884	8032	8039	8155	8264	8383							
1885	8506	8015										
No guns made 1886 until 1889												
1890	12651	12883										
1891	14275											
1892	No guns made											
1893	17218											
No guns made 1894 and 1895												
1896	20105	20106										
1897	20100	20107										
1898	20108	20109	20110									
1899 No guns made												
1900	20111	20112	20113	20114								
1901	20115	20116	20119									
No guns made 1902 and 1903												
1904	20117	20118										
1905	20120											
No guns made 1906 and 1907												
1908	20121	20122										
1909	20123											
No Guns made 1910 and 1911												
1912	20047	20048	20049									
1918	20050	20051	20052 to 20056 but no certainty all guns were built									

Footnote 1

Gun number 7634 ordered by George Gould was the first screw breech gun 1882, (action and breech plug all in one.)
Gun number 8155 was first double gun ordered by RPG.
Gun number 12883 was a double gun. Gun number 14275 was a double gun. Gun number 17218 was a double gun.
Gun number 20052 bought by William Berry of Inverness.

Footnote 2

Holland and Holland punt gun numbers may have been reserved in the Numbers Book but never manufactured.

Appendix 2

Holland and Holland Punt Gun Bore Sizes

Approximate numbers built by type and size. Holland and Holland records are unclear as to how many were manufactured

Gun type	Gun Bore Size							Number built
	One inch and					two inch	size unknown	
	an eighth	an quarter	three eighths	a half	seven eighths			
Single early record. Presumed Muzzle-Loader							1	1
London pattern with Clayton bars			1	19		3	6	29
Screw Extractor attached to stock	1	2	1	2	1			7
Single Gallwey lever with separate breech plug		1		11			3	15
Payne-Gallwey double punt guns				4				4
Single top lever with separate breech plug				13				13
Total	1	3	2	49	1	3	10	69

John Bishop would welcome any further information on Holland punt guns.

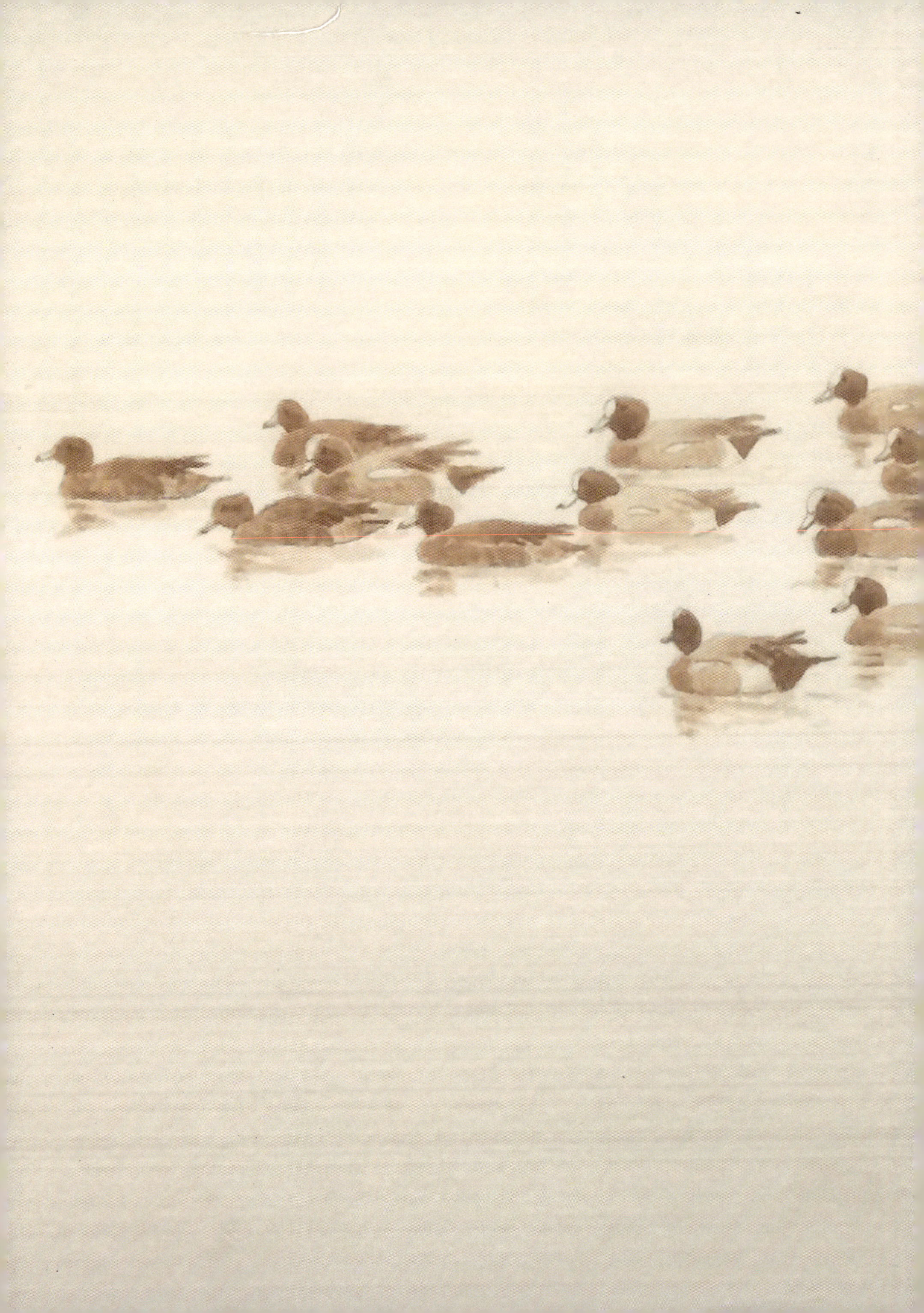